KILLING OF
TUPAC
SHAKUR

Cathy Scott

PLEXUS, LONDON

First, to the memory of my grandmother, Esther Rose (1901-1990),
a Carmel, California artist with an intellect far too early for her time.
Second, to the grieving mothers who have lost their sons to gangsta violence:
My sincere sympathies to you all as you struggle to make sense of
their deaths. And last, to the memory of Tupac Shakur: May
he live on through his music, films, and legend.

All rights reserved including the right of
reproduction in whole or in part in any form
New edition revised and updated 2009
Copyright © 2009, 1999, 1997 by Cathy Scott
Published by Plexus Publishing Limited
25 Mallinson Road
London SW11 1BW
www.plexusbooks.com
First printing 2009

British Library Cataloguing in Publication Data

Scott, Cathy
The killing of Tupac Shakur. - 2nd ed.
1. Shakur, Tupac, 1971-1996 - Death and burial 2. Rap
musicians - United States - Biography 3. Murder - Nevada -
Las Vegas
I. Title
364.1'523'09793135

ISBN-10: 0-89565-437-0
ISBN-13: 978-085965-437-1

First published by Plexus Publishing in 1997
Published by arrangement with
Huntington Press, Las Vegas, Nevada

Cover photo: Corjuni / Katz / Outline (front cover)
Aaron Mayes (author photo)
Cover design: Philip Gambrill
Printed in Great Britain by Bell and Bain

CONTENTS

ACKNOWLEDGMENTS

MANY PEOPLE (and a loyal Siamese) stood by me as I finished this manuscript. To coin the words of Tupac Shakur, "You are appreciated."

First, to Anthony Curtis at Huntington Press and his staff, including Bethany Coffey and Len Cipkins, and particularly editor Deke Castleman, for believing that the killing of Tupac Shakur was a Las Vegas story that needed to be told and that I was the one to tell it, and for their incredible editing, focus, and dedication to the manuscript – you steered me and the words in the right directions and made it better.

To the Las Vegas Metropolitan Police Department, notably Lieutenant Wayne Petersen and detectives Brent Becker and Mike Franks, for their interviews, but, especially, Sergeant Kevin Manning for putting up with my many questions and allowing me to flesh out the story.

To Geoff Schumacher (formerly my boss at the *Las Vegas Sun*) for giving me time off to work on the manuscript, and to the *Sun*'s daytime copy desk – Rob Langrell, Linda Wrzesinski, and Sal DeFilippo – for their endless good humor and encouragement; and to photographers Steve Marcus, Marsh Starks, and Aaron Mayes for their images.

A special thanks to the *Las Vegas Sun*'s online department for its innovation in packaging the daily Tupac stories. I especially thank Jennifer Whitehair for her hard work.

To my attorney Vickie Pynchon for her legal counseling and a lifetime of friendship that began in grade school where we had early aspirations in "Sisters of the Pen" of one day becoming writers.

To Kevin Doty, esquire, and Kent Lauer with the Nevada Press Association for their advice.

To Frank Alexander, a fellow Tupac author and former bodyguard, for his time.

To my sources, who, for obvious reasons, I won't name. And to one in particular – you know who you are – a thank you from the heart for reading every word I write, for understanding the role of a journalist, and for being my friend.

To my fellow newswomen and newsmen, allies and sterling journalists all: Kevin Powell for his sensitive description of the man, not just the rapper; Tonya Pendleton for her insights into the world of rap; Rachael Levy for forever being the devil's advocate and making me a better reporter; Charlene "Charlie" Fern for forcing style, style, style at my first daily paper; *Las Vegas Review-Journal* columnist John L. Smith for his confidence in my abilities; syndicated cartoonist Mike Smith for his steadfast support; Muriel Stevens for her sound literary advice; Myram Borders for her Las Vegas history; "Kayaking" Steve Waterstrat for his friendship; Teresa Hinds for listening and loaning me mystery writer Bill Moody – her then-fiancé – so I could pick his brain; and the *Sun*'s executive editor, former Nevada Governor Mike O'Callaghan, for believing in me.

To my family, most of whom were long-distance boosters: my son Raymond Somers Jr. for his never-failing encouragement and blessings; my mother, fellow writer Eileen Rose Busby, who taught me I could achieve whatever in life I chose; my father, James Melvin Scott, whose writing of his own book at 85 spurred me on to pen my own; my big brothers, Jon Scott for his continued faith and J. Michael Scott for his scholarly and brotherly advice; my sister Sally Scott for passing on to me her love of literature; and my twin sister Cordelia Mendoza for always being there.

To Tupac Amaru Shakur, may he rest in peace.

And, finally, my gratitude to a Grossmont College instructor whose name I no longer know and who is still unaware of the impact he had on a sophomore in his creative writing class when he told her she had talent.

AUTHOR'S NOTE

I'VE ENDEAVORED TO uncover the truth surrounding the killing of Tupac Shakur. Perhaps no one will ever know for certain who pulled the trigger, although police have said they know who did it. What is known is this: the gunman has gotten away with murder.

Not since John Lennon was cut down on the streets of New York City has a major entertainment figure been murdered at the pinnacle of his popularity. As in the Lennon killing, Shakur's death resonated far beyond the world of musical entertainment. Unlike the Lennon killing, Tupac's murder has yet to officially be solved.

From the start, my goal has been to separate fact from fiction in the tremendously high-profile case. Much of the information I've gathered and presented here has never been published before. In some cases, I've identified errors previously reported and replaced them with the facts as I've learned them and know them to be true.

This book is based on interviews, research, and observations that began the day Tupac was shot. I've gleaned information from a prodigious paper trail, including county, city, police, and legal documents and records. I've perused hundreds, if not thousands, of newspaper and magazine articles. In piecing together the events of September 7, 1996, and the continuing aftermath, I have diligently and painstakingly checked and rechecked the facts. I'm a police reporter by trade; it's my job to get it right.

I've interviewed more than 200 people about the case. More than 100 are cited. Some of my sources provided background information only and their names have not been included in the text. Although I've had many conversations with Shakur family members and their attorneys, agents, and assistants, Tupac's mother, Afeni Shakur, decided not to submit to an interview. Instead, I've included the few published comments she has made about Tupac's death.

The Las Vegas Metropolitan Police Department, known as Metro, was forthcoming at times and less so at others. In the past, Las Vegas cops have been notoriously tight-lipped – all the way up the chain of command to the highest levels. Long-term former Sheriff John Moran (now deceased) consistently refused to talk to reporters; even when he retired in December 1994, Moran declined to give a final interview, standing his ground and closing his door to the press one last time. It is a Las Vegas tradition to snub reporters.

That attitude carried over into the administration of Sheriff Jerry Keller, who was at the helm of the department when Tupac was murdered. Although Keller did talk to the media, he often became openly indignant and critical of reporters when the questions got too tough.

And although homicide detectives and others close to the Tupac Shakur case were understandably reluctant at times to discuss certain aspects of the Shakur case, they eventually provided enough details to allow me to construct an accurate portrayal of the events surrounding the criminal investigation.

LVMPD officers, however, drew the the line when it came to speaking with out-of-town reporters, purposely fielding only questions from local newsmen and women, whom they knew. As a result, the *Las Vegas Sun*'s newsroom, where I worked at the time, received calls from dozens of reporters from all over the world who had been stonewalled by Las Vegas police.

When a major story breaks in a newspaper's hometown, local reporters and editors often shine in the national spotlight. The world was watching the Tupac Shakur case unfold daily; the Las Vegas Sun was ahead of the curve each day, beating the competition in its quest to break the news. After all, this was our town and our story. We weren't about to let the national papers gobble it up and take it away from us. During the first week of coverage, the Sun assigned three reporters to the story, but the shooting investigation was all mine.

My pursuit of this story turned up a fascinating and convoluted sequence of events surrounding not just the shooting, but Tupac himself and the world in which he lived. I piece them together for you here, in the pages that follow.

This book is an accounting of the events. The language is raw and the drama could have come straight from the wildest movie. It didn't. This is not fiction. The players in these pages are real. This is a true, violent, and sad story of an unsolved crime, based on the facts. It is the story of the killing of Tupac Shakur.

PROLOGUE

SINCE THE SEPTEMBER 1997 release of *The Killing of Tupac Shakur*, I have received thousands of e-mails, letters, and telephone calls from fans of Tupac asking for more information about his murder.

Much has been learned since the first release of *The Killing of Tupac Shakur*, which is the reason for this updated and expanded edition. This new version is an attempt to further flesh out the facts surrounding Tupac's slaying. Included in this second edition are the events in more detail with fresh interviews. Hopefully, when you finish reading it you will be more informed and more enlightened.

Thanks to you all for your cards, e-mails, letters, and phone calls. While I may not always openly express it, I greatly appreciate your feedback. I also try to keep readers informed on my website at http://www.cathyscott.com/.

1

THE KILLING OF TUPAC SHAKUR

THE FREEWAYS crisscross Vegas, Nevada in the heart of the Mohave Desert in Clark County. Highway 95 connects Las Vegas to Reno in the north and Phoenix in the south. But the major artery in and out of the Vegas valley is Interstate 15; to the southwest is Los Angeles, to the northeast, Salt Lake City. I-15 is widely believed to be the get-away route used by murderers the night Tupac Shakur was cut down in cold blood.

Saturday, September 7, 1996, wasn't just any night in Las Vegas. It was the evening of the championship boxing match between heavyweights Mike Tyson and Bruce Seldon. The town was packed with fight fans, including wall-to-wall celebrities. Las Vegas nears peak capacity almost every weekend of the year, but this fight, a premier event, had sold out all the hotel and motel rooms in the region and gridlocked the Las Vegas Strip.

It would end up being a deadly fight night.

Vegas is famous for its boxing events, which have been magnets for high-spending action ever since Sonny Liston's 1963 first-round knock-out of Floyd Patterson. Muhammad Ali, Larry Holmes, Roberto Duran, Sugar Ray Leonard, Evander Holyfield, Mike Tyson, and a long list of great fighters have turned Las Vegas into a world-class mecca for boxing. Heavyweight bouts traditionally surround Las Vegas with an electrifying aura that rarely materializes during other events. Fights can gross more than $100 million, especially when Tyson's name is on the ticket.

On this particular night, Mike Tyson was expected to win back the heavyweight championship he'd lost six years earlier to Buster

Douglas in Tokyo. High rollers eagerly flocked to the desert at the invitation of the casinos to attend the fight as an opening act to a weekend of gambling and partying. The night was ripe. A high level of expectation and excitement was in the air.

"Nothing brings customers to Las Vegas like major heavyweight boxing, and Mike Tyson is the biggest draw in boxing, so it's a big special event for this town," explained Bill Doak, marketing director for the MGM Grand, where the fight was being held.

Rob Powers, spokesman for the Las Vegas Convention and Visitors Authority, echoed those sentiments: "The exposure Las Vegas will get will be incalculable in terms of media exposure."

Little did he know just how true those words would be.

Everything at the MGM Grand that night spelled H-O-L-L-Y-W-O-O-D, from its upscale stores and gourmet restaurants to the red-carpeted Studio Walk leading to the Garden Arena where two fights – one a boxing match, the other a brawl – would take place that night.

Tupac (pronounced "TOO-pock") Shakur, one of the most notorious emcees on the rap music scene, was among the many celebrities who assembled at the MGM Grand for the heavyweight bout. Six months earlier, Tupac and fellow gangsta rap artist Snoop Dogg had attended the Mike Tyson-Frank Bruno fight at Caesars Palace.

In town for the Tyson-Seldon match-up, besides Tupac Shakur, were the Reverend Jesse L. Jackson Jr., an avid fight fan and a familiar face on the Las Vegas Strip on fight weekends, as well as rapper MC Hammer, television star Roseanne, basketball player Gary Payton, hip-hop's Too Short, and rapper Run DMC.

They, along with 16,000 spectators in the arena and millions more sitting glued to the pay-per-view cable channel, watched as Tyson dismantled Seldon in exactly 109 seconds. The spectators barely had time to settle into their seats before they found themselves getting up again and filing out of the arena. Afterward, some spectators remained in the stands for a few minutes, booing the boxers. Fans dubbed it the "Gyp on the Strip." It marked Tyson's fourth comeback victory.

Tupac had taken in the fight with Marion Knight, known as "Suge" (pronounced "Shoog," short for his childhood nickname of "Sugar Bear"). Suge had co-founded and owned Death Row Records, Tupac's recording label. They sat ringside in $1,000 seats – some of the best seats in the house – with Tupac sitting in section 4, row E, seat 2. In the margin at the top of the stub was handwritten "Tupac." Even though Death Row had earlier purchased 12 tickets, which included seats for the record label's bodyguards, only four tickets were used by Suge's crew that night: one each for Tupac, Suge, bodyguard Frank Alexander, and a friend of Suge's.

Sitting near Tupac were other celebrities, including actors Charlie Sheen and Louis Gossett Jr., former star baseball player Reggie Jackson, and Reverend Jackson.

It was later rumored that Tupac and Suge had gotten into an argument, as they went to take their seats, with several people who had been sitting in the seats reserved for Death Row. But witnesses and security officers at the fight have said that no such argument took place.

The song that played over the public address system during Tyson's walk from backstage into the ring was written by Tupac especially for Tyson. It was titled "Wrote the Glory" and, as of 2002, was still one of Tupac's unreleased songs. Another song, "Ambitionz Az a Ridah" from Tupac's *All Eyes on Me* album, was also written for Tyson. At the beginning of the song, Tupac says, "Yeah, I dedicate this to my nigga Mike Tyson. It's all good." Tupac was filled with pride as his good friend Mike walked into the ring and his own lyrics pounded the arena. (Before he was banned from boxing in the U.S. for a year in 1999, Tyson for the second time used Tupac's "Wrote the Glory" as a fight song.)

After the fight, Tupac and Suge, along with members of their entourage, were making their way through the casino toward the entrance of the hotel when they got into a scuffle with a then-unidentified black man whom police would later learn was 21-year-old Orlando Anderson of Compton, California. This fight-outside-the-fight became enormously significant in light of the events that followed.

Tupac, according to the Compton Police Department's account, looked at Orlando and said, "You from the south?" Then Tupac lunged at Orlando, dropping him. Others in Tupac's group joined in. Once they had Orlando down on the ground, they kicked and stomped on him. A few minutes later, hotel security guards broke up the tussle.

Bodyguard Frank Alexander said he, too, helped break it up by shoving Tupac against a wall.

"Orlando Anderson was just standing there [in the hotel]," Frank told me in a telephone interview. He said Orlando was standing near a hotel security guard.

"Sal [Suge's friend] whispered into Tupac's ear and Tupac took off running," Frank continued. "Tupac ran up to Anderson and swung at him. Anderson swung back and a chain fell off of Tupac's neck. Tupac bent down to pick up his necklace. I went down as he did and grabbed Tupac and put him against the wall."

After security guards broke up the encounter, Tupac, Suge, and their crew immediately left. They headed for the lobby of the MGM Grand, then to the valet area in front of the hotel. They walked south on the Strip toward the Luxor hotel-casino, where the group were staying and where they had parked their high-priced cars. It's a 15-minute walk.

Las Vegas police were called by hotel security for backup. No one from Tupac's group was stopped or questioned by security or police. Tupac and his group, as recorded by surveillance cameras, simply walked away. No report was filed by Las Vegas police. After the scuffle, Orlando was seen on videotape talking to LVMPD and security officers. He was standing up and did not appear to be injured. Security guards offered him first aid. He declined. They also asked him to go with them downstairs to the security office to file a complaint. He declined.

This question has never been answered: Even though Orlando declined to file a complaint, why didn't police file a police report? In the state of Nevada, victims don't have to file a complaint for charges to be filed against a perpetrator. Suge was later imprisoned for violating parole because of his involvement in the scuffle, so obviously, authorities felt a crime had been committed. And security guards were witnesses. Yet no crime or incident report was ever filed.

Meanwhile, back at Luxor, a block south of the MGM, Tupac went to the room he was sharing with his girlfriend Kidada Jones, Quincy Jones's daughter, which Suge Knight had booked for the weekend.

Then, Tupac changed his clothes from a tan designer silk shirt and tan slacks to a black-and-white basketball tank top, baggy blue jeans, and black-and-white leather sports shoes. Around his neck on a heavy gold chain hung a large, round, solid-gold medallion. It wasn't the medallion Suge had given him when he bailed Tupac out of prison a year earlier. That one featured a diamond-studded Death Row insignia of a hooded prisoner strapped into an electric chair. The medallion Tupac wore to the fight was the size of a paperweight – and probably just as heavy – picturing a haloed and winged black man wrestling a serpent with one hand and holding a gun in the other.

Tupac didn't pack a weapon that night. He left his hotel unarmed. He also didn't wear a flak (or bullet-resistant) jacket or vest. Tupac's friends said he sometimes wore a Kevlar vest out of fear of being shot. But not that night. He always felt safe visiting Las Vegas. After all, it was a party town and he was going there to "kick it" and watch his homey Iron Mike kick butt. Besides, a flak jacket would be too hot in the desert heat. That's what he told Kidada when she packed his clothes earlier that day in California. It would turn out to be a fatal decision, but one to which Tupac didn't give another thought as he and his girlfriend prepared to leave for Vegas.

But to one of Suge's bodyguards, Tupac said otherwise. Frank Alexander, Tupac's personal bodyguard for the weekend, said, "There is a bodyguard who is a close friend to me, and Tupac told him he didn't feel good about going to Vegas and that he felt like his life was in danger. He didn't say it to me. But he did say it to this particular bodyguard." Alexander declined to name the bodyguard.

Still, it was rare for Tupac to wear a flak jacket, issued by the record company. Alexander said that "Tupac only wore it one or two times."

While waiting for their cars in the Luxor valet area, Tupac and his crew were videotaped on a tourist's camcorder, smiling and chatting casually with a couple of women. Kidada Jones remained in their hotel room upstairs.

When the cars were delivered a few minutes later, the group piled in again and drove to Suge Knight's Las Vegas residence in the southeastern valley, on Monte Rosa Avenue in the Paradise Valley Township. The Las Vegas subdivision boasts some of the oldest estates in the Las Vegas valley and is home to many of the wealthiest and most powerful Las Vegans.

Las Vegas Metropolitan Police Department Sergeant Kevin Manning, who led the homicide investigation, said the group went to Suge's house to relax. But Frank Alexander told me they went to Suge's specifically so Suge could change his clothes.

Then, Sergeant Manning said, the group planned on attending a benefit party at a Las Vegas special-events night spot, located at 1700 East Flamingo Road, known then as Club 662, where Tupac was to perform with Run-DMC. After his fight with Seldon, Tyson also planned to make an appearance at the nightclub, which Suge ran.

At about 10:00 p.m., the entourage left Suge's house and headed back to the action. Tupac rode shotgun with Suge behind the wheel of a car Death Row had just obtained: a $46,000 1996 black 750 BMW sedan, with darkly tinted windows, chrome wheels, leather upholstery, and a sunroof. The music was cranked up on the car stereo (this particular BMW model is known for its superb sound system). They were in a party mood as the caravan of luxury cars – a Lexus, a BMW wagon, a Miata, and a Mercedes Benz – carrying friends and bodyguards, followed closely behind.

Alexander, a former Orange County Sheriff's Department reserve deputy (now an author and producer), was the only bodyguard riding in the caravan. The rest of the dozen or so private security guards were waiting for the group a few miles away at Club 662. Frank was sitting in the driver's seat of a Lexus owned by Kidada Jones, behind Suge and Tupac's BMW. At the last minute, Frank decided to drive Kidada's car instead of his own. Frank's personal handgun was in his car, which he left in the Luxor parking garage. That had left Frank, the only bodyguard with Tupac, unarmed.

The group cruised four-mile-long Las Vegas Boulevard, commonly called the Strip, which was jammed with the kind of stop-and-go traffic that is the norm for a Saturday fight night. The sunroof of the BMW was opened and the windows rolled down. Suge and Tupac were hollering above the hip-hop blaring from the car's speakers. Tupac and his crew, easily recognized, were turning heads on the Strip. A photographer shot a frame of Tupac and Suge sitting in the black BMW. The photo would later garner between $800 and $5,000 each time it was sold for publication in entertainment and business magazines to air on TV tabloid and news shows. It is also pictured on the cover of this book. It was the last photo taken of Tupac alive.

At 11:05 p.m., Suge Knight was stopped on the south end of the Strip by a Las Vegas bicycle cop for playing his car stereo too loudly and for not having license plates displayed on the BMW. (That's when the photo of Suge and Tupac sitting in the BMW was taken.) The officer asked Suge to get out of the car and open the trunk. Suge did. He and the officer talked. A few minutes later, the officer let Suge go without ticketing him. Tupac and Suge laughed about it as they rounded the corner onto Flamingo Road, heading past Bally's hotel-casino toward Club 662, just two miles away.

They never made it.

***

None of Tupac's bodyguards, including Frank Alexander, and associates armed themselves before leaving for Club 662. The other bodyguards, all former or off-duty cops, including LVMPD police who were moonlighting that night, had been hired to guard Tupac and his entourage during their stay in Las Vegas. For out-of-state security officers to carry guns, Nevada law requires them, in advance, to obtain temporary concealed-weapons permits. According to Frank Alexander's account of the events that night, that advance permitting had not been done.

After Tupac and the bodyguards arrived in Vegas, they were disappointed to learn that the proper permits allowing them to carry firearms had not been applied for by Wrightway Security, a firm used by Death Row Records that hired only off-duty cops. A Las Vegas attorney for Death Row informed the bodyguards before the Tyson fight that they would not be legally allowed to arm themselves while guarding the Death Row entourage in Nevada. That left them as little more than unarmed rent-a-cops.

If they'd been caught packing weapons without permits, the police could have charged them and they could have faced stiff penalties. The majority of the security guards were accustomed to carrying sidearms. But not that night.

While they may have felt the same as Tupac, that they were going to a party in a town far removed from the street-gang violence long associated with Los Angeles, they had to make a hard choice. In the end, on the advice of Suge's attorney, the bodyguards left their guns behind.

Had the group decided to ignore the law, they no doubt could have walked undetected into the MGM Grand Garden that night with guns if they'd wanted to. According to John Husk, executive director of the MGM's arena operations, "There were no metal detectors used at the Mike Tyson fight on September 7."

Las Vegas police were out in droves and private security was heavy at the Grand Garden Arena before, during, and after the fight. Sergeant Ron Swift, with LVMPD's Special Events Section, said officers were assigned inside the casino near the boxing arena to strengthen the hotel's own security force.

"On property, we had some officers augmenting hotel security at the event itself," Swift said. "We do it at every major fight, as well as at concerts, rodeos, and parades."

The arena was not the only place cops were assigned to provide a show of force that night. Special Events officers, working overtime, were stationed at the private gate to Suge's neighborhood, which Metro, because of a county ordinance, does not patrol. The home-owners associations of many gated communities in the Las Vegas Valley hire private security officers to patrol inside their walls. Las Vegas police were also contracted to be present at Club 662 after the fight. Overtime for the off-duty Metro officers was billed to Death Row Records.

"[Death Row] asked us to do it," Sergeant Swift said. "My only con-cern at the time was traffic and public safety. If a company comes in and asks for extra security, we provide it. Death Row requested it for-mally from Metro."

One officer said that Death Row also had asked that African-American cops only be assigned to work Club 662 and Suge's house. "The request was made for only black police officers," the source said. "As far as I know, we complied."

But Swift couldn't confirm it, saying, "I've never heard that Knight requested black officers. The request may have come in, but I didn't hear about it." Still, the same source revealed that a black sergeant, along with six to eight other black officers, were assigned to the party at Suge Knight's house following the fight.

Tupac felt safe as he rode in the BMW toward Club 662 – Suge was driving, friends and bodyguards were nearby, and Las Vegas cops were stationed at the house and the club. In fact, the event at Club 662 was sponsored by LVMPD Officer Patrick Barry, a retired profession-al boxer, to raise money for Barry's Boxing Gym on Vanessa Drive in the southwest area of the Las Vegas valley. Tupac, Run-DMC, and Danny Boy were scheduled to perform at the charity event, intended, ironically, to raise money to keep children away from violence. Club 662's marquee advertised the event as Barry's Boxing Benefit, pro-duced by SKP (Suge Knight Productions). A line started forming out-side the club at 5:30 p.m. Hundreds of people paid $75 each to get in.

Barry's Boxing Benefit, organized by Las Vegas attorney George Kelesis, who once represented Suge, was also intended to help Tupac stay out of prison by fulfilling a court order and condition of probation in one of his criminal cases, in which he was ordered to perform community service in lieu of jail time.

The convoy was headed east on Flamingo Road when it stopped for a red light at Koval Lane, a busy intersection only a half mile from the Strip accross from the Maxim Hotel. One driver in the caravan pulled up a car length ahead to the right. Another car stopped directly behind them; in it were rapper Yafeu "Kadafi" Fula and two associates, Outlawz rapper Malcolm "E.D.I." Greenridge and bodyguard Frank Alexander. Another car was behind theirs. Riding in it, along with a couple of other people, was Tupac's friend Chris "Casper" Musgrave. Still another car was in front of the BMW at the stoplight. The sidewalk and street were busy with pedestrians.

The BMW was boxed in.

Four young black women, sitting at the same intersection in a Chrysler sedan to the left of the BMW, turned, smiled at Suge and Tupac, and caught their attention.

A moment later, a late-model Cadillac with three to four black men inside pulled up directly to the right of the BMW and skidded to a stop. A gunman sitting in the back seat on the driver's side stuck a weapon out of the left-rear window of the white Caddy, in full view of the entourage. The gunman tracked Tupac from the back seat.

Suge and Tupac saw the Cadillac but had no time to react.

Suddenly, the sounds of the night were shattered by the *pop, pop, pop* of a killer inside the Cadillac emptying a magazine from a high-powered semiautomatic handgun. At least 13 rounds were sprayed (that's how many bullet holes and casings investigators counted) into the passenger side of the BMW. Five bullets pierced the passenger door; some shattered the windows.

Startled and panicky, Tupac tried frantically to scramble into the back seat through the well between the front seats. But he was seatbelted in. In doing so, he exposed his middle and lower torso to the gunfire and took a round in his right hip. Suge grabbed Tupac, pulled him down, and covered him. He yelled, "Get down!" That's when Suge was hit with a fragment in the back of his neck.

Tupac was plugged with bullets at close range. Three rounds pierced his body. One bullet lodged in his chest, entering under his right arm. Another went through his hip, slicing through his lower abdomen, and ended up floating around in his pelvic area. Yet another bullet hit his right hand, shattering the bone of his index finger and knocking off a large chunk of gold from a ring he was wearing on another finger. (Tupac wore three gold-and-diamond rings on his right hand that night.) The gunfire nailed Tupac to the leather bucket seat. Glass and blood were everywhere.

Suge was grazed in his neck from the flying shrapnel and glass fragments. A fragment lodged in the back of his skull at the base of his neck. Bullets also blew out two of the BMW's tires.

The gunfire ended as quickly as it had begun. The shooting of Tupac Shakur, executed in cold blood, was over in a matter of seconds.

"You hit?" Suge asked Tupac.

"I'm hit," Tupac answered.

Frank Alexander said, "All I saw was the position of the shooter. He was in the back seat. I saw the arm of the shooter come out. I saw a silhouette of him, which was a black person wearing a skull cap, a beanie cap.

"I ran up to the back of the BMW. I got to the trunk of the car. Then the car [Suge's] took off and made a U-turn. I was shocked the car moved. There was no way to have seen all of that gunfire and then for someone to still be alive. The Cadillac made a right turn on a green light. It was the only car making a right turn." Frank ran back to his car, jumped in, and followed Suge.

Some reports and LVMPD sources said members of the entourage immediately returned fire. Although no other casings were found, police said revolvers may have been used, which leave no tell-tale shells behind.

Sergeant Manning admitted, "We did hear reports that gunfire was returned, but we were unable to validate it. There was no evidence."

Two LVMPD bicycle patrol officers were on a call concerning a stolen vehicle on the second floor of the parking garage at the Maxim when they heard the first shots fired at 11:17 p.m. Officer Paul Ehler and his partner immediately hopped on their mountain bikes and pedaled toward the street, where they heard more gunfire. They saw the black BMW driver about to flee the gunman.

The driver of the Cadillac, in the meantime, floored it and fled. The Caddy made a right turn onto Koval Lane and vanished. It happened so quickly that by the time the bicycle cops arrived seconds later, there was no trace of the Cadillac. The shooter and his associates escaped under the cover of darkness.

Other drivers who witnessed the shooting stopped and stared, dumbfounded. Shocked drivers maneuvered their cars around the BMW, driving over the crime scene and the spent bullets. Horrified pedestrians milled about the busy sidewalks.

Paul Gillford, a sound man for a syndicated TV show broadcast live from the Imperial Palace, was just getting off work and was on Koval Lane at Flamingo when the shooting took place. He said he, too, watched as all the cars left the scene in different directions.

At least six cars behind Tupac tried chasing the Cadillac as it sped south on Koval Lane, away from the scene. The rest of the crew stayed with Tupac and Suge.

Suge panicked. He knew he had to find a doctor for Tupac, and fast. Tupac looked like he was dying, bleeding to death. Suge was splattered with both Tupac's and his own blood. Tupac's breathing was labored and shallow. But his eyes were opened wide and he was alert.

Suge had a flip Motorola cellular telephone with him, resting on the sedan's console, but he didn't use it to call 911 for help. With adrenaline pumping and Tupac bleeding heavily as he sat slumped in the front seat, Suge somehow managed to make a U-turn in the heavy traffic, even though his car now had two flat tires. But the sedan had a powerful 4.4-liter V-8 engine, so Suge floored it and got out of there, flat tires and all.

"[The bike cops] saw about ten cars pull U-turns and head west on Flamingo at a high rate of speed," then-Sergeant Greg McCurdy told the *Las Vegas Sun*. Not all the cars stayed with Suge, though, once they saw they were being followed by the cops. Three followed him all the way to the Strip.

Both bicycle cops were pedaling fast, tailing the BMS. Why one officer didn't follow Suge while the other stayed behind at the shooting – the scene of the crime – was more than surprising. The officers said it was because they didn't know what had gone down at that point. They'd heard shots being fired, but they had made a split-second decision not to stay and secure the crime scene. They felt it was more important to follow Suge, one of the victims, not a suspect, and his entourage. It would prove to be the first of several questionable decisions made early on in the criminal investigation. One of the first lessons taught to cadets is to secure a crime scene until investigators arrive. The bike officers did not.

The scene of the shooting wasn't secured for at least 20 minutes while cars and pedestrians trampled over the evidence. No one will ever know how many potential witnesses left that scene when no officers were there to hold them for questioning.

One of the bike cops, in pursuit of Suge and his entourage, radioed dispatch and called for backup: "Shots fired. I repeat, shots fired. Possible victims. This unit in pursuit of vehicle. Need assistance. Leaving the vicinity of Koval and Flamingo, proceeding westbound."

As Suge made the U-turn, he hollered to Tupac, "You need a hospital, Pac. I'm gonna get you to a hospital right now."

"*I* need a hospital?" Tupac said. "*You* the one shot in the head. Don't you think you need a hospital?" He started moaning, but managed to utter, "Gotta keep your eyes open."

With three cars full of friends and associates still following closely behind, Suge, for some reason, headed back to the Strip. Bike officer Paul Ehler continued pedaling as he radioed for backup and medical assistance. Fifty yards up Flamingo, Suge's car became snarled in traffic. He frantically weaved the BMW in and out of the left-turn lane and over the median, then floored it.

Suge and Tupac made it onto the Strip. The BMW's rims caught the center divider as Suge turned left onto the boulevard, running a red light and giving the car its third flat tire. Suge then straightened out the steering wheel and drove south down Las Vegas Boulevard. He weaved in and out of the busy traffic for a quarter of a mile, running another red light at Harmon Avenue. There, exactly a mile from the shooting scene, Suge Knight's BMW got caught up on the median, then lunged back on the street, coming to a grinding halt in the middle of the busy intersection on the Strip.

That's when the Strip got really crazy.

Sirens from patrol cruisers, ambulances, a fire department rescue unit, and the highway patrol screamed as every available unit converged on the scene.

Bodyguard Alexander said that when Suge's BMW "turned into the intersection of Harmon, everyone else in the entourage was stuck at a red light," half a block behind him. When the light turned green, he said, they headed into the intersection.

Cops started yelling at everyone in Tupac's entourage, ordering them to "get out of your vehicles" and "get your faces on the ground," to lie flat on the pavement with their hands behind their heads. The police held some of the group at gunpoint, witnesses said. Even Suge Knight, bleeding from his head wound, was ordered to lie face down, with legs spread apart, on the street until the police figured out what was going on.

Alexander said it went down like this: "The only person who was face down on the pavement when I got there was Suge. Suge was spread out on the ground. I identified myself as a bodyguard and told them Suge was a victim and not part of the shooting. Then they let him up."

Blood was everywhere. The BMW's front leather seats were soaked with it and Tupac's cotton shirt was solid crimson.

By the time the paramedics arrived, the cops had things under control. They let the members of Tupac's entourage get up off the street, one by one, and sit on the curb of the Strip sidewalk while they waited for general-assignment and homicide detectives to arrive. As police sat them down on the curb, they admonished them not to discuss the shooting with each other. The moment they let him up, Suge ran to the BMW, to Tupac.

When the paramedics arrived, the mortally wounded Tupac was being lifted out of the front seat by Suge Knight and Frank Alexander. They placed him on the ground.

Tupac was conscious, but short of breath, as the emergency-response teams prepared to rush him and Suge, who was still bleeding from his neck injury, to University Medical Center, Las Vegas's county hospital, about three miles away.

"I can't breathe. I can't breathe," Tupac kept repeating. Then, he crossed his hands over his body and was still.

At that point, Tupac was still alert, with his eyes open, watching what was going on around him. He was lifted onto a gurney and put into the ambulance.

Frank Alexander described it, "I tried getting in the ambulance with Suge and Tupac. A motorcycle cop pushed me back, off of the ambulance, and told me to get away. That's how I ended up staying [at the scene]. Suge was in the ambulance alone with Tupac." Suge climbed in and sat on a bench next to the gurney. Just as paramedics were closing the back doors to the ambulance, witnesses heard Tupac quietly say, "I'm dyin', man."

His words were prophetic: Tupac Amaru Shakur would succumb to his wounds six days later.

2

THE AFTERMATH

YAFEU FULA WAS A rapper in the group the Outlawz Immortalz (since renamed the Outlawz), who backed up and toured with Tupac. Yafeu, whose on-stage name was "Kadafi" and whose friends called him "Yak," was in the car with Frank Alexander and Malcolm Greenridge, directly behind Suge's BMW, when the shooting occurred. Fula's car stayed with the BMW as it careened down Flamingo Avenue and the Strip. He was questioned by detectives at the scene, then rode several hours later to University Medical Center where Tupac was being treated.

While on his way to the hospital to check on Tupac's status, Yafeu Fula used a cell phone to call his mother, Yaasmyn Fula, and tell her what had happened. He said, "Call Afeni and tell her Tupac's been shot."

Yaasmyn Fula called her good friend Afeni Shakur and broke the news that Tupac had been gunned down and that it looked bad.

By the time Afeni Shakur was contacted by Yaasmyn, it was morning in Stone Mountain, Georgia, about 20 miles northeast of Atlanta, where Afeni lived in a home Tupac had purchased for her through Death Row Records. Afeni notified other family members. Then, accompanied by Tupac's half-sister Sekyiwa Shakur and cousin Deena, she caught the earliest flight available to Las Vegas.

They arrived in the afternoon and checked into Room 1039 of the Golden Nugget Hotel on Fremont Street in downtown Las Vegas. They left for the hospital, about four miles from downtown on West Charleston Boulevard.

The official death watch had begun. For the next six days, Tupac's family, friends, and fans kept a 24-hour vigil by his side.

Just hours earlier, after Tupac and Suge had arrived at the hospital by ambulance, Suge was admitted and placed in a regular hospital room. Tupac was taken to the trauma center's intensive-care unit, where a medical team prepped him for what would be his first of several emergency procedures and surgeries.

Outside, a crowd had gathered, including local and out-of-town reporters.

A few hours after Tupac's arrival, hospital spokesman Dale Pugh walked outside and held a news conference. He told the waiting reporters, "[Tupac's] had a right lung removed, he's back in his [private] room, and he remains in critical condition. He has been conscious. He is under a lot of medication, so he's pretty sedated at this time. He's severely injured. Suffering multiple gunshot wounds is obviously a terrible insult to the human body, so he's required intensive care, and he is receiving that right now."

Tupac was, indeed, in grave condition. Before undergoing the first surgery, he was placed on a ventilator and respirator. The next day, still on life-support machines, he was put in a drug-induced coma. Allowed in his room to see him in five-minute increments that first day, along with family members, were Suge Knight, Mike Tyson, MC Hammer, actress Jasmine Guy, Kidada Jones, and the Reverend Jesse Jackson Jr. Later in the week, the Reverend Al Sharpton visited Tupac's bedside. The trauma unit allows just two people in a room at one time. Visitors other than family are allowed to visit every three hours, five times a day, for 20 minutes each. Tyson stood up reporters at a news conference the Sunday after the Seldon match, but he made it to Tupac's side that same day. Tupac remained in a coma.

The same Sunday morning, Reverend Jackson, together with local Reverend James Rogers, then-president of the Las Vegas office of the National Association for the Advancement of Colored People, local Baptist minister Willie Davis, and NAACP assistant to the president, the Reverend Chester Richardson, attended services at the Second Baptist Church in West Las Vegas. There, Reverend Jackson gave a sermon about Tupac.

"Before you condemn Tupac for calling women bitches and ho's in his music," Jackson told parishioners, "you need to understand and know about the background of this man and where he came from. He was raised by a woman who was on crack. He didn't have a real mama. Don't condemn him for talking about his mama and for talking about women." Jackson asked churchgoers to pray for Tupac's recovery. Children and teenagers in the congregation cried as he spoke about the gravely injured rapper.

After visiting four other churches in West Las Vegas, which is known as "the Westside" and is the largest African-American community in Las Vegas, Reverend Jackson stopped by the hospital to visit Tupac. The civil rights leader first met Tupac when he was 12. Reverend Davis drove with Jackson to the hospital's trauma unit, where Jackson stood with Davis and prayed for 15 minutes at Tupac's bedside.

Outside, plainclothes gang-unit detectives assigned to the hospital kept a watchful eye on the usually quiet side streets surrounding University Medical Center.

MC Hammer drove up in his dark-green Hummer and parked on the street in front of the hospital's trauma center. Unaccompanied, he walked silently, with his head down, past reporters, ignoring their questions. He sat in the waiting room for about 30 minutes, waiting his turn to visit Tupac.

That Sunday, less than 24 hours after the shooting, T-shirts with Tupac's image were already being sold on the corner of D Street and Jackson Avenue in the heart of the Westside.

***

Homicide detectives and crime-scene analysts finished their work at the scene as the sun was rising early Sunday morning, then returned to their offices to work on their reports. Sergeant Kevin Manning wrote up a one-page press release and faxed it to the local media:

LAS VEGAS METROPOLITAN POLICE DEPARTMENT MEDIA RELEASE

September 8, 1996
Event #: 960908-2063

SGT. KEVIN MANNING
HOMICIDE SECTION
PHONE: 229-3521

September 8, 1996: At approximately 11:15 p.m., LVMPD patrol officers were at the Maxim Hotel on an unrelated call when they heard several shots being fired from Flamingo Road and Koval Lane. The officers looked to the area of the shots from the Maxim parking garage. They saw several vehicles and numerous people in the street. Several of the vehicles made a U-turn from eastbound Flamingo to westbound Flamingo, leaving the area at a high rate of speed.

The vehicles were stopped at the intersection of Las Vegas Blvd. and Harmon. Bike patrol officers were first at the scene and discovered two men suffering from gunshot wounds. Medical assistance was requested and the two victims were transported to UMC-Trauma.

The victims have been identified as Tupac Shakur, 25, and Marion Knight, 31. Shakur was the passenger in the vehicle and received several gunshot wounds. He was still in surgery and the injuries were considered serious. Knight received a minor wound to the head and was expected to be treated and released.

The investigation so far has determined that the Shakur and Knight group had attended the Tyson fight and were headed for a local nightclub. The group consisted of approximately 10 vehicles that were traveling in a loose convoy. As the vehicles approached the intersection of Flamingo and Koval, a late-'90s, white, 4-door Cadillac containing four people pulled up beside the Shakur/Knight vehicle and one of the people in the Cadillac started shooting into the Shakur/Knight vehicle. The suspect vehicle then fled south on Koval.

Anyone with information in regards to this incident is urged to call Secret Witness at 385-5555 or Metro Homicide at 229-3521.

Two detectives, Brent Becker and Mike Franks, waited outside Suge Knight's hospital room early Sunday morning to interview him about what he saw during the shooting. Suge claimed to be too busy with visitors passing through his room to talk to police. Suge instructed a nurse to ask the detectives to come back later. But at eleven o'clock Sunday morning, Suge was released – *before* the detectives returned to the hospital to take his statement. Suge went home to his Las Vegas estate without giving a witness statement to the police.

Two days later, on Tuesday, three of Suge Knight's attorneys – David Chesnoff and Steve Steiner from Las Vegas and David Kenner from Los Angeles – made arrangements with detectives to meet at homicide headquarters on West Charleston Boulevard, about four miles west of the hospital. All three lawyers are criminal defense attorneys. Under the circumstances, it didn't seem unusual for Suge to seek their help since, at the scene, he was treated like a suspect, not a victim, and ordered face down on the pavement. It was the same day that then-Sergeant Greg McCurdy, a department spokesman at the time, updated reporters on the status of the investigation with this missive: "We have nothing."

Meanwhile, back at homicide headquarters, Sergeant Manning said detectives had "many conversations with the attorneys" in setting a meeting with Knight, Knight's attorneys, and homicide investigators in attendance. "We've had contact with his attorney, but as of yet haven't seen him," Manning said. The lawyers told detectives that Suge was still recovering from his shrapnel wound. But their biggest fear, attorneys told detectives, was that Suge would be inundated by the press before and after the meeting. To guard against this, neither the time nor the location of the meeting was released to the media beforehand.

Sergeant Manning and detectives Franks and Becker waited three hours on Tuesday, September 10, but the foursome never showed. The investigators grew impatient and went home for the night (unless there's a homicide, a detective's day ends promptly at 4:00 p.m.). One of Suge's lawyers later told the detectives that they did go to homicide headquarters that evening, but not until after 6:00 p.m., when no one was there.

The next day, on Wednesday, September 11, four days after the shooting, Suge Knight and his attorneys again made arrangements and did finally meet with police at homicide headquarters. Two detectives and one sergeant – the team assigned to Tupac's shooting – interviewed Suge for less than an hour (one detective said it was for 30 minutes while another said 45). The interview took place in a small conference room off the front lobby in the single-story complex.

Suge offered little, if any, new information, investigators said. He told them he "heard something, but saw nothing."

"We were hoping he would tell us who shot him," Sergeant Manning said. "He didn't give us anything beneficial. Nothing he said helped us."

Manning said the only real evidence investigators had was "the number of bullet holes in the passenger door of the BMW."

Las Vegas attorney David Chesnoff criticized the detectives' short interview of his client, saying, "They didn't ask him in-depth questions. It was like they didn't want to know the details."

Sergeant Manning issued a news release the day after homicide's interview with Suge Knight, dated Thursday, September 12, 1996.

LATEST INFORMATION REGARDING THE LESANE P. CROOKS (AKA TUPAC SHAKUR) AND MARION H. KNIGHT (AKA SUGE) SHOOTING UPDATE

On the evening of 9/11/96, the attorneys for Marion "Suge" Knight made arrangements for Knight to be interviewed by LVMPD homicide investigators.

Knight made himself available for the interview, but was unable to give the investigators any information that would help in determining a motive, nor was he able to help identify possible suspects.

The investigation is at the same juncture. Investigators are hopeful someone will be able to provide information [of] substance.

A $1,000 reward is available for information leading to the arrest and conviction of the suspects. Anyone with information is urged to contact Secret Witness at (702) 385-5555 or LVMPD homicide at 229-3521.

Police said that a large reward would have prompted someone to come forward. Just $1,000, they said, wasn't incentive enough for witnesses to talk.

"We were hoping that there would be some type of reward that would be offered as an incentive for someone to come forward, but that's not happened and no one has really come forward since the night of the incident," said then-homicide Lieutenant Larry Spinosa.

Meanwhile, Tupac Shakur remained in a coma. A doctor treating him would only say that he had a 50-50 chance of survival. However, Doctor John Fildes, chief of trauma surgery at University Medical Center's trauma unit, elaborated, telling a reporter that the gunshot wounds Tupac suffered usually proved fatal. But he emphasized that Tupac had passed a critical phase.

"Overall, of all comers with a gunshot wound in the chest that passes through the blood vessels connecting the heart and lungs, only one in five survive," Doctor Fildes said. "The majority die in the first 24 to 48 hours from shock and bleeding during the treatment and surgery phase."

For victims such as Tupac who survive the first 24 hours, the chances of survival would be more than one in five. He said patients with wounds similar to Tupac also "die during the second major risk period, after five or seven days, when difficulties in oxygenation or the presence of infections or other complications arise." Fildes emphasized that he wasn't personally attending to Tupac, but simply commenting on the chances of survival for someone suffering such injuries. Fildes, in 2002, was the director of the trauma center.

University Medical Center at the time had the only "stand-alone" trauma center west of the Mississippi, with a trauma resuscitation area, angiography room, and three operating rooms. A 14-bed trauma intensive-care unit, where Tupac was being treated, adjoins the resuscitation and operating areas. Tupac was in good hands and was receiving the best of care, but, as Fildes put it, his chances were 50-50.

In an article printed in the *New York Daily News* on Wednesday, September 11, Doctor Fildes said, "It's a very fatal injury. Statistically, it carries a very high mortality rate. A patient may die from lack of oxygen or may bleed to death in the chest."

Tupac underwent two surgeries to stop the internal bleeding. The second was to remove his right lung, a measure doctors said was the only way to stop the bleeding. Still, the bleeding persisted; Tupac's doctors were stumped. A third surgery was scheduled, but Tupac died before it could be done.

It was Friday the 13th.

***

Patricia Cunningham, a radio reporter and correspondent for Sheridan Broadcasting, sat down inside the hospital and talked with Billy Garland, Tupac's father, and Kidada Jones, Tupac's girlfriend. Patricia, looking to interview for a radio piece she was working on, had been introduced on Monday, September 9, to Garland by a black minister from the Las Vegas community. She'd visited with Billy for a while, then left. She returned the next day and again met with Billy Garland. While she was sitting in the trauma center's waiting room with Tupac's father, Kidada walked up to them. She had just been to Tupac's room in the intensive-care unit.

Kidada declined to be interviewed by Patricia. "We're not speaking to the media," she said.

Still, Cunningham ended up driving Kidada Jones and a bodyguard to a hair salon that day.

"Kidada asked me if I knew where to buy hair products for black people," Patricia said. "I told her, yes, there were a couple of places." Kidada asked if the shops were within walking distance from the hospital or if she should take a taxi. Patricia offered to drive Kidada to the shop in Westside for the hair products. Kidada told her she also wanted to buy a CD player so she could play Tupac's music for him in his room. Billy Garland instructed one of Death Row's bodyguards to accompany Kidada.

Kidada, the unidentified bodyguard, and Patricia headed to a beauty-supply shop and an indoor swap meet. "As I sat in my van and waited for Kidada and her bodyguard to come outside from the store," Patricia said, "I thought to myself, 'No wonder Tupac got shot.' The people around him were too trusting. They weren't careful. They knew I was a radio talk-show host and a reporter, but they only knew what I told them. It occurred to me that they didn't know anything about me. I could have been anybody."

Earlier in the week, throughout the six days Tupac was in the hospital in a coma, one by one visitors filed in, past the security guards, to his room in intensive care. Once Tupac passed, no one, however, including Suge and Kidada, was allowed in.

One person Patricia did not see during the week at the hospital was Tupac's mother.

"I never saw Afeni Shakur," Cunningham said. "I was at the hospital all day for several days. I never saw her come into the hospital. I don't know when she came to see him. But it wasn't when I was there."

According to the coroner's report, it was Tupac's mother Afeni who made the decision not to revive her son. His heart kept failing and doctors kept reviving him. The decision was made that if Tupac's heart failed once again and he stopped breathing, doctors would not try to bring him back, according to the coroner's report.

Afeni Shakur explained her decision to ABC's *Prime Time Live*. "I really felt it was important for Tupac," she said, "who fought so hard, to have a free spirit. I felt it was important for his spirit to be allowed to be free. So I rejoiced with him, with the release of his spirit. I rejoiced then and I rejoice now – when I'm not crying."

Patricia Cunningham went to the hospital the day Tupac succumbed to his injuries. When she drove up, Kidada was outside, sitting on the curb, talking to Tupac's aunt. "I had my son with me," Cunningham said. "He said, 'Mom, that's Kidada Jones, Quincy Jones's daughter.' I didn't know whose daughter she was till then. We went inside. I said, 'Hi, Kidada. How're you doing?' She said, 'Okay,' but she looked angry, upset. I said, 'How is he doing today?' There's not been a change, has there?' She said, 'I don't know. I'm not allowed to say. You'll have to speak to the family about that.' She sounded like someone had pulled rank and said, 'You're just the girlfriend. You're not family.'"

Once Tupac had passed, Kidada ran outside, in tears, to the hospital parking lot. She was videotaped up by a TV cameraman running out of the hospital. "It was so sad," Patricia Cunningham said. "It broke my heart to see her like that."

As the news of his death spread across the world, more and more of Tupac's friends filed into the trauma unit. The scene inside the hospital waiting room was more than somber. Milling around the entrance, on the street and in the parking lot, was a crowd of roughly 100 or more fans. Danny Boy, a teenage rapper and rhythm-and-blues singer with the Death Row label who was said to be Suge's next hit maker and Tupac's protégé, broke down and crumbled to the sidewalk outside University Medical Center. It was in reaction to hearing the bad news that Tupac had died. Danny Boy was the only man at the hospital that day who openly wept for Tupac. He sat on the curb at the double emergency doors to the trauma unit. An unidentified friend of Tupac's sat down next to Danny Boy, put his arm over his shoulder, and tried to comfort him. Danny Boy appeared to be inconsolable.

A nurse said evening-shift employees scheduled to work that night called in sick because they were afraid to walk through the crowd. Dozens of security guards and police officers, including gang detectives, surrounded the area, but no problems ensued. Not in Las Vegas, anyway. A bloodbath had already begun, however, on the streets of Compton, California, in retaliation, police there said, for Tupac's shooting.

The driver of a black Lexus pulled up to the hospital, stopping in a no-parking zone in front of the trauma center. Danny Boy cried as he was embraced by one of several men who got out of the car.

It was Suge Knight.

When Suge was notified by telephone that Tupac had died, he was at his Vegas home, having a meeting with his bodyguards, including Frank Alexander.

Suge, six-foot-four and weighing about 300 pounds, was wearing a crisp-white T-shirt, black jeans, and brand new white-leather designer sports shoes. He was smoking a cigar. He opened the front passenger door and got out of the car. Holding the cigar in his right hand, he slowly sauntered from the curbside, strolling past Metro gang cops, fans, and a handful of reporters and photographers. After hugging Danny Boy, he walked through the automatic glass doors to the trauma center's security desk in the lobby.

Few people appeared to recognize him. They just stood quietly by and watched. His demeanor told them he was important, but they couldn't place him. Only one photographer, Marsh Starks, took a photo as Suge approached the hospital to pay his respects, first to his friend Tupac, then to Tupac's mother, Afeni. Suge looked right through the photographer, giving him a blank stare, and kept walking. His face was devoid of emotion.

Suge had the air of the linebacker and bodyguard he used to be as he somberly walked by. He appeared unconcerned for his own safety, despite rumors circulating that there were three contracts on his head and that he, not Tupac, had been the intended target of the shooter.

What no one knew then – except for the cops – was that Suge had gone earlier that day to register as a felon in the state of Nevada. As a convicted felon, he was required to tell his parole officer whenever he left California and, within 48 hours of arriving in Nevada, he was mandated by law to register with the LVMPD. On the sixth day after Tupac was gunned down and just hours before he succumbed to his wounds, Suge was fingerprinted, had his police mug shot taken, and was added to the state's convicted-felon registry. His Las Vegas attorney, David Chesnoff (law partner of mob-attorney-turned-mayor

Oscar Goodman) had called Suge to remind him that he needed to be registered.

At the hospital, Suge walked up to the security desk and told the officer on duty, who was planted at the entrance of the trauma unit, that he wanted to go to Tupac's room. The guard told him no one except family was allowed in. Suge told him he was "Marion Knight." The security officer drew a blank when he heard his name. "I'm sorry, sir. If you're not family, I can't let you in."

The guard, who was black, later told me that he didn't know at the time who Suge was. "I felt bad that I couldn't let him in," he said. "He seemed frustrated."

Suge said nothing. Then he learned from others that Tupac's body was no longer at the hospital, that it had been removed.

Radio correspondent Patricia Cunningham was inside the waiting room when Suge Knight and his entourage arrived. "Suge walked up to the security desk and he said he was Marion Knight and asked to go back [to Tupac's room]," she said. "They turned him away. Then he said, 'I'm Suge Knight.' They looked at him like, 'Who's that?' They didn't know who he was. He looked so hurt and devastated. He left."

Later, Suge talked to Afeni Shakur and told her not to worry, that he and Death Row Records would take care of her financially. He told her that he and Tupac had made a promise to each other: The family of whoever died first would be taken care of by the other.

Tupac's mother told Suge that if there was to be a memorial service, she wanted everyone to wear white, not black. Afterward, in a home-video documentary about Tupac's life titled *Thug Immortal*, Afeni said, "Tupac has gone to a better place. He's free now. Nobody can do nothing to him."

Deputy medical examiner Ed Brown was called at 4:15 p.m. by the in-charge nurse on duty and informed that Tupac Shakur had died. Ten minutes later, Doctor Brown arrived at the ICU building. He went straight to Tupac's bedside to examine him. "I found no apparent life signs, and trauma was observed to the right hand, right hip and right chest under the right arm, apparently caused from gunshots," he wrote in his report. The doctor walked outside the room to interview Afeni Shakur for his report. When he was finished, Brown returned to Tupac's private room. He tagged Tupac's toe. With the help of a nurse, he placed Tupac's nude body in a plastic body bag and sealed it with Coroner's Seal No. 855971.

But Tupac's body wasn't taken through the front entrance of the trauma center. Hospital personnel didn't want a mob scene on their hands. Instead, according to a hospital security officer on duty that afternoon, Tupac's body, on a gurney and in a body bag, was wheeled to the elevator banks in the trauma unit and taken upstairs, to the third floor. The guard said no one even noticed the gurney as attendants waited for the elevator doors to open. Once upstairs, Tupac's body was wheeled down a hallway to a parking-lot exit at the back of the hospital. From the back parking lot, an unmarked mortuary van took his body to the medical examiner's office three blocks away.

Meanwhile, upon being turned away, Suge walked toward the exit door and out of the trauma unit, unable to see Tupac one last time. He was followed by the same group of men he had arrived with. They all got into Suge's Lexus and drove away. No one spoke. Gang officers on the street appeared relieved once Suge was gone.

Word began to circulate that the coroner had used the back entrance of the hospital to remove Tupac's body. About the same time, Danny Boy walked to the front of the hospital to the driveway used by ambulances. He sat down on the curb with a friend and sobbed again. A crew member put his arm around him and comforted him. They stayed there for about 15 minutes.

Some of the fans who'd been keeping the hospital vigil left for the coroner's office, where Tupac's autopsy was about to begin.

"We had them [fans] at our back doors. We had them driving by. We had them calling. It got ridiculous," said Ron Flud, who, at that point, had been the Clark County Coroner for 13 years and, before that, had been a cop with the North Las Vegas Police Department.

Besides fans, black ministers also knocked on the coroner's office door. The coroner explained: "We had local ministers show up and say, 'Suge wanted us here.' First of all, as far as coming into the office, only the next of kin has any kind of control over the body. And the only reason you let them in is to identify the body. Tupac had already been identified [by his mother]. We're dealing with evidence, and we're very protective as to who is going to be around. Nobody goes into the autopsy except who we control. There were requests to be there from all kinds of people – medical personnel, cops, firefighters. We said, 'Why?'"

Flud, of course, would not let them or anyone else in, other than detectives and coroner's office personnel. Allowing them in was against department policy.

Reporters and photographers, meanwhile, waited outside the trauma unit for more than two hours for the hospital spokesman, Dale Pugh, to issue an official statement that Tupac had died. The media had been telephoned by Dale's office saying that Tupac had succumbed to his wounds and was dead. Reporters and photographers rushed to the hospital.

One of those waiting outside was Kevin Powell, a freelance rap journalist on assignment for *Rolling Stone* magazine. Kevin had befriended Tupac after interviewing him many times over several years. Powell looked sad as he stood by, notebook at his side, silently watching the group of mourners. Powell, a cast member on the MTV original series *The Real World* in 1992 and host and writer for MTV's documentary *Straight from the Hood*, had earlier described Tupac as his friend and said he didn't think Tupac was going to die. Powell called him tough, especially after surviving a shooting two years earlier in Manhattan. The Tupac Kevin knew was a fighter.

Reporters continued to wait, as they're accustomed to doing at crime scenes, hospitals, and courtrooms. Finally, they were told that Dale Pugh wouldn't be coming out after all. A hospital employee told me that Pugh felt he might be putting himself in danger by walking outside the hospital amid members of the press and waiting fans.

Pugh, however, later told me, "I never had a plan to come down and talk to the news media. Our decision was made. We knew how we were going to handle it if [Tupac] passed away. Our efforts were to *call* everyone in the press. We'd had so many telephone calls concerning it. The media from around the world was calling, besides [receiving] calls from fans. The hospital was deluged with calls about Tupac.

"Our main thing was to inform the local media that he had died and then return telephone calls. That's how we handled it because of the volume. I don't think we've ever in the history of this hospital held a press conference, nor will we probably ever do that. That's not the way we choose to handle that kind of thing."

Many hospitals, especially in California, hold press conferences to respond to high-volume inquiries about famous people. That way, they're responding to everyone at the same time without having to return every call. Not in Las Vegas at that time. Since then, when another celebrity, actor and model Lauren Hutton, was seriously injured in October 2000 in a motorcycle accident, the hospital set-up a hotline, with a recording giving periodic updates on her condition.

"To have celebrities here is not unusual," Dale Pugh said. "We've had [lots of them]. I remember one out-of-state politician who was here. Bob Stupak [a flamboyant casino mogul who was critically injured in a 1995 motorcycle accident] was here – that's well-known. Brent Thurman, the National Finals Rodeo rider who died, was here. In none of those instances did we hold any sort of press conference. We did individual news interviews."

As it turned out, it was a peaceful and somber crowd – mostly mourners – who stood vigil for Tupac outside the hospital that last afternoon and into the evening. No one appeared to be threatening. Cars slowly drove by the hospital as word of Tupac Shakur's death spread the news across the TV, radio and internet airwaves. Some passengers in the cars threw gang hand signs at the people standing outside, but no one reacted. Tupac's lyrics blared from car stereos.

Tupac's futile six-day battle to survive marked the end of a lifetime racked with emotional and physical struggles, first on the streets and later on the entertainment scene.

His death rocked the gangsta rap world to its core. Black leaders called for peace among the rappers, and politicians, including then-Vice President Al Gore's wife, Tipper, during a visit to Las Vegas, denounced the violence in gangsta-rap lyrics. (Tipper Gore, past head of the Parents Music Resource Council, was instrumental in creating and lobbying for Parental Advisory Stickers on CDs and tapes.)

Gang member Marcos, a friend of Tupac who declined to give his last name, made a telling statement while standing outside the University Medical Center in Las Vegas the day Tupac died. "We know who did it," he said. "I'm just saying that whoever did this is going to get found. The people who find him, I don't know what they'll do, but they'll take care of it in their own way. I mean, the pay back, it's already started." He didn't name names. The week after Tupac Shakur was shot, bullets riddled the gang-infested streets of Los Angeles, particularly Compton, as drive-by shootings broke out at a record pace. Southern California police noted 12 retaliation shootings – three deadly – the following week.

Spelled out in an affidavit written by Compton Police Detective Tim Brennan is a shot-by-shot account of a five-day bloodbath in Compton prompted by Tupac's shooting. War was declared between two notorious Compton gangs, the South Side Crips and the Mob Pirus. Both of the gangs were said to have strong ties with the Las Vegas shooting, namely Suge and Tupac with the Mob Pirus and Orlando Anderson with the South Side Crips. (Tupac always adamantly denied any gang affiliation; police have said otherwise.)

If the Compton PD's account is to be believed, on September 9, 1996, even before Tupac died, three separate Blood sects convened at Lueders Park, a gang hangout in Compton, where the plan for retaliation for Tupac's shooting was hatched. Compton police were told by their informant that five targets for drive-by shootings were chosen. At 2:58 p.m. on East Alondra, the first retaliation shooting took place; the victim was Darnell Brim, identified by police as "one of the leaders of the Southside Crips." He was shot several times, suffering injuries to his back and alleged to be one of the men in the Cadillac from which Tupac was shot. During the Alondra Street drive-by, a 10-year-old bystander, Lakezia McNeese, was shot and critically injured. She survived.

On September 10, George Mack, identified as a "Leuders Park Piru," and Johnnie Burgie, were shot in front of 713 North Bradfield Street, a known hangout for Pirus. They both survived. Also on September 10, Gary Williams, brother of former Death Row Records security employee George Williams, was shot while on the corner of Pino and Bradfield streets. He, too, survived his wounds.

On September 11, Bobby Finch was shot to death while standing outside a house on South Mayo. Compton Police told Las Vegas detectives that Finch was believed to be a passenger in the Cadillac from which Tupac was fatally injured. Finch, not a gang member himself, was a bodyguard who grew up in the same neighborhood as the Southside Crips, according to Compton Police Captain Danny Sneed.

On September 13, Tyrone Lipscomb and David McKulin were shot at while in front of 802 South Ward. They both survived. The suspects in this case, Compton police said, were believed to be members of the Bloods. Also on September 13, Mitchell Lewis, Apryle Murph, and Frederick Boykin were shot while in front of 121 North Chester. All three survived. Three Bloods members were alleged to have done the shooting while on foot.

All the shootings, as outlined in the Compton PD's affidavit, were believed to be retaliatory acts following Tupac's Las Vegas shooting.

Two months later, the lone witness to the shooting, Yafeu Fula, was murdered in New Jersey. Six months later, East Coast superstar rapper Biggie Smalls, under contract to Bad Boy Entertainment, rival to Death Row Records, was shot to death in a drive-by shooting in Los Angeles that was eerily similar to the one that claimed Tupac's life.

Meanwhile, Death Row Records, Tupac's label, started to unravel. Suge Knight, CEO of Death Row, jailed two months after Tupac's shooting for a parole violation, was sentenced to nine years in prison for his role in the fight with Orlando Anderson at the MGM Grand just hours before Tupac was shot. At the time, the FBI and IRS were looking into Death Row's books and its associations. In the aftermath, the slayings of the two hottest hip-hop stars stirred criticism of the rap world and made record companies uneasy, but the murders didn't hurt sales or deter fans; it was just the opposite. Both Tupac and Biggie's final albums went to No. 1 on *Billboard*'s record charts. Tupac's last album *Makaveli* and Biggie's album *Life After Death...'Til Death Do Us Part*, both released posthumously, broke all-time sales records, generating talk that the two rap superstars were worth more dead than alive.

The latest retaliation shooting occurred April 3, 2002 when Alton "Bungry" McDonald, 37, a former production manager for Death Row Records, was shot to death as he filled up his car at a Shell gas station in Compton. A truck pulled up and one or more people got out and opened fire. McDonald was hit several times in his upper body and died at St. Francis Medical Center in Lynwood. The killers got away. Police found large-caliber handgun casings around the gas pumps. In the hours following the shooting, the Los Angeles County Sheriff's Department sent a gang-enforcement team to search for suspects and stem further violence. Authorities said a man who had been with McDonald ran from the scene. The car McDonald was driving at the time of the shooting was registered to a former Compton police officer, Reggie White, who reportedly served as head of security for Suge Knight. McDonald was in the entourage the night Tupac was gunned down in Las Vegas. He was also involved in the videotaped brawl at the MGM Grand hours before Tupac was killed and could be seen in the footage dressed in white.

All the while, Las Vegas police continued to investigate Tupac Shakur's murder. But critics, including Tupac's mother, her attorney, and witnesses, complained about the LVMPD's handling of the case from the first moments following the shooting.

3

THE SCUFFLE

THE MIKE TYSON-Bruce Seldon match was supposed to begin at eight o'clock sharp that Saturday night, September 7, but it started about 15 minutes late. Then, Tyson knocked out Seldon in the first round in less than two minutes.

Tupac Shakur, Suge Knight, and two others who attended the fight, met up with the rest of their entourage outside the MGM Grand Garden's doors, where the match was held. The group walked out of the arena and into the casino. Tupac was spotted leaving the Grand Garden by freelance video cameraman Cornell Wade, who worked for a Las Vegas-based video services company that was filming celebrities for TV shows. That night Wade was contracted by Black Entertainment Television (BET). The BET reporter Wade was working with had trouble getting out of the crowded arena. And as the cameraman stood outside the exit waiting for her, he recognized Tupac as he walked through the turnstiles and out of the arena.

Wade was in the midst of interviewing Louis Gossett Jr. when he spotted Tupac. Unlike Gossett, Tupac wasn't one of the celebrities Wade was assigned to film. But he thought to himself, *What the heck. I'll [film] him anyway.* He wrapped up his interview with Gossett and walked a few steps toward Tupac. He said, "I'm with Black Entertainment Television. Can I ask you about the fight?"

"Sure. No problem, man. Go ahead," Tupac replied as his record producer, Suge Knight, stood quietly in the background, behind him.

Wade put a mike in front of Tupac and switched on the camera. "What'd you think of tonight's match?" Wade asked.

Tupac looked straight into the camera lens and said, "Did y'all see that? Fifty punches. I counted. Fifty punches. I knew he was gonna take him out. We bad like that – come outta prison and now we runnin' shit."

It was the last interview of Tupac's life.

Later, when the reporter learned that Tupac had been at the Tyson fight and had been shot afterward, she commented to Wade, "I wish we would have gotten video of him."

"I did," Wade told her. "I got it." He handed the tape over to BET, even though he undoubtedly could have sold it to the TV tabloids for an exorbitant price. The short interview aired for several days on an untold number of national TV news programs.

At 8:45 p.m., as Tupac, Suge, and their friends were winding their way through the casino on their way to the street, they ran into Orlando Tive Anderson, from Compton, California. A fist fight broke out.

Exactly what had precipitated the fight is still not completely known. But there were rumors that Anderson, also known as "Little Lando" and "Land," had tried to grab a large gold medallion with the Death Row Records insignia from the neck of one of Tupac's friend. As a result of whatever prompted the beef, Tupac and the group jumped Anderson. There were also reports that Tupac and Orlando had exchanged heated words earlier in the evening, inside the Grand Garden as they waited for the bout to begin, and that they caused the beef outside. Anderson and his friends were said to be sitting in the front-row seats reserved for Tupac and Suge when the entourage walked in to watch the fight. (Those rumors later proved to be false when Orlando could not produce a ticket stub for police and told them he had come to Las Vegas "to gamble." There was no evidence that Orlando had been inside the Grand Garden Arena.)

Hotel security guards quickly converged on the scene and broke up the altercation with Anderson and broke it up.

After the run-in, Tupac and his crew hurriedly left the scene while an unnamed MGM Grand security guard called in Las Vegas police, already on premises to work the fight. The officers talked to the security guard and the victim (Orlando), whose identity they didn't establish. The cops offered to take the then-unnamed victim to the MGM Grand's basement security office to fill out a police incident report and sign a complaint. But Orlando said no. He told them he was okay and didn't want to press charges. Because he refused, and appeared to be uninjured except for some bruises, the officers did not even write down his name before letting him go.

In the state of Nevada, if a victim of a crime declines to file a report, police can let the victim go. That's the law. But if they think there's probable cause to pursue the case – based on visible injuries, for example – they may file a police report. In this case, they chose not to.

Metro Police Lieutenant Wayne Petersen defended security's failure to identify the victim. "No victim, no crime," he explained. "In a misdemeanor battery like this one, if the victim chooses not to fill out a crime report, we can't force him to. It's not unusual at all. It happens all the time. And we certainly aren't going to generate more work for ourselves and take a report if the victim is not willing to cooperate. In court, to prosecute, you have to have the victim's testimony."

But in this case, a bigger crime may have been avoided by pursuing the case and questioning Orlando Anderson further: Anderson is widely believed to be the shooter in Tupac's murder.

The scuffle between Tupac and Anderson was captured on MGM Grand security videotape. The murky recording shows seven to eight men – Tupac, Suge, their paid bodyguards, and other members of the entourage – throwing the then-unidentified black man to the casino floor, then stomping on and beating him.

"They kicked the holy shit out of him," said a police source who viewed the entire unedited version of the surveillance videotape. "They beat him up pretty bad."

But because the original videotape was grainy and indistinct, it was difficult to tell exactly what was going on, according to homicide Detective Brent Becker. "It's like a pile of people," he said.

On Wednesday, September 11, Metro Police issued a third news release. It said:

"The LVMPD homicide investigators have viewed a surveillance tape provided by the MGM Grand. The tape depicts an altercation between Tupac Shakur, some of his associates, and an unknown person. The altercation was broken up by security. Shakur and his people left the area. The unknown person was then interviewed by MGM security and LVMPD patrol officers.

"The unknown person was asked if he wished to file a report, but he declined. It does not appear that the person or the patrol officers knew that Shakur was the other person in the altercation. The unknown person was still with security and patrol officers when Shakur and his associates left the building.

"Investigators have no reason, at this time, to believe that the altercation has any connection to the [Tupac] shooting.

"The videotape will not be released since it appears to have no evidentiary value to the shooting incident."

No "evidentiary value" just hours before a homicide shooting? In retrospect, the decision was premature and possibly, indeed, evidentiary. The tape, in fact, was later released, made public, and used against Suge Knight to put him in prison for violation of parole.

Why didn't the police and security officers detain Tupac Shakur and members of his entourage for questioning after the attack on Orlando Anderson? Though the official statement denies it, surely those first on the scene knew that Tupac was involved. Was it Suge and Tupac's celebrity status that allowed them to walk away from an obvious crime? Was it Suge's business connection to Metro? After all, off-duty Metro officers at that very moment were being paid time-and-a-half wages by Death Row to patrol Suge's house and club. Later, just 15 minutes before the shooting, Suge would again be treated preferentially when he was stopped, but not cited, for failure to display a license plate on his car and for playing his music too loudly. Did the polite police behavior stem from the fear of offending a celebrity? Police say no.

Contrary to the claim in the police news bulletin that the videotape would not be released, it was subsequently relinquished by LVMPD. While continuing to adamantly deny the beating was related to Tupac's homicide, detectives released the tape to Fox's *America's Most Wanted* TV show. Later, it was subpoenaed by the Los Angeles Superior Court for Suge Knight's parole-violation proceedings, where it became public record.

Another surveillance tape shows an agitated Tupac and his friends storming through the casino at the MGM Grand. Suge can be seen running behind Tupac, trying to catch up, with members of their entourage following behind. Tupac is seen slamming his hand against an MGM glass entrance door as he angrily leaves the casino for the valet area.

After the existence of the surveillance tapes became widely known to the media, Sergeant Manning dismissed the scuffle, saying, "It appears to be just an individual who was walking through the MGM and got into an argument with Tupac. The man probably didn't know who he was dealing with. He probably didn't know it was Tupac Shakur." Later, of course, we found out differently.

The victim "wasn't dressed like everyone else," an investigator said. "The subject was wearing a ball club shirt, like a team jersey, and wasn't dressed up like Shakur and his group." In other words, he didn't look like he fit in with Tupac and his flashy West Coast crew, who were wearing expensive clothes and jewelry.

At some point, and privately, the investigators changed their thinking. The videotape of the scuffle became evidence. What had been a minor fight-night encounter turned into an event of enormous significance in the grand scheme of the investigation.

"Any of those incidents leading up to Tupac's death obviously are of interest from an investigative standpoint," Lieutenant Peterson later said. "[But] we don't have a case. We've got no evidence linking [Orlando Anderson] to this [murder]."

The surveillance videotape was forwarded to the evidence vault for storage several months after the murder.

After the shooting, homicide detectives scrambled to learn the identity of the victim in the MGM Grand altercation by talking to the officers who responded that night. Only the man's first name, "Orlando," could be recalled. That was enough, according to police. How the first name of a young black man could have been enough information for Metro detectives to contact the Compton Police Department with wasn't revealed and is still unclear. Perhaps they had more than just his first name. Compton police gang officers were able to give Las Vegas police the name of "Orlando Anderson" and shared information that Anderson was allegedly tied to the Los Angeles Southside Crip street gang. Police in Compton quickly dispatched a photo of Orlando, a mug shot from their files. The photo was shown to the officers and security guards working at the MGM Grand on September 7 to see if they could identify him. They could. They positively identified Orlando Anderson as the victim of the beating.

Just as the MGM Grand hotel videotape was obtained by LVMPD, investigators could have easily confiscated videotape from Excalibur, where Compton police say Orlando Anderson stayed that weekend. Detectives could have viewed surveillance videotape from the Excalibur parking garage to see whether Orlando was captured getting in or out of a white Cadillac. Or they could have looked to see who Orlando, in town, police say, with fellow gang members from Compton, was hanging out with and what cars they were getting around in. Las Vegas police didn't do any of that.

The vibe Compton police were getting from LVMPD homicide detectives was that they, for whatever reason, weren't interested in solving Tupac's murder. A raid that took place just four days after the shooting confirmed, police say, Compton officers' suspicions that Orlando was involved in some way.

It happened like this. On Wednesday, September 11, Los Angeles-area police raided a Compton house, responding to reports that the men inside had weapons. When officers arrived, they found Orlando Anderson and four other alleged Crips members standing in the front yard of the house. Anderson reportedly ran inside, followed closely by police. Upon questioning, he claimed he didn't live at that address, that he lived next door, even though police said a high school diploma bearing his name hung on a bedroom wall. Inside, investigators discovered an AK-47 assault rifle, a .38-caliber revolver, two shotguns, a 9-millimeter M-11 assault pistol, and ammunition. Police confiscated the weapons. But because Orlando insisted he didn't live in the house and police had no real evidence to prove otherwise, they let him go.

Even so, in the days following, police began focusing on Orlando Anderson as a possible suspect in Tupac's murder, as well as in an unrelated L.A.-area killing. Both Las Vegas and Compton police said they'd received several tips accusing Orlando of being connected to the Las Vegas crime. One tip, given to Compton police on September 13, held that a reputed member of the Bloods identified the man who shot Tupac as Orlando Anderson.

An affidavit signed by Compton Police Detective Tim Brennan, dated September 25, 1996, and unsealed in February 1997 in Los Angeles Superior Court, read: "Informants have told police that Southside Crips were responsible for the Las Vegas shooting [of Shakur]. There is also an ongoing feud between Tupac Shakur and the Bloods-related Death Row Records with rapper Biggie Smalls and the East Coast's Bad Boy Entertainment, which employed Southside Crips gang members as security."

Bad Boy Entertainment has adamantly denied it hired Crips members.

"We have no knowledge of security being provided by Crips or other gang members," Bad Boy spokeswoman Maureen Connelly said in a released statement. "Bad Boy Entertainment employs full-time security personnel and they [are] supplemented by off-duty members of the Los Angeles police force."

The accusations by Compton police were damning evidence against Orlando. Even so, he remained free. And Orlando, through his attorney, denied any involvement. Edi M.O. Faal, Rodney King's one-time attorney, represented Orlando. Although he admitted Orlando was the man assaulted at the MGM Grand by Tupac and his entourage, Faal denied that his client had any involvement in Tupac's murder.

Anderson also strongly denied any connection to Tupac's death. But Compton police remained convinced and unwavering that Shakur's murder was the result of a Bloods-Crips feud. What was frustrating, Compton police sources say, is having evidence against Orlando and watching LVMPD detectives ignore it.

In mid September 1996, Los Angeles police organized a massive predawn sweep of Bloods and Crips neighborhoods – in Lakewood, Long Beach, Compton, and L.A. It was a 45-location gang sweep. The action would go down two weeks later, in October. The raid was organized after three people were killed in 12 shootings in the Compton area the week following the Tupac shooting, Compton Police Captain Steven Roller told reporters. He described the violence as possible retaliation for Tupac's murder.

As part of the operation, Los Angeles and Compton police mapped out an early morning raid, which included plans to serve a search warrant at Orlando Anderson's house. Las Vegas homicide detectives Brent Becker and Mike Franks were notified and invited to be there so they could question Orlando. They arrived in L.A. the day before the raid.

On October 2, approximately 300 Los Angeles-area police and federal agents, most clad in riot gear – black masks, helmets, combat boots, and bullet-resistant vests – raided 37 homes, including Anderson's. LVMPD Detective Becker talked with Orlando Anderson outside the house he shared with relatives, while Los Angeles-area police searched inside the house.

Becker, sitting in his car while Anderson stood nearby, said he talked casually with the young Compton resident about the MGM surveillance tape of the scuffle between Tupac, Suge, and other Death Row Records associates. Becker told me he questioned Orlando only about the scuffle at the MGM the night Tupac was shot, and said he didn't touch on the homicide that followed.

Later in a CNN interview, Orlando accused Las Vegas police, specifically Detective Becker, of telling him he was a suspect in Tupac's murder. "I want to let everybody know – you know what I'm sayin'? – I didn't do it," told CNN. "I been thinkin' that maybe I'm a scapegoat or somethin'."

Appearing on CNN with Orlando, his lawyer Edi Faal said, "This young man is almost acting like a prisoner now. He is very careful where he goes. He is very careful when he goes out."

Becker and his supervisors maintained that Anderson was merely asked about the fight that was captured on the casino surveillance tapes, and that Orlando was reading more into the encounter with Becker than was there. Becker later said it must have been his simply talking with a Las Vegas detective that had made Orlando nervous.

LVMPD homicide Lieutenant Wayne Petersen defended Becker and strongly denied Anderson's allegation. "When Brent went to Los Angeles to talk to Anderson, he asked Anderson questions only about the fight at the MGM," Petersen insisted. "He never asked him about the homicide. If he wanted to ask him questions about the homicide, he would have had to read him his Miranda rights." Becker told Petersen that "Anderson asked [him] if he was going to take him back to Vegas, and Becker's response was, 'Why should I?'"

The Los Angeles police raid of gang houses netted 23 arrests, including Anderson's, on various weapons and drug-possession charges. Also confiscated from one of those arrested was a Death Row pendant (it has yet to be revealed by police which suspect the pendant was taken from). Orlando Anderson was held for questioning in connection with a 1994 murder, as well as for questioning by Las Vegas Metro police about the scuffle at MGM. But Compton police said they didn't have enough evidence on the 1994 gang-related murder to hold Anderson. He was released the next day without being charged.

LVMPD detectives, too, had decided not to charge Orlando Anderson with a murder, this one of Tupac Shakur.

The scuffle at the MGM Grand had serious legal ramifications and repercussions for Suge Knight. He ended up being charged with a serious infraction of probation for an earlier conviction.

On October 18, 1996, a warrant for Suge's arrest was issued for failing to submit to periodic drug tests, one of the conditions of his probation.

On Tuesday, October 22, 1996, 45 days after the Tyson-Seldon and Shakur-Anderson fights, Suge surrendered to Los Angeles police for violating probation, to which he was sentenced in 1995 after pleading no contest to assaulting two rappers at a Hollywood recording studio. (In 1992, brothers George and Stanley Lynwood, two aspiring rappers, used a telephone at Suge's studio without first asking permission. Suge walked in and caught them. He beat one of them with a gun, and threatened to kill them both. He also forced the brothers to remove their pants. The Lynwoods filed a police complaint against Knight. Suge was convicted on assault charges and sentenced to probation.) Suge was jailed without bail. In early November, he was in court to answer charges that his involvement in the MGM Grand altercation was also a violation of his probation.

The small neighborhood of Compton, a largely African-American suburb in South Central Los Angeles, is where Suge Knight grew up (the youngest of three, with two older sisters) and where, cops say, he became affiliated with the Bloods street gang. Suge sports a tattoo that reads "M.O.B." which some say stands for "Member of the Bloods"; others say its for "Money Over Bitches" (one of Knight's known mottos); still others say it stands, simply, for "Mob," as in the Mafia. The letters "M.O.B." also coincide with numbers 662 on a telephone number pad. The significance is in the name Club 662, the nightspot Tupac and Suge were heading to the night of the deadly shooting.

After Orlando Anderson's October arrest in the L.A. gang sweep, several people who were arrested with him told Compton police that Suge had been the intended target.

In an affidavit filed November 5, 1996, with Los Angeles Superior Court Judge J. Stephen Czuleger, probation officer Barry Nodorf recommended that Knight's probation remain revoked, and that the defendant remain locked up pending a formal violation hearing.

Judge Czuleger viewed the MGM Grand security videotape in his courtroom. The tape shows a man identified as Suge Knight pushing down another man and kicking him.

"There are compelling reasons to believe that another probation violation has occurred," probation officer Nodorf said in his seven-page report.

"This fact, coupled with the defendant's potential threat to the community and the possibility of his being a flight risk, leaves the probation officer with no alternative but to make the recommendation" that the defendant remain in jail, where he would spend four months awaiting the hearing's outcome, he said.

Suge's attorney, David Kenner, denounced the report. "The allegation that Suge Knight beat someone up at the MGM is meritless," Kenner told reporters.

Knight is visible on the tape, but his actions are obscured by other people and objects. According to Nodorf, however, a hotel security guard identified Knight as one of the aggressors in the scuffle. Suge said he was trying to "break up the rumble."

His assertion, oddly enough, was backed by Orlando Anderson, who testified during Suge's probation violation hearing that Suge was the only one who helped him that night. Earlier, however, in another court proceeding, Anderson identified Suge as one of those *involved* in the scuffle. When pressed, Orlando couldn't give a reason why he flip-flopped his testimony, later naming Suge as the one who came to his rescue.

Had someone gotten to Orlando? If so, was it Suge? That's what investigators speculated. but wouldn't say for the record and never produced any evidence thereof. Someone, they privately surmised, was persuasive enough with Orlando to make him do an about-face in his sworn testimony. Suge Knight sat in the defendant's chair with a smile on his face while Anderson testified.

The judge was not impressed. He sentenced Suge to nine years in state prison

4

THE INVESTIGATION

AS FAR BACK as anyone in the Las Vegas Metropolitan Police Department can remember, the Tupac Shakur murder case is the biggest Las Vegas has ever seen. (Since then, the Ted Binion homicide case is said to be one of the largest and most notorious; that, and mob cases before it.) Even though it's one of the largest and most highly publicized, the killing of Tupac Shakur will no doubt never be solved. Even the former lieutenant of the homicide section, Wayne Petersen, who took over the homicide bureau shortly after Tupac died, does not believe the murderer will be captured, nor will the case ever be prosecuted.

It's an investigation the LVMPD probably wishes never came its way, for more reasons than the obvious; the murder of a famous young man. The handling of the investigation has been criticized from start to finish by participants and observers alike who contend the police haven't done everything they could or should have.

According to authorities, it has not been for a lack of effort, but rather, for lack of cooperation from just about everyone involved: witnesses, Tupac's friends and associates, Suge Knight, and even police from other departments and jurisdictions.

Back in 1996, seven homicide teams – made up of a sergeant and two detectives – rotated on an on-call basis at Metro. Each three-man team investigated an average of 25 murder cases a year. (Tupac's was one of 207 homicides within the Las Vegas valley and one of 168 within the jurisdiction of the Las Vegas police that year. The 1996 numbers marked a record year for the highest number of homicides ever for the valley, up 38 percent from the 150 total cases the year before. In LVMPD's jurisdiction, which includes Las Vegas and unincorporated areas of Clark

County, there was a 25 percent jump – from 1995's 134 to 1996's 168 cases.) The night Tupac was shot, the team on call consisted of Sergeant Kevin Manning, Detective Brent Becker, and then-active Detective Mike Franks, all veteran investigators but not veteran homicide cops.

Brent Becker worked in the robbery section before being moved to the homicide bureau. At the time of Tupac's murder, he'd been working the homicide detail for about two years. His partner, Mike Franks, had been working in homicide for four years. Before that, Franks had worked in the narcotics unit with Manning. (Mike Franks retired in February 2001, at 53-years-old, after 30 years on the force, many of them spent tracking the mob and trying to solve murder cases.) In a record homicide year, the Tupac murder case would prove to be one of the most remarkable the team had ever seen. Sergeant Manning, early in his police career, was a part of LVMPD's first street narcotics unit. He'd also worked in the gang detail. When Tupac was shot, Manning, although he'd had experience as a supervisor in other units, had been a homicide sergeant for just a year-and-a-half.

The Clark County Sheriff's Department merged with Metro in 1973 and became the Las Vegas Metropolitan Police Department, or LVMPD. Franks and Manning had been hired by Metro and Becker by the sheriff's department before the two departments merged.

"Brent was one of my trainees [at Metro] when I was a training officer," Manning said. "I worked with Mike in narcotics. We're all friends."

Overseeing the Shakur murder investigation was Lieutenant Wayne Petersen, who joined the Las Vegas Metropolitan Police Department on August 27, 1979. Petersen was promoted to sergeant in 1988 and served stints in patrol and the detective bureau before moving to Criminal Intelligence for two-and-a-half years. There, in 1994, he was promoted to lieutenant. In late 1996, shortly after the Tupac shooting, Petersen was put in charge of the homicide section. During his tenure there, he oversaw the investigations of 600 homicides, including Tupac's. In November 2001, at 47, he left the homicide unit after five years for the department's traffic bureau.

The homicide bureau at the LVMPD are a somewhat casual bunch.

It's an elite group; working homicide is a sought-after assignment. But Las Vegas detectives don't dress the part. They don't wear white shirts, neckties, and black slacks like many of their counterparts in other cities. Here in the desert, they're more likely to be seen wearing golf shirts and Dockers.

Manning, Becker, and Franks were called to the scene at Las Vegas Boulevard and Harmon Avenue about an hour-and-a-half after the shooting. The homicide lieutenant at the time, Larry Spinosa, was out of town; otherwise he would have been there too.

In the days and weeks following the homicide, the team interviewed a couple of dozen people who were friends or associates of Tupac, some of whom were part of the entourage, and they talked to "literally thousands of people" about the case, Manning said.

Throughout the investigation, police say, witnesses uniformly refused to cooperate. The detectives were frustrated from the very beginning, stunned by the number of witnesses who claimed not to have seen the assailants, or anything else for that matter.

The witness statements were pretty similar: "I didn't see nothin'. I didn't know nobody. I wasn't even there," Lieutenant Wayne Petersen commented, mocking the language.

No one on East Flamingo Road that night, including Suge Knight, admitted to seeing anything that aided investigators in their efforts to find the killer or accomplices. Police assumed that Suge, who was driving the car and sitting next to Tupac, would probably be their best eyewitness. They were wrong.

Petersen said, "He's obviously a prime witness in this, also a victim, and we've gotten no cooperation from him. We believe we know who's responsible for this. The problem we have with this case is we don't have anyone willing to come forward and testify to it. The gangsta-rap mentality that they don't want to talk to police is definitely hurting this case."

Sergeant Kevin Manning agreed. "He doesn't care. It's the code of that mentality. They just don't care."

"Every September," Lieutenant Petersen said later, "on the anniversary of Tupac's death, worldwide media call asking what's going on with the case. I always have to tell them, 'Nothing.' We had a lot of people in position to see a lot of stuff, and all we ever had was a description of a hand sticking out of a window with a gun. None of them wanted to be seen as cooperating with the police."

When Suge Knight was asked by an ABC *Prime Time Live* reporter whether he would tell the police who killed Tupac if he knew who it was, he answered slowly, but directly, "Ab-so-lute-ly not. I mean, because I don't know. It's not my job. I don't get paid to solve homicides. I don't get paid to tell on people."

"There's a potential for God knows how many witnesses that night," Lieutenant Petersen commented. "It was a Saturday night. It was a fight night. It was close to the Strip. How many hundreds of people were at that intersection? Say there were a hundred. Nobody was able to provide us with an accurate description of the shooter and the vehicle? The best anyone on the scene could tell investigators was that the Cadillac was light-colored, probably white.

"Most of the witnesses said the car was white. How many white Cadillacs are there in this town?"

Investigators were also given what they called "misinformation" by "unreliable sources" who said that everyone in the Cadillac was wearing masks. But that didn't correspond with what the lone cooperative witness, Yafeu Fula, told police in a brief interview immediately after the shooting. Yafeu said the gunman's face was not covered.

Early in the Shakur investigation, Sergeant Manning told a reporter, "The shooting was not a random act of violence."

But that's about all investigators seemed sure of. Perhaps most frustrating, the members of the entourage were close-mouthed about the shooting, claiming they saw only the Cadillac and not the assailants. Several bodyguards were in the group, and their lack of detailed information took LVMPD investigators by surprise. After all, they were being paid to protect Tupac and Suge.

"It amazes me," Manning said, "when they have professional bodyguards who can't even give us an accurate description of the vehicle.

You'd think a personal bodyguard would have seen something. It's a murder, and the people closest to the scene should be able to help us, but they say they didn't see anything. So far they haven't enlightened us as to a suspect or a motive, and that's the bottom line."

The night of the shooting, about eight detectives were on the scene, Petersen said, including general-assignment detectives, a watch commander, and patrol officers "trying to deal with the mass of witnesses and the large crime scene." One crime-scene analyst was called because "it was an attempted homicide," said Lieutenant Brad Simpson, who oversees Metro's criminalistics section. "[Tupac] didn't die right away, or we would have sent two technicians. We approached it as an attempted homicide, so we only sent one senior crime-scene analyst."

That's not how it usually works, Simpson said. "On average," he explained, "there are a minimum of two, probably three, criminalists on a homicide scene. One is a crime-scene supervisor and one a senior crime-scene analyst, which means they've been on [the job] for at least four years. Their job is to collect the forensics evidence. In the Tupac Shakur case, they would look at the bullet holes in the vehicle, the trajectory of the bullet holes hitting the car and him, blood-splatter evidence, which shows the direction of high-velocity wounds. They would photograph the crime scene, taking overall views. They would probably go back within a week to take an aerial shot to get a better perspective of what's going on. They would diagram the crime scene."

An aerial photograph, however, was never taken. (Aerial photos are used for court. If there's an arrest, photos of the street will be taken from a helicopter. The police didn't take an aerial photo that night "because it was dark," Sergeant Manning said.)

A Metro K-9 (canine) team was dispatched to the Strip and Harmon Avenue to search for a gun police believed may have been thrown into the center divider. Later that night, however, they learned that the shooting had actually taken place a mile away. So the dogs were sniffing for 15 minutes in the wrong place at the wrong scene. A helicopter (LVMPD had three at the time) wasn't used in the investigation to search for the shooter's Cadillac. By the time the police realized where the shooting had taken place, too much time had elapsed to dispatch a helicopter. They figured the getaway car was long gone.

When investigators learned that the gunman had fled south on Koval Lane, detectives checked to see if any shootings had occurred in that area; there were no reports of any. And no fights or disturbances were reported involving black men in a Cadillac.

A Nevada Highway Patrol sergeant and six troopers arrived at Harmon where Suge's BMW had come to a halt, blocking the Las Vegas Strip to through traffic.

"We got a call that shots were fired on the Strip that there was a shooting in progress," Nevada Highway Patrol trooper Steve Harney said. "When we first arrived, we shut everything down. We have to shut everything down in case there are any bad guys around."

Ironically, Suge's route had taken the BMW almost all the way back to the MGM Grand where, because of the Tyson-Seldon fight, state troopers' presence was already heavy.

"Look at how many additional people were there because of the fight. So many officers responded because there were hundreds working that night. We have what's called an operational plan," Harney said. "Any time there's a major event on the Strip, the hotels involved hire additional officers, and we provide traffic control. When there's a shooting, it's a simultaneous notification to Metro and the highway patrol. We stayed on all night."

Bicycle patrol officer Michael McDonald, who at the time was working the swing shift as a LVMPD cop and served as an elected Las Vegas City Councilman by day, was called to the scene as backup. "We rolled on it as soon as we heard they had a shooting going on," McDonald explained. Officer McDonald and his partner, Eric Holyoak, were on the north end of the Strip near the Circus Circus casino.

"I was at a car stop," McDonald said. "You just start rolling. You don't have time to think about it. I didn't even finish the stop. I gave [the driver] his stuff back, his license and registration, said 'See you later, bye,' and I was outta there."

He said officers knew right away that it was Tupac Shakur bleeding to death inside the BMW.

By the time McDonald had arrived on the scene a few minutes after the BMW stopped, "the whole cavalry had arrived," McDonald said. "There must have been 30 or 40 patrol cars. When we got there, the ambulances were just leaving."

"I had to calm the bodyguards down," McDonald continued. "They were saying, 'Man, we have to go to the hospital with Pac.' They were freaking out. Their friend had just been shot. They were upset. I talked to them. I told them that if they didn't calm down, the cops were going to have to cuff them and take them in. I made sure they didn't mingle. The detectives don't want the witnesses to speak to each other. I told them, 'You guys have to understand, the quicker you talk to the detectives, the quicker you're outta here.' I said, 'You can do this here or you can do this downtown.' They calmed down. After the detectives talked to them, they all jumped in their cars and went to the hospital.

"They were in three cars. Their cars were parked in the middle of the street, right next to the median. When the BMW came to rest, it was in the middle of the intersection at Harmon and the Boulevard. It was facing kind of southeast, turned to the left, cocked, like Knight was in the middle of making a left turn when he was stopped. It had four flat tires. The rims were bent from going over the curbs."

No one knows where Suge was trying to head by attempting a left turn onto Harmon from the Strip.

Dispatch had called detectives from general assignment to investigate before a homicide team was called in. General assignment detectives arrived and tried to interview the witnesses. But the scene was chaotic. Everyone on the street knew it was Tupac. He was easily recognized by music and film fans. A large crowd had gathered. People had begun charging the car, trying to rip off the side-view mirrors, wire-rimmed hubcaps, door handles – anything they could grab. The cops yelled at them to get back and threatened to arrest anyone who got near the car. A few officers had to physically keep people back. At the very least, it was the scene of an attempted homicide and the car held crucial evidence. The police, including officers McDonald and Holyoak, secured the perimeter, protecting the crime scene, until investigators and the lone crime analyst were finished working it.

Malcolm Payne, chief photographer for the *Herald Dispatch* newspaper in South Central Los Angeles, was on assignment in Las Vegas covering the Tyson fight. He had returned to his hotel room at the Aladdin Hotel across the street from where the BMW came to a stop. He looked out his window to the street scene below.

"I saw the yellow tape and police and realized there had to be a murder or something," he said. "I grabbed my camera and went down there."

When he got to the street, he asked what had happened. "A little boy told me, 'Tupac got killed.' He said, 'That's the car he was riding in.'

"Immediately, what went through my head was the scene out of 'Bonnie and Clyde.' The car was all shot up. I said to myself that this was history and I was going to shoot it. So I pulled out my camera and started taking pictures. Tupac was like a legend, and it was his last ride, you know?"

Payne began shooting photos of the car, riddled with bullet holes, and of the witnesses from Tupac's entourage as they were being interviewed by detectives. Yellow crime-scene tape separated the witnesses from the crowd gathered on the street. The street was closed; police had blocked off the Strip to through traffic.

"The ambulance was gone," Payne said. "I got a shot of some of the guys [Tupac's entourage]. They were upset. I shot them sitting on the sidewalk. The police had them blocked off with yellow tape. They kept them there for quite some time, at least two hours. Their cars were right there, on the side [of the road].

"When I got there the street was blocked off. You had plainclothes, uniforms, and the guys who ride around Vegas on bicycles. And they'd brought out a dog team. Somebody told them the gun was thrown out in the median, so they had the dogs out searching in the median for the gun. It seemed like the police were trying to do a thorough investigation at that crime scene. They were really trying to find the gun. They were tearing that car up too."

Payne turned out to be the only still photographer at the crime scene. The police took photographs, but theirs weren't for public consumption, and have since been locked away in a file cabinet inside LVMPD's photo lab with a "420" [murder] label.

When the detectives arrived, then-officer Michael McDonald said, they investigated three different scenes: the location of the shooting at Flamingo and Koval; the spot where Suge made the left turn from Flamingo onto the Strip; and the center divider where Suge's car stopped for good. They also backtracked to make sure there weren't any bullet casings strewn elsewhere.

"Everybody locked down the scene. When you know it's a blatant homicide, you lock the scene down till detectives can get there. You put cones over the casings, cordon off the crime scene, put the tape up, keep witnesses from talking to each other. We were there for hours, way into overtime," McDonald said.

Once the street was reopened to one lane, officers stopped some drivers to question them. They were looking for witnesses. They found none. Reports that cops were stopping only black male drivers were untrue, said Nevada Highway Patrol Trooper Steve Harney and LVMPD bike cop Michael McDonald, both of whom were there when motorists were being stopped. "We do not do that," state Trooper Harney said. "When we did stop people to question them, we stopped everybody. It wasn't just black male adults. We treat everybody the same."

Unlike the location where the BMW came to rest, the shooting scene at Flamingo and Koval in front of the Maxim hotel wasn't secured right away, police said.

"It made it tougher to investigate," Sergeant Kevin Manning later admitted. "Within a relatively short period of time, that scene was secured enough so that there was still evidence present. But if any of it had been moved, like cars hitting it, how do we know?"

State trooper Steve Harney added, "You've got to understand, when it's a shooting, unless it's in a house, if you're on an interstate or a busy street, you're not going to have as much preservation of evidence."

When the K-9 unit arrived, the officer and his dog went to work a mile away, where Suge and Tupac ended up, *not* at the crime scene where the shooting actually had taken place. At that point, police were under the wrong impression that the gunfire had erupted on the Strip. Had police immediately talked with members of Tupac's entourage, they might have told them that the Cadillac had fled, and which way it had gone. But by the time the general assignment detectives arrived and began questioning witnesses, not only had enough time gone by for the Cadillac to flee without a trace, but the entourage members were irate.

Detectives were surprised when Tupac's friends who'd witnessed the shooting wouldn't talk. They weren't willing to give up any information at all after the patrol cops had thrown them face down on the street's blacktop. They made it very clear afterward that they were angry with the way officers had treated them. Though Metro police called it "standard procedure," when its officers treated potential witnesses to the highest profile murder case in the history of the department like suspected criminals, they forever alienated the all-important members of the entourage, including Suge Knight. All hope of establishing cooperation from the witnesses vanished within those first few minutes. Las Vegas police gained nothing and lost everything.

Suge Knight described the actions of police toward him that night like this: "The police jacked me up like a '57 Chevy." Needless to say, Suge wasn't talking either.

Detectives eventually questioned witnesses from the first crime scene about the actual shooting. Witnesses talked some, but not a lot — and there were inconsistencies. Some told detectives the Cadillac had California license plates. Others said Nevada. No one was sure. In addition, there were early reports that the shooters were women, but according to LVMPD Lieutenant Larry Spinosa, that's not what the police ultimately concluded. People on the street that night may have been referring to the women who were in the Chrysler sedan near Suge's BMW when the shots were fired.

A young Tupac, in the days of stogies (blunts), 40-ouncers, bandanas, non-designer underwear, and less-defined abdominal muscles. (Trilobite)

Good times – Tupac partying after the 1995 Soul Train Awards ceremony. (Trilobite)

Bad times – Being led to jail by NYPD officers after being arrested for sexual abuse in Manhattan. Tupac later said, "Before I made a record, I never had a record." (AP/Wide World Photos)

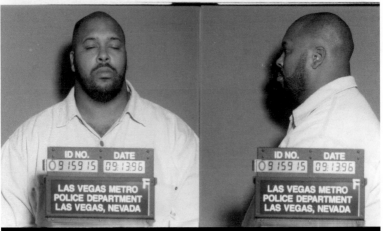

Top: *Suge Knight arrives at the hospital after Tupac's death to pay his respects to Afeni Shakur. (R. Marsh Starks/Las Vegas Sun)* Above: *Mug shot of Suge taken earlier the same day when he registered in Las Vegas as an ex-felon.*

Bad Boy Entertainment's rapper Biggie Smalls (left) and CEO Puffy Combs on the set of one of the last videos they shot together. (Trilobite)

The scuffle at the MGM Grand. Top left: *a frame from the video surveillance tape of the attack in the casino.* Above: *minutes later, Tupac storms towards the MGM entrance.* Top right: *Orlando Anderson is later identified as the beating victim.*

Club 662, where Suge and Tupac were headed, is located two miles farther east on Flamingo. (AP/Wide World Photos)

Aerial photo of the BMW's course. (1) The shooting occurred at the corner of Koval Lane and East Flamingo Road. Suge made a U-turn and headed west on Flamingo, to (2) the corner of Flamingo and Las Vegas Boulevard, where he clipped the median making a left turn onto the Strip. At point (3), the intersection of Harmon Avenue and the Strip, the BMW finally came to a stop. (Jason Cox)

Top: *Members of Tupac's entourage wait to be questioned by homicide detectives at the corner where the BMW came to rest. (Malcolm Payne)* Above: *Homicide Sergeant Kevin Manning presides over the only news conference about the investigation conducted by Las Vegas police. (Steve Marcus/Las Vegas Sun)*

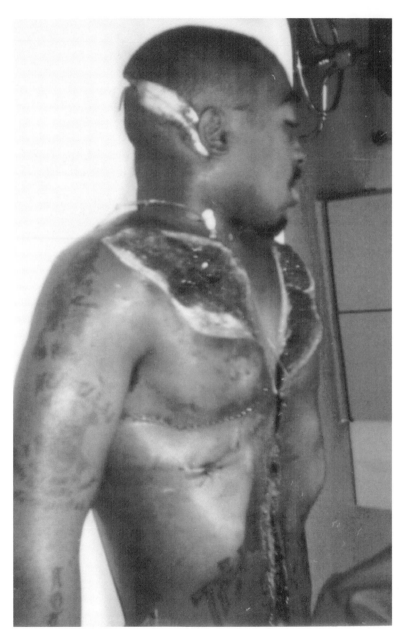

The photo – Tupac Shakur on the coroner's autopsy table.

According to Sergeant Kevin Manning, when detectives arrived at the scene of the shooting, the four women were still there. They were escorted to an interview room at Metro Police's headquarters downtown, in Las Vegas City Hall on the second floor at Stewart Avenue and Las Vegas Boulevard. The women, all from California, were not planted at the intersection to set-up Tupac and Suge, nor were they used as distractions while the gunman drove up in the Cadillac, Manning insisted. It was a coincidence. The women told police they didn't see the shooter. Five years later, their names have not been released to protect them, homicide Detective Brent Becker said.

Becker agreed that the women were not vital to the investigation. "They were just people in the mess," he said. "They're just like everybody else who was on the street that night. There were a lot of women nearby. There's no significance. I'd sure hate to hear about four women getting jammed up because someone thinks they're strong witnesses."

Most of the witnesses, including bystanders on the street, told the officers it looked like there were four men, all African-American, inside the four-door Cadillac. Witnesses also told police that no one in the Cadillac had gotten out of the car and that the shots were fired from inside the car, from the back seat on the driver's side. Some later reports had one gunman getting out and tracking Tupac, aiming directly for his side of the car, but police said that was not the case.

And then there were the eyewitnesses who were in the cars behind Tupac when the shooting erupted. Several from Tupac's entourage were taken downtown by general-assignment detectives early the next morning for questioning, according to Becker, instead of being interviewed on the street. Bodyguard Frank Alexander and rapper Malcolm Greenridge, who were in the car behind Tupac and Suge, both told police they didn't see anything and were allowed to leave. Later, they recanted their stories, telling the *Los Angeles Times* that homicide detectives had never asked them if they could identify the shooter.

Then there was 19-year-old Yafeu Fula, the member of Tupac's back-up rap group, Outlawz Immortalz. He was the third man in the car with Alexander and Greenridge. He was interviewed briefly on the street that night by homicide detectives. He told them he would probably be able to pick out the shooter from a photo line-up of suspects. Police took his name and telephone number. He was the best eyewitness police talked to that night. Of all the potential witnesses to the shooting, only Yafeu Fula claimed to have seen anything. But officers let him go without interviewing him in-depth. It would turn out to be their last opportunity to question him.

Within 48 hours of the shooting, on the following Monday, Las Vegas police called what would be their only news conference on the subject of Tupac Shakur. The national media, as well as local print, radio, and broadcast reporters and photographers, attended. What made the conference unusual were the entertainment reporters standing shoulder to shoulder with the hard-news reporters who are accustomed to following and reporting homicides.

Sergeant Manning, along with then-Sergeant Greg McCurdy from LVMPD's Public Affairs Office, held the news briefing on the lawn next to the executive-park building on West Charleston Boulevard that houses homicide's offices. With cameras and mikes aimed at him, Manning, visibly nervous, stood in the shade of the trees to avoid the blazing midday sun. By afternoon, the temperature had soared to nearly 100 degrees.

The sergeant read a brief statement – his original press release of the shooting – then fielded questions from reporters. For some, it would be the only opportunity they would have to speak directly to the lead investigator on the Tupac case. Most of the reporters' questions were about the assailant; some asked about Tupac's condition. One asked about the gun.

"We have not and will not make any comments about the gun. It's the only real physical evidence we have," Sergeant Manning said, referring to information that ballistics uncovered from the shell casings and bullets. "I know what's out there [in the media]. Semiautomatic would be accurate. Glock [a semi-automatic Glock pistol] has been mentioned. We don't know where the Glock is coming from. We have never said that."

In response to a reporter's question, Manning addressed the rumor that Suge Knight, not Tupac, was the intended target. Reporting anything differently, he said, "is not based on the facts of the case."

"The gunfire hit the passenger on the passenger side," he continued. "I assume the passenger was the target."

Several reporters walked up to Manning after the news conference and handed him their business cards, asking to be faxed or called if anything new were to come up. The homicide sergeant wasn't happy "dealing" – as he called it – with reporters, especially national ones. They were a nuisance and didn't serve his purposes. Later, Manning complained that interruptions from reporters were what was keeping him from investigating Tupac's murder. Still, according to sources, when the national magazines and newspapers came out with ample quotes from and photos of the sergeant, he went from newsstands to magazine racks, buying up souvenir copies for himself.

The feeling at LVMPD toward the media has sometimes tended toward disdain and mistrust. When reporters call to ask about a crime or an internal investigation into misconduct by an officer, they're often met with remarks like, "That's old news; why are you asking about that?" or "That's not a story." The thinking inside Las Vegas's homicide unit (and, for that matter, other units within the LVMPD) is that they should only answer questions from reporters if it serves LVMPD's investigative purposes. Considerations of the "public's right to know," often with even the most basic information, have traditionally taken a back seat. It's a tough system for many local reporters to work through.

Over the next few weeks, with international media attention focused on the shooting and death of Tupac Shakur, detectives Becker and Franks would go on camera only once, making an appearance on the Fox Network's *America's Most Wanted* program. But Sergeant Manning wouldn't allow his homicide team to be interviewed on camera – or off, for that matter – by *Unsolved Mysteries* when producers from Burbank, California, came to town to produce their own segment about the murder.

"They can't help us," Manning explained. "It would be of no use to us in our investigation." The decision was made despite the fact that *Unsolved* at that point had reported to have more viewers than *America's Most Wanted* and a better "solve rate." According to an *Unsolved Mysteries* producer, one of the reasons detectives declined was because *Unsolved* also airs what the producer called their "ugga bugga stories," such as UFO sightings and tales of spontaneous human combustion, sandwiched between true unsolved crime stories. *America's Most Wanted* reports only crime and missing-person's cases.

Regardless of the real reason for LVMPD's non-participation, it turned out to be a lost opportunity. After the *Unsolved Mysteries* piece aired on March 14, 1997, without cop interviews, the show received hundreds of tips. One, from a woman who said she was told twice by her friend that he had committed the murder, appeared to be solid. The woman, living in a Southern state, was afraid to give her name. An FBI agent who was in the *Unsolved Mysteries* studio when the program aired interviewed the woman and spent a lot of time with her on the phone. Las Vegas police were not in the studio, having declined when asked to go to Burbank to be on hand in case any solid tips were called in.

LVMPD detectives had one willing witness, 19-year-old Yafeu Fula, a rapper from New Jersey. He'd witnessed the shooting from his seat inside the car behind Suge's and said he'd be able to pick the gunman out of a photo line-up. But instead of detaining him until they could question him in-depth, police let Fula go.

Almost immediately after being allowed to leave Las Vegas, Fula contacted David Kenner, Death Row Records' attorney. Kenner played hard to get with Las Vegas investigators for two months. Promises to set-up a meeting between detectives and Fula were made but never kept.

It may have been fear that had prompted Fula to enlist Death Row's lawyer to keep him from being interviewed. After all, had he talked and identified the shooter, he would have been a snitch; people would have found that out during the trial of whomever he fingered, if not before. Furthermore, just telling police he had seen the suspect's face had been risky.

Fula, it turned out, had good reason to be frightened. Two months almost to the day after Tupac was shot, Yafeu Fula, the lead witness to the shooting, was forever gagged, murdered in New Jersey.

Detectives' hopes for a break in the case were raised four months after the death of Yafeu Fula when Frank Alexander and Malcolm Greenridge, bodyguards who were in the car with Fula, came forward, telling a *Los Angeles Times* reporter that they might be able to identify the shooter. The pair, however, criticized Las Vegas police, claiming detectives had never asked them if they'd be willing, in the future, to look at photos of possible suspects when investigators questioned them the night of the shooting.

Both men said they had come forward six months later because they were tired of hearing Las Vegas police say that an arrest had not been made because of uncooperative witnesses. They also said that LVMPD detectives had not contacted them since their initial questioning the night of the shooting. Like other witnesses, the pair complained that they were offended that night by the tactics of the cops who had made them feel like suspects, then held them half the night before questioning them.

Frank Alexander said he was taken to Detective Brent Becker's unmarked police car and questioned for "I'm guessing it was at least 30 to 45 minutes," Frank said. "Then the other guys, some of them didn't want to talk. I couldn't say which ones. There were six of us – Malcolm, Yak [Yafeu Fula], Kastro, me, K-dove, and Trebon. K-dove and Trebon were Suge's guys, two of his homeboys."

Sergeant Manning said Frank Alexander and Malcolm Greenridge might be able to help detectives crack the case, while also saying that if they did, they'd be changing their stories from what they had originally told detectives. According to Manning, when Alexander was asked on the night of the shooting if he could identify the gunman, he replied, "Absolutely not." Greenridge, when asked by detectives if he could identify the gunman, answered, "Nope." Alexander's original taped interview was 13 pages long after it was transcribed; Greenridge's was 11. Their answers mostly consisted of general descriptions of the night's events, without too many specifics.

"They never said they could identify a shooter," Manning said. "Nowhere during the [initial] taped interview did they say they could recognize or identify anyone in the vehicle, the shooter or otherwise." Manning noted that he found it curious the pair had complained to a *Los Angeles Times* reporter that they were harassed by police, while at the same time saying they had never been contacted by detectives. "So which is it?" Manning asked.

But Alexander told me, "It wasn't that we weren't interviewed by police. It was that there was never any follow-up, no line-up. We wanted to see the shooter brought to justice. It took them until that time for it to happen, after the *Los Angeles Times* article came out in February of 1997."

Detectives Becker and Franks traveled to California after the *Los Angeles Times* story appeared so they could re-interview Alexander and Greenridge. Alexander met with the detectives at an Orange County restaurant, where he told them the *Los Angeles Times* story had been "exaggerated." He also denied saying he could identify the shooter, Manning said. At the restaurant, Alexander viewed suspects from photographs – what cops refer to as a photo line-up – but he couldn't pick out the gunman.

Greenridge, interviewed the same day as Alexander at another location, also told Becker and Franks that he could not identify the shooter. He told the detectives he didn't even want to look at the photos.

"We re-contacted them and Greenridge stated, 'I still say I didn't see anything,'" homicide Lieutenant Wayne Petersen said. "These guys are responsible for Shakur's safety and well being, and the shooting goes down and they don't get an accurate description of the vehicle. When bullets are flying, who knows what they saw? If anybody out there did see it and didn't tell us what they saw that night or within a reasonable period after, then they basically screwed us out of a prosecution."

Lieutenant Petersen emphasized that even if the pair had said they could positively identify the assailant, defense attorneys would ask them, "How does your recollection of what happened get better six months after the event?"

"All it did was cause a lot of problems," Manning said afterward, "problems with everybody thinking we didn't do what we were supposed to do, and having us have to chase Frank Alexander and Malcolm Greenridge down."

The investigators called it a wasted trip and a waste of their time. They ended up back where they had started.

The aggravations weren't all coming from the outside. During the first week of the investigation, detectives thought they found help from one of their own in identifying members of Tupac's entourage videotaped during the scuffle by the MGM Grand's surveillance cameras.

"They [homicide] got a call from a young black Metro patrolman," an anonymous police source said. "He told them he knew some of the people and could help identify some of them. It turns out he didn't identify any of them. They think he came in to see what they had. He left homicide and got into a brand-spanking-new Lexus."

The source said that "investigators believed he might have been a snake, an informant for those wanting to plant someone inside the investigation."

Besides the possible betrayal by one of their own, Las Vegas police also had to watch their backs with out-of-town police officers, as well, who might have alliances with gang members.

"Every step of this investigation everybody had to be careful," the same police source said. "These guys [rappers] employ tons of cops. When this thing hit here, right away the Los Angeles agency down there called and said, 'Hey, we want to help.' All they wanted to do was pick their brains for information."

An LAPD detective, who spoke on the condition that his name not be used, said he didn't believe it was that Las Vegas and Los Angeles-area police didn't trust each other, but that they had to protect inside information.

"Those kinds of things go on all the time between agencies," he said. "Everybody's protecting their information. These are high-profile cases and nobody wants to make a mistake. I don't know if there's distrust [from LVMPD]. When all your witnesses live in Los Angeles, it makes it difficult logistically to investigate it in Las Vegas."

New York City police also had called homicide detectives in Las Vegas looking for information. Sergeant Manning, too, had telephoned NYPD to talk about the first time Tupac was shot, in Manhattan in 1994.

"We talked to numerous people in New York," Manning said. "The thing that was interesting, every time I talked to someone in New York, I asked, 'Whose case is this?' I talked to someone who said it was his case, then I'd call back and someone else would say it's their case. I finally asked a lieutenant to help straighten it out. I couldn't believe they had all these guys in charge of this [one] investigation. The funny thing was, they stopped calling me back after that. Most of them seemed to be on fishing expeditions rather than trying to find out [information] for their investigation. I couldn't hazard a guess why."

On the other hand, another police source said, "Compton [police], without even asking, sent a six-man investigative team made up of L.A. County Sheriff's Department and Compton PD [to Las Vegas]. They were very helpful. They shared information as to who in law enforcement to be leery of, who was working for [various] gang members." The officers spent two days with homicide detectives in Las Vegas.

A law-enforcement agent elaborated on the dynamics of protecting police investigations from infiltration: "In traditional organized-crime investigations, the old La Cosa Nostra [Mafia] kinds of investigations, police always had to be leery of outside officers until they knew the answers, because that was a very common way for bad guys to get information. If you're a successful bad guy, you try to develop sources in the good-guy community, that being law enforcement. It's a possibility [in the Tupac investigation]. It's always been that way."

The fact that it was still that way during the investigation into

Tupac's murder was underscored by a peculiar incident in Los Angeles in March of 1997. Detective Frank J. Lyga, an undercover police officer wearing civilian clothes and driving an unmarked police car, radioed his fellow officers that he was being followed and harassed by a motorist who, it turned out, was also an out-of-uniform off-duty cop, Officer Kevin L. Gaines.

The *Los Angeles Times* reported that the confrontation began with Lyga and Gaines staring each other down at a red light. It then escalated into a verbal confrontation.

An unnamed source close to the investigation told the *Los Angeles Daily News* that Gaines had rolled down the window of his car.

He told Lyga to quit staring him down or he would shoot him. That's when Lyga reportedly drove away and radioed dispatchers that he was having trouble with the motorist. A few blocks later, the officers were again next to each other at a traffic light.

Gaines pulled a handgun on Lyga, who "feared he was about to be shot," Lyga told investigators. Lyga pulled his department weapon and fired twice, fatally wounding Gaines, LAPD Lieutenant Anthony Alba told the Associated Press. Gaines didn't know Lyga was an officer and Lyga didn't know Gaines was an officer until Gaines was taken to a hospital, where he died. The Gaines family later expressed serious doubts that Kevin Gaines had provoked the shooting because, they said, he wasn't the type.

After the shooting, it was revealed that Gaines, a six-year veteran of the LAPD, had been dating and living with Suge Knight's then-estranged wife, Sharitha Golden Knight (they have since divorced and Knight has remarried). The officer was driving Sharitha's car when the altercation occurred. It was also revealed that in an earlier incident, Gaines had reported to Internal Affairs that officers had pushed and cuffed him on August 16, 1996, during a search of a home owned by Sharitha Knight.

Kevin Gaines's widow, who was separated from her husband at the time of his death, hired Johnnie Cochran Jr., O.J. Simpson's former criminal defense lawyer, to investigate the shooting.

While the Suge Knight connection is intriguing, police have claimed that there was no harassment and that the Suge association was irrelevant.

False tips are a regular occurrence in any murder case. In a big murder case, they can become a serious nuisance, and the Tupac Shakur case was no exception.

On the morning of March 26, 1997, a man came forward and told homicide detectives that he'd seen everything and could identify the gunman. The man's story deteriorated during interviews, until he finally confessed that he wasn't even in Las Vegas at the time.

Sergeant Kevin Manning said a few "wackos" had called in to "confess." One man left a blow-by-blow confession with minute and descriptive details on the homicide bureau's voice mail. There was only one problem: he claimed he did it in December, two months *after* Tupac was killed.

Another "informant" who was in custody on another charge in Wisconsin swore to police there that he knew who shot Tupac Shakur. He gave the cops specific information on the investigation, "specifics we were looking for," Manning said. "Police there interviewed the guy. They did a diagram of the crime. He was supposed to be a witness. They faxed his statement to us." What police in Las Vegas got, however, was a script from the *Unsolved Mysteries* segment about Tupac's murder that aired in March 1997.

"He copied *Unsolved Mysteries* word for word," Manning said. "We continue to get hundreds and hundreds of calls from *America's Most Wanted* and *Unsolved Mysteries*. If they [callers] have too many details, how do we sort out the credible from the uncredible?"

That's why, Manning continued, police don't worry about incorrect and inaccurate information circulating because it helps them tell the real witnesses from the fakes.

Some evidence remains sacrosanct. The gun, for example. The only hard evidence police have is from the ballistics. And they don't give up that information to the media, because only the perpetrators and the cops know the truth. That piece of intelligence was useful when a tip came in on April 11, 1997, from FBI agents in Bakersfield, California. Sergeant Manning tells the story:

"We got a call from the FBI in Bakersfield who had a guy who said he was in the car with the shooter, but he would only talk to an FBI agent. No one else. No other law enforcement. So I said, 'Okay.' We gave them some questions to ask. It turned out to be nothing. The guy said he shot into the driver's side with an Uzi."

Police haven't disclosed what kind of gun was fired at Tupac. Sources say it was a Glock. Even if a gun were recovered, Manning said, "We would still have difficulty putting that weapon in the actual shooter's possession. By now it's been too long. Even with fingerprints, it wouldn't be too useful."

In fact, he added, "Even a confession wouldn't solve the case, without concrete physical evidence."

Reports that there was more than one gunman were not true, Manning noted. Also, reports by a cub reporter in one local newspaper that the gunman had gotten out of the car to shoot Tupac were unfounded, he said. The security guards and some of the members of the entourage had gotten out of their cars, and witnesses in the confusion might have thought that one of *them* was the shooter, Manning said.

Richard Fischbein, the Manhattan attorney administering Shakur's million-dollar estate and representing Tupac's mother, said in a telephone interview, "It's an outrage that the Las Vegas police are sitting around waiting for a suspect to come to them. I believe that had [Afeni] been anyone else, they would have had the courtesy to call her, to keep in contact to tell her what is going on.

"Afeni's comment is, it's not going to bring her son back if they catch the killers or they don't catch them. On the other hand, it would be nice if the Las Vegas Police Department tried, because that would be the right thing to do. It would show that it doesn't matter who you are – if you get shot, the police are going to be there to do something about it."

But homicide Lieutenant Petersen took issue with the statement, saying that it was Shakur's mother who, when contacted by detectives, had refused to talk to *them*.

"The first time we contacted Mrs. Shakur, she would not talk to us. All other contacts were made through her attorney," Petersen said.

Interestingly, officers had had ample opportunity to interview Mrs. Shakur. She was at the hospital off and on during the six days Tupac was on life support. According to family members and friends, detectives never approached her.

A local radio personality intimated that it was prejudice and not a lack of cooperation that prevented an early resolution to the case. Louis Conner, a DJ for KCEP (now known as Power 88 on FM 88.1) radio in Las Vegas, whose on-air name is LC, said that if Tupac had not been a gangsta rapper, police might have worked harder to solve the case. LC said he played Tupac's music the remainder of the day Tupac passed away "as a tribute to him." He said he doesn't understand why police haven't made more progress in their investigation.

"It's unfortunate that Metro Police have not been able to make an arrest in the Shakur case," LC said several months into the investigation. "Maybe they're out of manpower, I don't know. I don't think it's a black-and-white issue. I think it's what Tupac represented, what he rapped about in his music. I think that makes it another type of prejudice. A lot of prejudices and stereotypes went into this case, and that's one of the things holding up the investigation process. I think they're working on it. They're just going about it at their own pace."

Sway, a disk jockey on San Francisco's KMEL radio station, agreed that police could have done more in attempting to find Tupac's killer.

In an interview from his San Francisco studio, Sway elaborated, saying, "This is hard for me to believe – that somebody as visible as Tupac can, during prime time in Las Vegas, just get massacred on the Strip. It doesn't seem like that's possible in 1997 without somebody knowing something.

"I don't think the powers that be give a damn that another little ghetto kid gets killed in the streets. It's not important to them to solve this case. I think they feel it's another headache killed in the streets. It doesn't serve their time and energy to solve the case of Tupac Shakur. I think it's just another day in America. If it was one of theirs, the killer probably would have been convicted and sentenced to death by now. From what Tupac represented to them, they probably thought it didn't matter as much."

Orlando "Little Lando" Anderson's name surfaced early in the investigation, when it was determined that he was the one attacked by Tupac and members of his entourage at the MGM Grand just hours before the mortal drive-by shooting. And police have said Anderson was associated with the Crips, the rival street gang to the Bloods, with which Suge Knight has allegedly been affiliated since he was a teenager. Detectives, however, stopped just short of calling Anderson an actual suspect.

"We're not ruling anybody out at this time," Lieutenant Petersen said, "but for us to say he's the only suspect is incorrect. There are people out there who believe Marion Knight is a suspect."

Homicide detectives don't keep lists with names of suspects, Petersen said. It's others, he explained, not the cops, who have called Orlando Anderson a suspect. On the record, anyway.

Police treaded lightly for another reason, a good one: Police would be putting his life in danger. "I'm getting tired of everybody calling Orlando Anderson a suspect," Detective Becker said, "because if he gets killed, well..." then his voice trailed off.

While Las Vegas police said no one would come forward and point a finger at the gunman, they, too, refused to officially name the shooter even while they said they knew who did it.

Sergeant Manning said, "We'd like to solve every case. In this particular case, there's personal pride and organizational pride involved. We'd love to put handcuffs on somebody. Once again, it comes back to this: until somebody has the courage to take the witness stand and put themselves in front of the prosecution and defense attorneys to answer hard questions, the case is at a standstill. This isn't like you have fiber evidence and hair evidence. You're talking about a drive-by shooting that leaves very little evidence behind."

Then-Compton Mayor Omar Bradley told me in his first interview about the case that Compton cops expressed to him their disappointment in LVMPD's handling of Orlando Anderson after they detained him during the gang raid in L.A. Officers told the mayor the word on the street with gang members was that Anderson was involved.

"Officers don't like to criticize each other publicly," Bradley said. "But they did criticize Las Vegas police privately.

"We arrested someone [in the Shakur case]. The Las Vegas police didn't want him. Compton police thought he was the one. I think the Compton police did their job."

Bradley said he was surprised that Orlando "was not further scrutinized by the Las Vegas Police Department. I don't understand why the Las Vegas police didn't pursue the case. It doesn't seem as if the investigation is proceeding."

When told that Las Vegas investigators felt they didn't have enough evidence to charge Anderson with Shakur's murder, Bradley said, "Evidence is something that prosecutors would decide, isn't it? Did Metro submit their case to the district attorney?"

The answer to that question is a resounding no; the case was neither submitted to a grand jury nor to the district attorney's office so that they, and not the police, could make the final determination as to whether there was enough evidence to seek an arrest and prosecute.

Wayne Petersen, the lieutenant in charge of the homicide division of the Las Vegas Metropolitan Police Department at the time of the shooting, defended that position with this: "We believe we know who is responsible for this. The problem we have with this case is we don't have anyone willing to come forward and testify to it. The gang, gangsta-rap mentality that they don't want to tell the police is definitely hurting this case. We don't have any more than rumor and innuendo. It's all these unconfirmed sources saying that, yes, Orlando Anderson did it, but there's no witness there [at the scene] who can testify to it. It's the old talk on the street, everybody claiming they heard that Orlando Anderson did it. We have no evidence linking him to this."

Petersen summed it up like this: "Getting away with murder happens all the time. The general public would probably be alarmed to know how often people get away with murder."

However, a source close to the investigation revealed in October 2001 that Orlando Anderson, despite "official" denials, was, in fact, considered a full-on suspect by police when he was alive. They believed him to be, the source said, Tupac's murderer.

"Orlando Anderson was the likely suspect [shooter], but wasn't alone in the car," the source said. "There have been no new leads and the case is just sitting there until or if something comes up that they can follow-up on. With the people involved in that case, gang members and rap dopers, it will be a hard case to get any more information on. [Homicide investigators] know who was involved with [Tupac's] death, but probably will never be able to prove it."

Compton police, too, having sources deeply ingrained in the area's street gangs, are adamant that Orlando was the shooter. Compton detectives were unimpressed with LVMPD homicide detectives' interview of Orlando, referring to it as "elementary," a Compton source said. After Las Vegas Sheriff Jerry Keller learned of Compton Mayor Bradley's criticism of his department, Keller called the chief of police in Compton. The chief issued a formal apology. Mayor Bradley did not.

The list of questionable decisions in the Tupac Shakur homicide investigation is long.

Both bike cops who heard the shooting from the Maxim hotel's parking garage followed the BMW instead of splitting up, so one could secure the crime scene and the other could follow the BMW.

Detectives and a K-9 team were dispatched to the wrong location. It took a while, officers said, to figure out what was going on and where the crime had occurred.

No aerial photos were taken. LVMPD officers who responded to the bike cops' calls for back-up alienated all but one of the potential witnesses within a few minutes of the shooting.

Then, in another questionable move, detectives released Yafeu

"Kadafi" Fula, the only witness willing to cooperate. The decision becomes even more troubling in light of Fula's murder two months later, before police could interview him at length. When Metro needs prostitutes or transients or even out-of-towners to testify as witnesses or to issue statements against a suspect, they simply lock them up, because they're considered flight risks. Even though the other witnesses to Tupac's shooting were uncooperative, police did not feel they needed to detain their only willing witness, one who lived 2,300 miles away, in New Jersey. Yafeu Fula had slipped through their fingers, and they had no one to blame but themselves.

Las Vegas detectives, while saying they were doing the best they could to investigate the murder, admitted waiting for their phones to ring. Yet, when people did call in, they often chalked up the calls to fake leads from wannabe tipsters. When Sergeant Manning received 300 calls in one day about the Shakur case, he simply stopped answering his phone and let his recorder pick up.

The detectives assigned to the Shakur murder appeared on *America's Most Wanted*, but not *Unsolved Mysteries*. News stories historically prompt witnesses to come forward, and sometimes ferret out suspects. Publicity via the media gets the word out to the public, which, in turn, often helps solve crimes. Not only would LVMPD not take part in the *Unsolved Mysteries* segment, they declined to be on hand to take calls at the studio right after the *Unsolved* segment aired.

Finally, LVMPD police have said they believe they've known all along who those involved are, but they don't have enough evidence to press charges. If they do know who's behind the killing, any efforts they've made to capitalize on that knowledge have been ineffective.

5

ABOUT TUPAC SHAKUR

VIOLENCE WAS NOTHING new to Tupac Shakur. He grew up on the mean streets in housing projects in New York City, Baltimore, and Oakland. A product of those environments, as an adult he looked every inch the thug his songs insisted he was.

Tupac's head was clean shaven, his muscular frame covered in tattoos. Even after surviving an earlier shooting, he was able to maintain rippled abdominal muscles that resembled a washboard.

He was handsome, with boyish good looks and an engaging smile and manner. He had a sauntering but determined walk, a hard stare but soft eyes and long eyelashes – a look decidedly different from other rappers.

Over the years, Tupac had accumulated more than a dozen tattoos, although some were said to be temporary. The one on his left forearm said "OUTLAW." On his left upper arm, there was Jesus's head on a burning cross with the words "Only God can judge me." Also on his left upper arm was written "Trust Nobody." On his right upper arm was the word "HEARTLESS" etched above a bloody skull and crossbones, underneath which was written, in small print, "My only fear of death is coming back reincarnated." On his left shoulder was the head of a black panther.

Revealing his street allegiances, on his right forearm, in old English lettering, was the word "Notorious"; on the back of his right forearm was "MOB"; and on his right shoulder was the word "Westside."

Etched on the right side of his neck was "Makaveli," the moniker he used while performing with the Outlawz; on the back of his neck, the word "Playaz"; underneath that, "Fuck the World." On his back was a large cross and, below it, "Exodus 18.11" (the Biblical passage reads, "Now I know that the Lord is greater than all gods: For in the thing wherein they dealt proudly he was above them").

He also had the image of an AK-47 fully automatic assault weapon tattooed on his left upper chest just below a scar from a bullet wound. The tattoo splashed across Tupac's lower chest said "THUG LIFE" with a bullet in place of the letter "I." Above that was "50 NIGGAZ" positioned atop a rifle. This tattoo symbolized a black confederation among the 50 U.S. states. And splashing the word "Nigga" across his chest, he believed, would advertise it as an acronym, which he said meant "Never Ignorant Getting Goals Accomplished." "2PAC," his stage name, was tattooed above his left breast.

On his right upper chest was "2DIE4" below the profile of a woman's face: Some say it was Nefertiti, an Egyptian queen whose name means "The Beautiful One is Come"; others believe it was a portrait of his mother.

The images tattooed on his body represented the things Tupac held sacred.

Tupac also adorned himself with jewelry. He had a particular penchant for gold. Besides the solid-gold chains around his neck, and diamond and gold rings on the fingers of both hands, he wore diamond studs in his nose and ears and an 18-karat-gold Rolex watch on his right wrist.

Tupac wore jewelry like medals, badges of honor. Even the lyrics of Tupac's favorite passage, a borrowed poem, became a reality for him. To his director in his first movie, *Juice*, he recited Robert Frost's poem "Nothing Gold Can Stay." It read:

"Nature's first green is gold, her hardest hue to hold. Her early leaves a flower; but only so an hour. Leaf subsides to leaf. So Eden sank to grief, so dawn goes down today. Nothing gold can stay."

(Tupac, who was an avid reader, often quoted passages from a book or lines from a poem or lyrics from a song. His friends were used to it. He'd done it since he was a boy.)

Just before his death, Tupac had formed a new group made up of kids, which he named Nothing Gold. He planned to personally produce their songs, which would, he felt, send a positive message to teenagers.

Tupac was a talented singer-songwriter with five solo albums to his name. Additionally, he had contributed songs to soundtracks for several movies, including *Above the Rim, Poetic Justice, Supercop,* and *Sunset Park.* He was also a rising film star, having starred in the movies *Juice* (1992), *Poetic Justice* (1993), *Above the Rim* (1994), *Bullet* (1997), *Gridlock'd* (1997), and *Gang Related* (1997). The latter film wrapped up a week before the fatal shooting and was released on the first anniversary of his death.

Boston Globe movie critic Jay Carr described Shakur's acting abilities in a January 31, 1997 review. "Whatever else the late gangsta rapper Tupac Shakur was, he was a good movie actor," Carr wrote. "He was good in *Juice,* and he was the best thing in *Poetic Justice.* He's even more appealing as the soulful half of the strung-out buddy team alongside Tim Roth in *Gridlock'd.*"

Rap journalist Kevin Powell said Tupac acted with a moody intensity comparable to that of James Dean, whose acting career was also cut short, but by a fatal car accident.

Tupac had reason to be moody. His childhood had been far from easy.

Tupac's mother, Alice Faye Crooks, aka Afeni Shakur, and his father, Billy Garland, were in the late 1960s founding members of the national Black Panther Party, based in New York. Alice (not yet known as Afeni Shakur), while out on bail pending felony charges for conspiring to blow up department stores and police stations, dated Garland. She'd earlier been married to Lumumba Abdul Shakur, but when she got pregnant (by Garland), Lumumba, a fellow Panther, divorced her a short time later.

In April 1969, she and 20 other Panther members were arrested. They were dubbed the notorious "Panther 21." Also part of the group was Tupac's future aunt, Assata Shakur (who began living in exile in Cuba in 1984). Alice found herself pregnant and incarcerated at the Women's House of Detention in Greenwich Village. Alice represented herself in court, *pro per,* delivering, according to Connie Bruck in a July 1997 article in the *New Yorker,* "a withering cross-examination of a key prosecution witness, who turned out to be an undercover government agent." Fourteen of the original 21 co-defendants, including Alice, were acquitted in May 1971, only a month away from Alice's delivery date of her baby boy.

On Wednesday, June 16, 1971, a son was born to Alice Faye. She named him Lesane. She and Garland parted ways soon after Tupac's birth. Garland, who had two other children from previous relationships, saw his son off and on until he was five, then lost contact. Garland wouldn't see him again until 1992, after he saw Tupac's picture on a poster advertising the movie *Juice.*

The Las Vegas Metropolitan Police Department's homicide unit lists Tupac's given name as "Lesane Crooks." Lieutenant Larry Spinosa said the family gave officers that name. The Clark County Coroner shows the rapper's name as Tupac A. Shakur with an alias of Lesane Parish Crooks. It is believed that his legal surname, Crooks, was his mother's maiden name.

Alice Faye married Jeral Wayne Williams, her second husband, when Tupac was a toddler. Later, when Williams changed his name to Mutulu Shakur, Alice Faye Williams became Afeni Shakur, and she gave her son the name Tupac Amaru, after a warrior and the last Inca chief to be tortured and murdered by Spanish conquistadors. Tupac means "Shining Serpent," which was an incan symbol of wisdom and courage. Shakur, which became his new surname, is Arabic for "Thankful to God"; it is a common surname chosen by members of the Nation of Islam when they join the Muslim religion. Afeni never legally changed her son's name to Tupac Shakur, but that's what he went by the rest of his life.

Tupac was born a fighter.

"It's funny, because I never believed he would live," Afeni told writer Veronica Chambers about her son in an *Esquire* interview. "Every five years, I'd be just amazed that he made it to five, that he made it to 10, that he made it to 15. I had a million miscarriages, you know.

"This child stayed in my womb through the worst possible conditions. I had to get a court order to get an egg to eat every day. I had to get a court order to get a glass of milk every day – you know what I'm saying? I lost weight, but he gained weight. He was born one month and three days after we [Panther 21 members] were acquitted. I had not been able to carry a child. This child comes and hangs on and really fights for his life."

After she was found not guilty, Afeni went on the speakers' circuit to talk about her experiences. But her celebrity was short-lived; Afeni found herself back on the welfare rolls, living in the ghetto.

She settled with her baby boy in the Bronx. Two years later she gave birth to Tupac's half-sister Sekyiwa Shakur. Sekyiwa's father, Mutulu, was also a Black Panther and a nationalist with the Nation of Islam. Mutulu called himself a doctor, claiming he had received a degree in acupuncture in Canada.

In 1986, Mutulu was arrested and charged with master-minding a 1981 Brinks robbery in which two Nyack, New York cops and a Brinks security guard were killed. Mutulu denied being involved in the hold-up. He was convicted anyway and is serving a 60-year sentence in a federal maximum-security penitentiary in Florence, Colorado. Mutulu was also convicted of conspiracy for his role in helping to break Assata Shakur, a family friend whom Tupac called "aunt," out of prison. Assata, also a Black Panther, then a Black Liberation Army leader, was convicted in 1977 of murdering a New Jersey state trooper and sentenced to life in prison. She escaped a few years later. She has been living in Cuba since 1984 and remains at large.

Mutulu went underground after the Brinks holdup in 1981 and wasn't captured until 1986. He was on the FBI's 10 Most Wanted List until his capture. Tupac was taught early by Mutulu not to trust law-enforcement officers. FBI agents would periodically go to Tupac's school to ask him if he'd seen his stepdad. Mutulu, who was close to Tupac, kept in touch while on the run.

Tupac's godfather, Elmer "Geronimo" Pratt, a deputy minister in the Black Panther Party, also wasn't around when Tupac was growing up. Pratt was sentenced to life in a California prison after his conviction for the murder of a white Los Angeles grammar school teacher when Tupac was an infant. Pratt's attorney at the time was a young Johnnie Cochran Jr., who went on to successfully defend former football star O.J. Simpson in the murder trial of Nicole Brown Simpson and Ronald Goldman. Pratt's case became, and remains, a famous civil-rights cause celebre for L.A.'s African-American community, because Cochran claimed racism. Cochran argued, and Pratt maintained throughout his incarceration, that Pratt was framed by law enforcement. After his conviction, Pratt was denied parole 16 times because he refused to renounce his politics or confess to a crime he said he didn't commit.

Geronimo Pratt walked out of prison in June 1997 after his conviction was overturned by an Orange County Superior Court judge, who declared that the Los Angeles County District Attorney's prosecution was unlawful and corrupt. His conviction was reversed on the grounds that the government suppressed evidence favorable to him at his trial, notably that the principal witness against him was a paid police informant. The decision was handed down midway through Pratt's 26th year in prison.

Tupac later said that he continued where Geronimo Pratt, Afeni and the Black Panthers, Mutulu Shakur, and Lumumba Shakur all left off. In his lyrics, Tupac referred to them as political prisoners.

Afeni and her two children eventually moved to Harlem to live with Afeni's new lover, Legs, and in homeless shelters and with friends and relatives. Legs, once linked to New York drug lord Nicky Barnes, was jailed for credit-card fraud and died in prison at 41 from a crack-induced heart attack.

Legs, Tupac later said, was the man who taught him about being a thug, an aspect of Legs's personality Tupac said he admired. He was also the only father Tupac ever knew, and now he was gone. "I couldn't even cry, man," Tupac told writer Kevin Powell. "I felt I needed a daddy to show me the ropes, and I didn't have one."

When Tupac was 10-years-old, a minister asked him what he wanted to be when he grew up. "A revolutionary," was his answer, because that was all he had ever known.

"Here we was, kickin' all this shit about the revolution and we starving," Tupac told Powell.

When Tupac was 12, something happened that would change his life: Afeni sent him to a Harlem theater group. He was a natural on stage. At 13, he played the role of Travis in *A Raisin in the Sun* at the famous Apollo Theater for a Jesse Jackson fundraiser. Tupac loved the limelight and enjoyed performing; through acting, he felt he could become someone worthy of respect. It changed the direction of his life and eventually got him out of the ghetto.

In 1986, when Tupac was 15, Afeni moved her family to Baltimore, Maryland. There, Tupac entered the prestigious Baltimore High School for the Arts, after his mother talked the school into taking him. It marked another major turning point; this time it meant going to a school far removed from the ghetto. While there, Tupac thrived, starring in several productions. He also started dabbling in rap.

Besides music, Tupac studied ballet, poetry, and acting. It was at the Baltimore school that he began calling himself an "artist." His classmates and teachers considered him talented. The thug in his personality hadn't emerged yet – at least he wasn't showing it.

Life at home, however, was still a hand-to-mouth existence. Afeni often didn't have the money to pay her utility bills and the electricity in their apartment was shut off most of the time. When that happened, Tupac, always the avid reader, studied outside by the light of the street lamps. He stayed at Baltimore High School for the Arts for two years. He told Kevin Powell, "That school was the freest I ever felt."

When a neighborhood boy was killed in a gang shooting during Tupac's junior year, 1988, Afeni put her kids on a Greyhound bus to spend the summer with a family friend who lived in Marin City, California. It turned out to be an area cops called the "Jungle," a small ghetto just below pricey hillside homes across the bay from San Francisco in affluent Marin County. Afeni didn't realize she was sending her kids to another gang-infested ghetto – the same as, or worse than, what they'd lived in for most of their lives. A few months later, after her friend called and said she was going into an alcohol rehabilitation center, Afeni joined her children in California, moving with them into a low-income federal housing project, the worst in the area. The family lived in the heart of the Jungle, in Building 89, Unit 1. Surrounded by neighborhood drug dealers, Afeni soon took on a cocaine habit.

Tupac, a skinny teenager, was taunted by the street drug dealers from whom his mother bought crack cocaine to feed her worsening habit.

"It'd be the shitty, dumb niggas who had women, rides, houses," Tupac told Powell. "And I didn't have shit... They used to dis me..."

And to writer Veronica Chambers, Tupac said, "Everybody else's mother was just a regular mother, but my mother was Afeni – you know what I'm saying? My mother had a strong reputation. It was just like having a daddy because she had a rep. Motherfuckers get roasted if you fuck with Afeni or her children. Couldn't nobody touch us."

Still, Tupac felt he could no longer handle his mother's crack habit. He moved out of her apartment and into an abandoned housing unit with a group of boys. They later formed the singing group One Nation Emcees. Even though he was a good student with a high grade-point average, Tupac eventually dropped out of high school at age 17 and, to survive, worked odd jobs, one at a pizza parlor. He also sold crack on the street to get by.

Tupac remembered crying a lot while he was growing up. Because his family had moved around so much, often to homeless shelters, he never felt like he fit in anywhere. He led a lonely existence. He didn't have any long-term friends and felt pressured to reinvent himself each time his family moved into a new neighborhood. He felt vulnerable living in the ghetto. Kids made fun of him, calling him "Tuberculosis" and "Tube Sock" because of his name, and "Pretty" because of his good looks. He told writer William Shaw he didn't have decent clothes and went to school "in the same things every day, holes in my jeans, the fucked-up sneakers. You don't want to be Tupac. You want to be 'Jack.'"

It was in the Bay Area that Tupac got into hip-hop music. He started writing poetry, then turned his poems into songs. He called himself MC New York. When he wasn't writing lyrics, Tupac spent his spare time reading. He couldn't get enough of books, movies, and music. He was hungry for knowledge.

It was there that he came into his own with his rap style, where he rhymed straight and to the point, where his lyrics became direct, where he learned not to pretend to be someone or something he wasn't. His family was still poor, still living in the ghetto; he admitted it and wasn't ashamed of it – keepin' it real, as he would often say.

In 1986, Tupac and his friends in the Jungle formed a rap group and named it Two from the Crew. They wrote songs, including "Lifestyles of the Poor and Homeless," "Let's Get It On," and "Get Ourselves the Girls." Their theme song and what would later become Tupac's anthem, was titled "Thug Life," so named because people in the neighborhood referred to the teenagers as young thugs. Tupac said his music showed how he and others like him lived. The lyrics about violence involving police, for example, were based on actual stories of what young black men faced in the ghetto. His thug-life image, for which he later became famous, was born.

"You were just giving truth to the music," Tupac later told San Francisco's KMEL DJ Sway. "Being in Marin City was like a small town, so it taught me to be more straightforward with my style. Instead of being so metaphorical with the rhyme, I was encouraged to go straight at it and hit it dead on and not waste time trying to cover things. In Marin City, everything was straightforward. Poverty was straightforward. There was no way to say 'I'm poor' but to say 'I'm poor.'"

He would not be poor much longer.

6

NEW YORK SHOOTING

ON WEDNESDAY, NOVEMBER 30, 1994, Tupac Shakur was ambushed and shot inside the lobby of a recording studio in Manhattan's Times Square. Tupac's team of criminal attorneys had been in New York with Tupac awaiting a verdict on sexual-assault charges against the rapper. Tupac's attorneys afterward said the shooting "looks like a set-up and smells like a set-up." Later, Tupac publicly blamed Biggie Smalls, who was upstairs in a recording session at the time, in helping to set-up the attack.

Earlier in the evening, Tupac had been invited by Ron G., a DJ in New York, to record with him. Tupac had agreed to do the recording for free, as a favor to the young rapper, whom he wanted to help out. (He usually charged other rappers a fee to record on their albums.)

Based on statements made to police by witnesses to the shooting, it went down like this. After finishing the taping session, Tupac was paged by a rapper named Booker, who asked him to tape a song with Little Shawn, an East Coast rapper. Tupac told him he'd do it that day, for $7,000. Booker agreed and told Tupac it was to take place at Quad Studios, at 723 Seventh Avenue between 48th and 49th streets in Times Square. While heading out to the studio, Tupac got a second call from Booker asking why he was taking so long. Then came a third call telling Tupac they didn't have the money to pay him. Tupac told Booker he wouldn't record unless he was paid, and hung up. Finally, Tupac got a fourth call from Booker telling him that Uptown Entertainment would take care of the fee, which would be waiting for him when he finished recording. Tupac headed for the studio. By that time, it was just after midnight.

At 12:16 a.m., according to Detective George Nagy with the NYPD's Midtown North 18th Precinct, Tupac, along with his manager Freddie Moore, his common-law brother-in-law Zayd Turner, and fellow rapper Randy "Stretch" Walker, and his half-sister Sekyiwa arrived at Quad Studios. They left their car in a parking garage at 148 West 48th Street. Then they walked the short distance, around the corner, to the studio on Seventh Avenue.

Nine minutes later, Tupac and his group arrived in front of the studio, a police report said. Standing on a small terrace overlooking 48th Street, for a smoke break, were a couple of teenage members of Junior M.A.F.I.A., a group Biggie Smalls was sponsoring. They hollered down to Tupac to say hello, then went back inside to tell everyone that Tupac had arrived.

Upstairs, it was a party atmosphere. It was a large studio, and a lot of people were there that night. Word had spread that Tupac would be recording there. People were excited in anticipation of the popular rapper's arrival. Also there to record, but on a different floor from where Tupac was scheduled to record, were Biggie Smalls and Puffy Combs. They were working on Biggie's "Warning" video. At the time, Quad had recording studios and equipment on five different floors.

Back on the street, on Seventh Avenue, as Tupac and the others approached the entrance to Quad Studios, they could see two black men, near the elevator, wearing Army fatigues, recognized by Tupac as gang garb worn mostly in the Brooklyn area; a third man, also black, was in the lobby, pretending to read a newspaper. Tupac and his group didn't think twice about the men.

Tupac pressed the intercom button. The four were buzzed in. As they walked toward the elevator, Tupac, according to the police report, was ambushed by the three men, including the man who had been standing just outside the lobby. Two of the three men pulled identical handguns, NYPD Detective George Nagy said.

They went straight for Tupac, ordering him to the floor and demanding he give up all his jewelry and money. When Tupac went for his own gun stashed in his waistband, they shot him. A round hit him in the groin area and passed through his thigh. That bullet cost him a testicle. Then the gunmen began beating him. They ripped his jewelry off him, then shot him again, hitting him in the chest. Tupac was shot five times: twice in the head, twice in the groin area, and once in his left hand. Freddie was shot once in his abdomen. None of the wounds were life-threatening. The men also snatched jewelry from Freddie Moore as they continued holding guns on the others, Nagy said.

All told, Tupac had $35,000 worth of gold taken from him. Stolen were a diamond-and-gold ring, a gold bracelet, and several heavy gold chains. Freddie had $5,000 worth of jewelry stolen, which consisted of a gold bracelet and several gold chains.

Two years later, in one of the last interviews he gave to *Vibe* magazine, Tupac spoke to a reporter about what it felt like to get shot.

"...The dude with the newspaper was holding the gun on [Stretch]. He was telling the light-skinned dude, 'Shoot that motherfucker! Fuck it!' Then I got scared, because the dude had the gun to my stomach. All I could think about was piss bags and shit bags.

"I drew my arm around him to move the gun to my side. He shot and the gun twisted and that's when I got hit the first time. I felt it in my leg; I didn't know I got shot in my balls. I dropped to the floor. Everything in my mind said, 'Pac, pretend you're dead.' It didn't matter. They started kicking me, hitting me. I never said, 'Don't shoot!' I was quiet as hell. They were snatchin' my shit off me while I was laying on the floor. I had my eyes closed, but I was shaking, because the situation had me shaking. And then I felt something in the back of my head, something real strong. I thought they stomped me or pistol-whipped me, and they were stomping my head against the concrete. I saw white, just white. I didn't hear nothing. I didn't feel nothing, and I said, 'I'm unconscious.' But I was conscious.

"And then I felt it again, and I could hear things now and I could see things and they were bringing me back to consciousness. Then they did it again, and I couldn't hear nothin'. And I couldn't see nothin'; it was just all white. And then they hit me again, and I could hear things and I could see things and I knew I was conscious again."

After they finished robbing Tupac, then Freddie, the would-be assailants stepped out of the lobby, still pointing their guns at the four, and backed away so they could continue watching them. Then they simply walked out the door and disappeared into the night. When they were gone, Tupac said, "Yo, I'm hit."

The four, with Tupac stumbling and bleeding from his wounds, stepped outside the small lobby and yelled, "Police!" As they walked back inside, they saw an NYPD squad car pull up. Just then, the elevator door in the lobby opened. Tupac got in. Zayd and Stretch followed him. Freddie, who also was bleeding from his gunshot wound, stayed downstairs with Tupac's half-sister and waited for an officer.

The three took the elevator to the eighth floor. When the elevator door opened, waiting for Tupac in the floor's reception area was Booker. Tupac yelled, "Call the police, call the police," even though he had seen a squad car downstairs. Biggie and Puffy were still recording on another floor.

Tupac got on the phone and called his then-girlfriend Keisha Morris (who later would become his wife). He said, "Call my mom. I've just been shot."

By this time, Tupac was becoming hysterical and no doubt was going into shock from his injuries. He began pacing back and forth. He looked at Booker and said, "You the only one who knew that I was coming. You musta set me up."

Booker was astonished and told him, "Yo, you buggin', Tupac. C'mon. Talk to me."

But Tupac kept repeating, "Call the police."

Reporters, as well as the police, showed up at the scene. Tupac was interviewed by newspaper reporters who quoted him as saying it was a set-up. Tupac also accused those with him of "dropping like a sack of potatoes" and not coming to his aid.

A lot of people were in and out of the studio that night, Tupac pointed out, many of whom were as bejeweled with gold as he was, but who were not robbed or shot.

Included in those present that night was record producer Andre Harrell. Tupac later accused Smalls and Combs, who now calls himself P. Diddy, of setting him up.

Jacques Agnant, the Haitian music promoter who introduced Tupac to the woman who accused him of rape, also had ties to Little Shawn, with whom Tupac was supposed to record with that night. Tupac later rapped about Agnant on his album *The Don Killuminati* with this: "About a snitch named Haitian Jack/Knew he was working for the feds... /Set me up."

Agnant filed a libel suit against Tupac's estate, Death Row, Interscope, the producer and engineer of the song, and the publishing company. However, the U.S. District Court in 1998 held that it was not defamatory for Tupac to accuse Agnant of being an undercover police informant. The court also held that Agnant could not recover monies from the Shakur estate for other statements made by Tupac because "they did not constitute libel per se."

Andre Harrell gave this account of the studio shooting to a *Vibe* reporter in April 1999: "Everybody was all excited about Pac comin' in, but we were starting to get antsy because he was supposed to get there at a certain time, and we wanted to see how this song with Little Shawn was going to set off."

When Tupac got off the elevator, "we were all standing in the hall," Harrell said. "Tupac was just bopping back and forth saying, 'I was set-up.' At first I didn't realize he had been shot, because he wasn't bleeding heavily from the head. It looked like he had had a fight. He said, 'It's not goin' down like that.' I was like, 'Yo, you shot. You need to sit down.' He told Stretch to roll him up a spliff [marijuana cigarette]. He was in a movie mode at this point. He did the whole James Cagney thing."

Harrell directed people inside the studio at the time to call 911. After an ambulance arrived, he told Stretch to ride with Tupac to Bellevue hospital so he wouldn't be alone. He didn't want anything more to happen to him. As paramedics were lifting him into the ambulance, Tupac flipped off a newspaper photographer, who caught the gesture on film.

Though he was shot five times and lost a testicle, the prognosis was good: He would live. He checked out of the hospital shortly after his surgery the next day, because he wanted to be in court for his sentencing on the rape conviction.

Officers wrote in their police report that Tupac was unarmed but carried a magazine, ammo for a 10-millimeter. Freddie, the report said, was armed with a 10-millimeter handgun.

A security guard had been on duty at the time of the shooting, but his whereabouts weren't mentioned in the report. It was never made clear whether the guard had been in the lobby or in another part of the building at the time of the attack. Later, another guard said a camera had been pointed at the door at the time of the shooting. Buzzers upstairs give personnel on any floor the ability to let people in to the lobby, he said. "It's pointed at the door so they can see who's there," the guard told me. "Then they're buzzed in."

That news was an integral piece of the investigation because it meant that whoever had shot Tupac had been buzzed in by someone inside. An employee later said that police did not confiscate the videotape from the studio's surveillance cameras. Instead, the investigation was abruptly halted and the case closed.

But what the New York cops at the time considered to be a break in the Quad Studios shooting came in October 1996, about a month after Tupac was killed. In a published statement, federal prosecutors in New York said that Walter Johnson, aka "King Tut," a 17-year career criminal, was a suspect in the 1994 shooting. Johnson was jailed in October 1996 and charged with 12 federal felony counts stemming from three armed robberies in Brooklyn. The charges didn't include Tupac's shooting, though law-enforcement sources told the *New York Daily News* that they were investigating statements he allegedly made to a confidential informant. "He [Johnson] said Tupac is a sucker," the informant told investigators. "He said Tupac is not a real gangsta and that he shot him." As of 2002, however, Johnson had not been charged in the case.

Investigators also told the newspaper the Johnson investigation could help solve Tupac's slaying. "We hope this will lead to a solution of the murder of Tupac," one source close to the investigation told the *Daily News*. LVMPD's Sergeant Manning could not recall talking to New York City police about the case, noting, "The only King Tut I've heard of is the one in Egypt." Manning did say he had spoken a few times to the NYPD detectives about the Manhattan shooting, but just briefly.

Some say Tupac was accidentally shot with his own gun when the attacker tried to grab it from him. There was no mention of that scenario, however, in the police report, which made no mention of Tupac being armed.

Stretch, before he was shot to death in Queens exactly a year later, told *Vibe* magazine that Tupac was armed that night and accidentally was shot with his own gun. "Tupac got shot trying to go for his shit," he said. "He tried to go for his gun, and he made a mistake on his own. But I'll let him tell the world that. I ain't even going to get into it all like that... He tried to turn around and pull the joint out real quick, but niggas caught him, grabbed his hand when it was by his waist."

Stretch said that Zayd had taken Tupac's gun from him before the police arrived on the scene so Tupac wouldn't be in possession of a firearm.

After the shooting, videotape shot from outside Quad Studios by a TV camera operator showed Puffy inside the downstairs lobby, in a baseball cap with a straw hanging from his mouth, staring at the camera and talking to several men. News footage also showed Biggie walking out of the lobby, closely followed by Puffy.

Tupac underwent surgery that night at Bellevue Hospital. The next morning, Biggie visited him. At that point, Tupac hadn't yet accused Biggie of being involved in the shooting.

The next morning Tupac, still recovering from surgery, checked himself out so he could be in court for his sentencing in his criminal trial. Rather than convalesce in a hospital, he stayed temporarily at actress and friend Jasmine Guy's New York apartment. A few days later, Tupac went to prison to serve out his sentence for the sexual-assault conviction.

Before his sentencing, Tupac had told *MTV News*: "If God sees it fit for me to spend some time in a cell, if he's brought me so far from hell to put me here and now he wants me to go to jail, I'll go. When I come out, I'll be reborn. My mind will be sharper. The venom will be more potent. They shouldn't send me there. You don't throw more gasoline on a fire to put it out."

During Tupac's incarceration, his album *Me Against the World* was released. For the first time ever, a jailed man had the country's No. 1 best-selling album.

While in prison, Tupac obsessed in his isolation and became convinced that Biggie and Puffy had helped set-up the Quad Studios ambush. The case, however, would never be solved.

Instead, just a month after the shooting, the New York Police Department closed its investigation into the shooting. No one would ever learn what had really gone down that November night. The NYPD ended its probe when, they said, Tupac opted not to cooperate with investigators.

"Calls were made to Shakur's lawyer, but they never responded," NYPD Detective Nagy told me. "His lawyer never called back. No one ever called back. Therefore, the case was closed."

NYPD police said that because Tupac had refused to cooperate, it meant the end of their case. "They were totally uncooperative... They more or less handled it in their own way," Nagy said. The officer, clearly frustrated, then went on to outline the police's attitude in a bold admission of the way things really are: "Why would a guy go out of his way to investigate a case when the guy who was shot didn't even care?" he asked. "Why are you going to try hard when you have a million other cases?" That was the attitude investigators on the case had at the time, he said. He noted that, to close a case, "you really need a valid reason. The boss has to sign off on it. This was a high-profile case. There had to be a valid reason to close it."

Even after Tupac was killed in Las Vegas, Nagy said, the Quad Studios case was not reopened. He explained, "You can reopen a case if somebody walks in and says, 'I shot Tupac.'" Without a willing eyewitness, there would be no one to testify against a suspected shooter and, therefore, no case, Nagy said.

Gregg Howard, Suge Knight's publicist until 2000, said the shootings were nothing more than the result of jealousy by immature rappers. Combs's attorney, Kenny Meiselas, on the other hand, said the record companies did not engage in petty jealousies among rappers and that Puffy was not involved in any way with the shooting.

7

ABOUT THE MUSIC

WHILE TUPAC'S FRIENDS in the Jungle rapped with him for the fun of it, they later said that rap had become Tupac's obsession, even as a teenager. Tupac got his foot in the door of the professional music world when he met Leila Steinberg, a young white woman, at a San Francisco park. They became fast friends and Tupac made her his manager. Leila, a part-time teacher at Bayside Elementary, a school near the Jungle, introduced Tupac to poetry readings.

Also a show promoter, Leila was already working with a rapper named Ray Love. She introduced Tupac to Ray. The two began rapping together as the group Strictly Dope. Tupac moved into Leila's house in Sonoma County, and his public life began.

Leila introduced him to Atron Gregory, the manager of the Grammy-nominated Digital Underground, a seminal Bay Area rap ensemble. One of the things that attracted Atron to Tupac was that Tupac's lyrics and rhymes were straight from the street. It was what Tupac called "keepin' it real, keepin' it street."

Tupac started out in 1989 at 18 as a roadie and tour dancer and worked his way up to rapper, debuting on the *Sons of the P* album. Tupac was a "humpty-hump" dancer on stage, performing while the singers, including Queen Latifah and Shock G, rapped. Shock G started letting Tupac rap on stage and eventually on an album. Tupac continued rapping with Digital Underground under the moniker MC New York, and went on a world tour with the group.

After the tour, Tupac rented his own apartment in Oakland. He'd earned enough money to buy a lime-green Toyota Celica. He also spent some money on firearms. His friends often visited his apartment to "kick it," listen to Tupac's music, smoke blunts, and handle his new guns. His personal arsenal included 12 gauges, a Glock 9, and an AK-47. Tupac felt he was on his way up. After all, he had the possessions to prove it. But he still went back to the Jungle regularly to visit his friends, proudly driving through the projects in his bright green car.

Soon, he'd recorded enough songs for a solo album, but he couldn't get a record company to release it. One of the labels that rejected him was Tommy Boy Records.

"He was funny, adorable, a real flirt," Tommy Boy Records president Monica Lynch told William Shaw for an article in *Vanity Fair*. "But as an artist, he wasn't there."

By this time, 1990, gangsta was in style, hot, especially in L.A. Dr. Dre was living there, and so were Snoop Dogg, Eazy-E, Ice-T, and Ice Cube. Gangsta had become popular with young West Coast whites as well as blacks. L.A. was the place to be. Tupac would get there eventually. In the meantime, other opportunities started to come his way.

While waiting for a record deal, Tupac went along with his friend Money-B on an audition for a movie called *Juice*, a coming-of-age drama. Money-B was trying out for the part of a punk named Bishop, but he didn't do well. Tupac asked to audition. The producer, Neil Moritz, agreed to let him read. He was "dynamic, bold, powerful, magnetic – any word you want to use," Moritz later said. "Tupac was it. We cast him right on the spot."

They shot Tupac's part in Harlem with Spike Lee's cinematographer, Ernest Dickerson, directing. Moritz congratulated Tupac after his performance and told him, "Ten years from now, you're going to be a big star."

"Ten years from now," Tupac responded, "I'm not going to be alive."

Juice marked another turning point in Tupac's life. He was not only a rising rap star, but a movie star to boot. In interviews for a video biography about Tupac, *Thug Immortal*, his friends said that before Tupac made his first movie, there had been a softer side to him. But while playing the role of Bishop, a street-smart hard-core thug, it was as if Tupac decided to *become* the character. He took on the persona of Bishop and began talking and acting tough. His friends said he wasn't really like that; he was just trying to look hard because he thought it was expected of him as a thug rapper. His friends later described him as a chameleon, becoming whatever he thought those around him wanted him to be.

It was about that time that Tupac had the words "THUG LIFE" tattooed across his midriff. He later claimed Bishop was just a reflection of one type of young black male during that particular time; he said that not all young black males were violent. He pointed out that the role of Lucky, who he played in the film *Poetic Justice*, was just the opposite, that of a young black man who was a parent, lived at home, and was working to get ahead. Still, Tupac appeared to identify more with Bishop than Lucky.

Atron Gregory, in the meantime, was trying to set-up a deal with Interscope Records, an independent label owned by department-store heir Ted Field (heir to the Marshall Field fortune) and Jimmy Iovine, a former John Lennon record producer. At the time, Interscope was in a partnership with Warner Music Group, a subsidiary of Time Warner. Interscope president Tom Whalley signed Tupac to Interscope. Interscope and Gregory sealed a deal for Tupac's debut album, *2pacalypse Now*. Released in 1992, it went on to sell $90 million worth of albums.

"Right away you could tell that this guy [Tupac] was different from the rest of the world," Whalley told *Vanity Fair*'s William Shaw. "I couldn't slow him down. I never worked with anyone who could write so many great songs so quickly."

Tupac's rap had a fresh voice, a fresh style on the gangsta scene. There was a softness behind his bad-boy persona. He had an emotional depth that was revealed in the more contemplative lyrics in his music. But beneath the surface, he was an angry young man, haunted by demons from his youth that surfaced in his tougher lyrics.

He demonstrated his unique range as a performer on *2pacalypse Now*. The record included militant lyrics depicting violence between young black men and the police, drawing on the gang culture of South

Central Los Angeles. The hit single "Brenda's Got a Baby," with its references to cops being killed, caused an uproar. Then-Vice President Dan Quayle singled out the album, criticizing it for its encouragement of violence, cop killing, and its disrespect for women. Quayle, in his war against the breakdown of traditional values in the entertainment industry, used Tupac as an example, saying that Tupac's lyrics had "no place in our society." Bolstered by the invaluable publicity, the CD catapulted Tupac's career into star territory. He was nominated that year for an American Music Award as Best New Rap Hip-Hop Artist.

In the video biography, *Thug Immortal*, writer Tony Patrick described Tupac as charismatic.

"There was something special about him," Patrick said. "You saw it in his records. I saw it a little bit more in his movies. He had that glow. He had that charisma. There was no one else who looked like him. He had the eyebrows. He had the cheekbones. You know, handsome. Sometimes when you saw him sitting there introspective, if you were a woman you wanted to go over there and ask him, 'Pac, what's wrong? What can I do for you, baby?' He had that special glow about him that attracted you to him right away."

While *2pacalypse Now* was still on the charts, Tupac's film debut in *Juice* hit screens around the country. *Juice* director Ernest Dickerson spoke to MTV about what it was like directing the rap star. Dickerson described Tupac as a thinking man.

"I think that he's very introspective," he said. "I mean, when we were shooting *Juice*, in between takes he would spend a lot of time by himself, writing. You know, he thinks a lot. He thinks about what's going on in the world, he thinks about what's going on in the neighborhoods, and he talks about it in his music. The thing that I really got from Tupac was that he was always thinking, always at work. His mind was always going."

In early 1992, after the filming of *Juice* wrapped up, Tupac and longtime friend Charles "Man-Man" Fuller moved from northern California to South Central L.A. Tupac began taking target practice at shooting ranges and working out with weights. His success continued to soar.

Tupac's critical acclaim for *Juice* led to his second movie role, co-starring as Lucky opposite Janet Jackson in *Poetic Justice*. Director John Singleton also praised Tupac's acting abilities. Singleton told *Vibe* magazine, "He's what they call a natural. You know, he's a real actor. He has all these methods and everything, philosophies about how a role should be played." (*Vibe* magazine has since published a collection of interviews titled *Tupac Amaru Shakur 1971-1996*.)

"When I saw *Juice*, Tupac's performance jumped out at me like a tiger. Here was an actor who could portray the ultimate crazy nigga. A brother who could embody the freedom that an 'I-don't-give-a-fuck' mentality gives a black man. I thought, *This was some serious acting*. Maybe I was wrong.

"During the filming of *Poetic Justice*, Pac both rebelled and accepted my attitude toward him as a director [and] advisor. This was our dance in life and work. We'd argue, then make up. Tupac spoke from a position that cannot be totally appreciated unless you understood the pathos of being a nigga, a displaced African soul, full of power, pain, and passion, with no focus or direction for all that energy except his art."

Writer Veronica Chambers was on the set of *Poetic Justice* at the invitation of Singleton, who'd asked her to author a behind-the-scenes book. In an *Esquire* article published after Tupac's death, she reported that "Tupac had a hard time following the rules."

"Half the time, there were no problems at all," she wrote, "but it wasn't unusual for Tupac to get high in his trailer, to be hours late to the set in the morning, or to get pissed off for what seemed like no reason at all. Once, toward the end of the shoot, Tupac was told he could have a day off. That morning, the producers decided that they would shoot publicity stills and called Tupac to the set. He arrived with his homeboys and began screaming, 'I can't take this shit. Y'all treat a nigga like a slave.' He stormed off to his trailer and promptly punched in a window.

"It certainly wasn't the first time a star has had a fit on a set. But Tupac was a young black male with more than a little street credibility. At the time, nobody knew how far he was willing to take his mantras about living a 'thug life.' There was indignation on the set about being blasted by some young punk, but there was also fear, fear both *of* Tupac and *for* Tupac. I believe this was a pattern of concern that those around him felt right up until his death."

In late 1993, Tupac, his stepbrother Mopreme (aka Maurice Harding), and three others recorded *Thug Life, Volume 1*. It was hard-core rap. The album went gold.

Tupac had escaped life in the ghetto, but he couldn't seem to get the ghetto out of his blood. As he experienced first-hand the tough gangsta life he rapped about, his personal rap sheet grew. Starting in 1992, when Tupac was charged with battery for slapping a woman who asked for his autograph, criminal charges and civil lawsuits loomed over him like a dark cloud. At one point, Tupac was scheduled for court dates in Los Angeles, Atlanta, New York, and Detroit, all within a two-week period. He was doing his part to live up to the bad-boy image he'd cultivated for himself.

Mopreme has said that when Tupac's second solo album with Interscope, *Strictly 4 My N.I.G.G.A.Z.*, was released in 1994 with a red cover, everyone assumed Tupac had become a member of the Bloods, since red is its color. While he sometimes hung out with Bloods, Tupac also on occasion hung out with Crips. But he came to be identified with the Bloods, especially after he signed on with Death Row Records, run by Suge Knight, whose connection to the Bloods ran deep. Tupac's affiliation came back to haunt him in the scuffle at the MGM Grand with Orlando Anderson, who police said was a member of the rivaling Crips.

In 1992, Tupac was involved in a civil wrongful-death lawsuit after a six-year-old boy was killed at a northern California festival celebrating the 50th anniversary of the Marin City neighborhood, or the Jungle, where Tupac had spent his teenage years. The boy was caught in gunfire between a member of Tupac's crew and a rival gang member. Interscope Records, under which Tupac was recording at the time, settled with the boy's family out of court for nearly a half-million dollars. While Tupac had to pay the half-million because of the civil court order, he never was criminally charged.

Then, on Monday, April 5, 1993, Tupac was arrested and accused of trying to hit a fellow rapper with a baseball bat at a concert at Michigan State University. The incident was triggered when Tupac got angry on stage and threw a $670 microphone that belonged to the group MAD. Rapper Chauncey Wynn publicly objected to Tupac's behavior. A near-riot broke out when the audience stormed the entertainers; security guards and police had to clear more than 3,000 people from around the stage.

Tupac testified he'd been clutching the baseball bat, which he said he used as a prop at the concert. He told the court he didn't hit or attempt to hit anyone and that the bat had simply scared the other rapper.

Tupac, 23 at the time, pleaded guilty on Wednesday, September 14, 1994, to a misdemeanor in exchange for prosecutors dropping felony assault charges. He returned for sentencing on Wednesday, October 26. He could have gotten up to 90 days in the East Lansing Jail. Instead, he was sentenced to, and served, 10 days in jail, and ordered to perform 35 hours of community service.

It would only get worse.

During a 1993 concert at a Pine Bluff, Arkansas nightclub, a woman named Jacquelyn McNealey was hit by a stray bullet. The bullet seriously damaged her spinal cord, leaving her paralyzed below the chest. After Tupac's death, she sued the nightclub and Tupac's estate, claiming that Tupac "was taunting the crowd. He created a riot-like atmosphere which ended up in a shooting," her lawyer argued. The judge had granted full damages of $16.6 million after Tupac's representatives failed to appear at the hearing. Richard Fischbein, attorney for Tupac's mother and his estate, told the Associated Press that Tupac had not been notified of the lawsuit or the judgment. The nightclub settled for $500,000. At the same time, the gunman was prosecuted and sent to prison.

On Sunday, October 31, 1993, Tupac was charged in the shooting of two off-duty police officers in Atlanta. Witnesses testified that Tupac and his associates had shot back at the plainclothes officers after they opened fire on Tupac's car. The charges were eventually dropped when it was learned that the cops, who'd been drinking, had initiated the shooting. The prosecution's own witness testified that the gun used by an officer to threaten Tupac had earlier been seized in a drug bust and was missing from a police evidence locker. It was damning evidence against the cops, enough to exonerate Tupac.

Tupac also served jail time for an altercation on the set of a music video. The fight involved Tupac and the video's directors, Albert and Allen Hughes. The brothers had fired Tupac from the cast of *Menace II Society* six months earlier because of Tupac's violent temper.

Tupac told his side of the story to *Vibe* magazine. "[The Hughes brothers] was doin' all my videos," he said. "After I did *Juice*, they said, 'Can we use your name to get this movie deal?' I said, 'Hell, yeah.' When I got with John Singleton, he told me he wanted to be 'Scorsese to your De Niro. For starring roles I just want you to work with me.' So I told the Hughes brothers I only wanted a little role. But I didn't tell them I wanted a sucker role. We was arguing about that in rehearsal. They said to me, 'Ever since you got with John Singleton's shit, you changed.' They was trippin' 'cause they got this thing with John Singleton. They feel like they competing with him."

A few months after the firing, Tupac ran into the Hughes brothers at a video taping. The three argued. "That's a fair fight, am I right? Two niggas against me?" Tupac later asked *Vibe*.

Tupac was eventually charged with carrying a loaded concealed weapon. He faced the possibility of a year in jail and a $3,000 fine. He was convicted of misdemeanor assault and battery on Thursday, February 10, 1994, and sentenced in March to 15 days in Los Angeles County Jail and 15 days on a California Department of Transportation road crew, which he reluctantly served. He later said he hated being jailed; he felt smothered. Rumors that Tupac had been raped by fellow inmates while incarcerated have never been substantiated. His friends adamantly say it never happened.

Tupac's most notorious criminal rap came when he was accused of sexually abusing a female fan. The woman alleged that Tupac and two pals had held her down while a fourth man sodomized her in a hotel room.

Tupac claimed it was a set-up. It all started when Tupac began hanging out with a Haitian-born music promoter named Jacques Agnant. On the night of Sunday, November 14, 1993, Agnant had taken Tupac to Nell's, a high-brow downtown New York nightclub, and introduced him to Ayanna Jackson, a 19-year-old Manhattan woman. As the story goes, Ayanna, on the dance floor, allegedly performed oral sex on Tupac, with more sex later that night in his hotel room.

Four days later, Ayanna returned to Tupac's hotel room at the Parker Meridien, a posh Manhattan hotel, to collect her belongings she had left behind after the encounter. The two ended up, again, in the bedroom. Ayanna testified during Tupac's trial that as she and Tupac were kissing, three men burst into the room, and Tupac and the men stripped off her underwear, then sodomized and sexually abused her. After she left the hotel, she filed a police report accusing the four of gang-raping her.

Jackson testified that Jacques Agnant and a friend of his, along with Charles Fuller and Tupac, were in the room when she was gang-raped. Tupac, Agnant, and Fuller were arrested and charged with sexual assault. Agnant's friend had left the room earlier (he was not charged with a crime). A prosecutor told the court that Tupac liked the woman so much, "he decided to share her as a reward for his boys."

All three beat the rape charges, although to different degrees: Agnant copped a plea to a misdemeanor, while Tupac and Fuller each were convicted of three counts of first-degree sexual abuse, meaning they groped and touched the victim without her consent. Tupac and Fuller were sentenced to two-and-a-half years in prison. Tupac and Fuller were acquitted of weapons charges; police had found two unlicensed handguns in the men's hotel suite. Tupac's lawyer, Michael

Warren, successfully argued that the weapons didn't belong to the pair. They also were cleared of sodomy charges, which, if convicted, would have required a prison term of up to 25 years. A jury rejected the woman's claim that Tupac had forced group sex on her. But they convicted him of the lesser sex-abuse charge. It meant prison time.

Tupac Shakur, inmate No. 96A1140, at 22, was sent to Riker's Island, a county jail, then to Down State Correctional Facility, a holding center near New York City, from February 28 to March 8, 1995, for a medical evaluation. Then he was bused to the Clinton Correctional Facility in Dannemora in upstate New York, 320 miles north of Manhattan. Considering he was not convicted of rape, Tupac's attorneys were stunned that the judge had shipped him to Clinton, nicknamed "Little Siberia," a maximum-security prison for men. (On June 3, 1845, Clinton's first 50 prisoners arrived in shackles, ankle-chains, and stripes. It was where New York sent its worst offenders.)

Meanwhile, in a highly unconventional ruling, at least at face value, a judge agreed to sever Jacques Agnant's case from Tupac and Charles Fuller's. Tupac later became convinced that Agnant was a government informer who'd set him up.

The verdict came a day after Tupac was shot five times in the lobby of the Times Square recording studio. He was in Bellevue Hospital when the verdict was to be read; he insisted on being released so he could face the jury. He wanted them to look him in the eye as they read the verdict. He went in a wheelchair, but had to leave early because he felt too sick.

For all his earlier legal troubles, it was the first shooting that became Tupac's most infamous event, the day before his sentencing. On Wednesday, November 30, 1994, Tupac was gunned down in the lobby of Quad Studios, a Manhattan recording studio in Times Square, assaulted by men police described as robbers. The case was never thoroughly investigated; it was closed shortly after it was opened.

While Tupac was recuperating from the attack in a New York hospital, Billy Garland, his biological father, paid him a visit. Garland told writer Kevin Powell, "I had to be there. He's my son. I've never asked him for anything – not money or nothing. I just wanted to let him know that I cared. He thought I was dead or that I didn't want to see him. How could I feel like that? He's my flesh and blood. Look at me. He looks just like me. People who I had never seen before immediately knew I was his father."

Tupac did 11 months of hard time at the Clinton Correctional Facility before Suge Knight posted bond, pending an appeal for the conviction. While incarcerated, Tupac married his girlfriend, Keisha Morris, an education student he'd dated for six months before being jailed. They met in June of 1994 at the Chippendale's club, now Capitol in New York. They spent time together in Tupac's bachelor pad – a large house outfitted with a swimming pool, big-screen TV, and pool table – in a pricey, secluded area of Atlanta, Georgia. For her birthday, that November 10, Keisha told *Sister 2 Sister* magazine, Tupac gave her a BMW 735. Later, he bought matching Gucci watches. He also gave her a large diamond in a platinum setting.

A female chaplain married them on April 29, 1995, in a prison ceremony. The marriage was annulled shortly after Tupac was released. Tupac later said it was a marriage of convenience that had seemed right at the time while he was in prison. But once he was out, his busy career and fast lifestyle got in the way of the relationship. He and Keisha parted as friends.

While in prison, Tupac continually told his friends he needed to get out. If he did, he vowed he wouldn't return to the thug lifestyle. He said he wanted to turn over a new leaf.

Death Row Records' Suge Knight sent Tupac a bullet-proof vest with "Death Row" and its insignia printed on it. Then Suge and his attorney, David Kenner, visited Tupac at the New York state prison. Tupac told Suge, "I want to join the family. Just get me out."

Suge and Kenner, apparently trying to capitalize on Tupac's desperation, presented him with a four-page handwritten record contract that committed Tupac to three albums for the Death Row family. In return? Knight and Kenner would get Tupac out of prison by posting the $1.4 million bond required for him to be released during the appeals process. Tupac signed. He also agreed to appoint Kenner, Death Row's long-time attorney, as his own lawyer.

On Thursday, October 12, 1995, according to the records department at Clinton Correctional, Tupac walked out of prison.

Some say it was only because Tupac was behind bars that he signed the contract with Death Row. Tupac was the breadwinner for his family – cousins, niece, mother, and half-sister. He had attorney fees and other lawsuits to settle. Death Row bailed him out, and not just out of jail, but financially as well. Friends and associates warned Tupac that he'd be selling his soul, that he'd be owned by Suge and Death Row, but Tupac signed anyway.

"Why they let me go, I don't know, but I'm out," Tupac rapped in a music video after his release.

Tupac was a free man. He was grateful to be out. Waiting for him upon his release was a private chartered jet that flew him from New York to Los Angeles. That same night, he was in a Los Angeles studio recording an album for the Death Row label. Within three days after his release from prison, he'd recorded seven songs. It marked the beginning of a torrent of songs – some 200 of them – Tupac would record between then and his fatal shooting 11 months later.

"There's nobody in the business strong enough to scare me," Tupac said during a *Vibe* interview. "I'm with Death Row 'cause they not scared either."

Tupac was openly grateful to Suge. "When I was in jail, Suge was the only one who used to see me," he said. "Nigga used to fly a private plane all the way to New York and spend time with me. He got his lawyer to look into all my cases. Suge supported me, whatever I needed. When I got out of jail, he had a private plane for me, a limo, five police officers for security. I said, 'l need a house for my moms.' I got a house for my moms.

"I promised him, 'Suge, I'm gonna make Death Row the biggest label in the whole world. I'm gonna make it bigger than Snoop ever made it.' Not stepping on Snoop's toes; he did a lot of work – him, Dogg Pound, Nate Dogg, Dre, all of them – they made Death Row what it is today. I'm gonna take it to the next level."

Tupac's Death Row Records solo debut, the double-CD *All Eyez on Me*, made $14 million in its first week in stores. It was the fastest-selling CD of 1996. With its 27 songs and titles such as "Shorty Wanna Be a Thug," "Wonda Why They Call U Bytch," and "Ratha Be Ya Nigga," it sold seven million copies.

Death Row was the world's premier rap label, producing more platinum albums than any other. And it wasn't just black youths from the ghetto who were buying the record. White boys from middle America were also lining up to hear his sound. The majority of fans and buyers of rap music are middle-class white youths; 70 percent of those who buy rap music are white. Not everyone, however, understood why so many were drawn to Tupac's music.

Richard Roeper, a columnist for the *Chicago Sun-Times*, called Tupac "a street-walking clown obsessed with guns, money, sex, and killing. His success isn't the story of someone rising above the thug life through his talent. It's the story of someone wallowing in it."

"As I write this," he continued, "I'm listening to *All Eyez on Me*. If I hear the words 'motherfucker,' 'bitch,' or 'nigger' one more time, I'm going to open the window and throw my little stereo into the sea. There's scarcely a mention of the word 'love' in any of the more than two dozen songs, but the aforementioned words appear more than 100 times apiece. It's a soundtrack for the '90s. Meet Tupac Shakur."

Tupac called Kevin Powell to the state prison while he was incarcerated. As he smoked one cigarette after another, he told the former reporter from *Vibe* magazine, "This is my last interview. If I get killed, I want people to get every drop. I want them to have the real story."

Tupac told Kevin that when he was first incarcerated, fellow inmates dissed him, "Fuck that gangsta rapper," they said. Tupac was insulted. He didn't like being recognized only as a gangsta rapper; he considered himself a fully-fledged rapper, one who was paving the way for others to follow. He said he rapped about life, which, in his world, included a lot of violence. He considered himself to be saddled with more responsibilities than others in his age group because people looked up to him, turned to him for answers. But there was a major problem: he'd been smoking so much marijuana and drinking so much alcohol that he was barely coherent. He called himself a "weed addict." Then he went to jail and was forced to get clean. Once off pot and booze, his mind had begun to clear. He talked to Kevin about two of his favorite themes: race and black-on-black violence.

"The real tragedy is that there are some ignorant brothers out here," Tupac told Kevin Powell. "That's why I'm not on this all-white or all-black shit. I'm on this all-real or all-fake shit with people, whatever color you are. Because niggas will do you. I mean, there's some foul niggas out there. The same niggas that did Malcolm X. The same niggas that did Jesus Christ. Every brother ain't a brother. They will do you. So just because it's black don't mean it's cool. And just because it's white don't mean it's evil."

Upon his release from prison, Tupac renounced the thug life (an acronym for The Hate U Give Little Infants Fucks Everybody), but his ambition for his career and passion for music were untamed. He was trying to keep the two elements of his career – movies and music – on track. He also was appealing his sexual-abuse conviction.

Tupac and Suge had become inseparable in the months after Tupac's release from prison. In between recording sessions, Suge took Tupac to Mexico and Hawaii. In return, Tupac brought a fresh star image, a charisma, to Death Row that the other rappers didn't have.

Tupac claimed that work had rehabilitated him. He used his performance in the movie *Gridlock'd* to prove it. "If nothing else," he said of his work on the film, "it'll just prove that I can show up to the set on time and still have an album that sells five million while I'm doing my shit. It'll just show that I work hard. Also, it'll show that I should not be in jail 'cause in the little bit of time I've been out, I've showed that I can be rehabilitated out here with everybody else. It's the money that rehabilitates me, not the jail." Tupac wanted people to know that he worked hard, that he wasn't a slouch.

But, as the world would later learn, Tupac was far from rehabilitated. He got out of prison swearing he was a changed man, but he quickly succumbed to the same gangsta lifestyle. Maybe worse.

Tupac became Death Row's artistic centerpiece, its biggest star. Along with him, Death Row became the hottest and biggest rap label ever.

In 1995, following the multimillion dollar success of his CD *Me Against the World* (with Interscope), and his co-starring role, with Mickey Rourke, in *Bullet*, Tupac founded a company, Euphanasia, to manage his film and music careers. Euphanasia (phonetic for euthanasia) was listed as his employer on the Clark County Coroner's report of his death. Months after his murder, the business was still operating. Seven months later, however, the telephone number had been disconnected and the office at 8489 West Third Street, Suite 1038, in Beverly Hills was closed.

A few months before his death, Tupac got engaged to Kidada Jones, daughter of Quincy Jones. They had known each other for just a few months. Once, Tupac had publicly criticized Quincy Jones for marrying Kidada's mother, Peggy Lipton, a white woman and former *The Mod Squad* star. Kidada, who had met Tupac at a nightclub, reportedly took a while to warm up to him because of that. After dating a short time, they moved together into a pricey Calabasas estate leased by Death Row. Tupac installed banks of video games and slot machines in an entertainment room for his friends and relatives who often stayed with the couple at their new digs.

Tupac's feelings about women were complex and contradictory. In a 1995 interview on MTV, he said his songs attacked loose women, but not all women. He told journalist Tony Patrick, "There ain't nothin' like a black woman." (He also rapped about his allegiance to his other "girlfriend," his favorite pistol.)

His feelings about children were, however, simple. In an *Esquire* article, Tupac talked about why he didn't want to have any.

"Procreation is so much about ego," he said. "Everybody wants to have a junior. But I could care less about having a junior to tell, 'I got fucked by America and you're about to get fucked too.' Until we get a world where I feel like a first-class citizen, I can't have a child. 'Cause my child has to be a first-class citizen, and I'm not having no white babies.

"There's no way around it unless I want to turn white, turn my back on what's really going on in America. I either will be in jail or dead or be so fuckin' stressed out from not going to jail or dying or being on crack that I'd just pop a vessel. I'll just die from a heart attack. All the deaths are not going to be from the police killing you."

During the last year of his life, Tupac's acting career was skyrocketing. Vondie Curtis Hall, star of TV's *Chicago Hope*, directed Tupac in the film *Gridlock'd* – which opened nationwide on January 29, 1997 – a dark comedy about survival adapted from Hall's semi-autobiographical screenplay. He told *Parade* magazine that Tupac had not been difficult to direct, despite his reputation to the contrary.

"When we cast Tupac, he'd just gotten out of jail, and a lot of people were leery of working with him. But he never caused problems," Hall insisted, "always coming to work prepared and on time. We never sensed that his luck was running out."

At the 1997 Sundance Film Festival in Park City, Utah, four months after Tupac was killed, actor Tim Roth talked about starring opposite the rapper in *Gridlock'd*.

"It was great [working with him]," Roth told a reporter for the *Park Record*. "I know him only from the set, so I didn't know his music and I hadn't seen his films, and he preferred that. When he came to meet me for the first time, he said, 'Please don't see any [films] if you haven't. Don't listen to the music. Don't see the videos. People are going to tell you things, and some of them are going to be true and some of them aren't, but try to come in with a clean slate.'

"He was very charming, very witty. He's a good actor, I think. My experience with him [was] we spent a lot of time laughing. I mean, we would get pissed off at each other and that's the normal way of things day-to-day, but we had a good time. A lot of stuff came out in the press, almost as though he deserved it when he died, but I look at him and think, 'Wow, that's a great actor.' If I saw the film and wasn't in it, just saw it, I would think, 'I would love to work with that guy.' So it *is* tragic. He was constantly writing. He would film during the day, then go off and direct videos, or produce videos, or be in the studio recording music or go off and write music. He was prolific."

Tupac played the straight man to Roth's crazy-junkie character.

"Comedy only works when you have somebody good and solid to fire your stuff off of," Roth told the *Park Record*. "Although Tupac was really funny in the film, he makes a really good straight man."

In an interview with *Mr. Showbiz* magazine, Roth said Tupac had a work ethic that surpassed others he had worked with: "He worked harder than any of us. He would be off directing videos at night and then go into the studio until four or five in the morning. Then he would be very tired and he would sleep as often as he could when there was down time. But he was very professional…"

"He talked about dying a lot," Roth said, "because he knew it would happen. He knew he wasn't going to live to a ripe old age. It just was not going to be what happened to him… He really wanted to get away from what was expected from him, from how people had pigeonholed him, and move on and do different things. That's why he was doing *Gridlock'd*. It was part of that change – which is a very adult emotion, so he was somebody who was really growing. He had all the talent to do that, and he had the power and the money to do that. But on the other hand, he couldn't keep his mouth shut. We'd talk about that, how exhausting it is to be that testosterone guy they want you to be on the street, then I would see an interview with him and he would talk about his life in a very mature way, and then I would see another interview with him and he would be getting in somebody's face. Like everybody, he had a very childish aspect and a very mature aspect. And they were in conflict. He knew there was no clear-cut way out of where he was at that time"

Roth's assessment was insightful. The conflict within seemed to stem from Tupac's prison-time perspective and the temptations and demands of the outside world. When he was in jail, he told reporters he was a changed man. But after his release, he reverted to his old ways, talking tough and throwing gang hand signs. In many ways he appeared harder than ever before.

While in prison, Tupac said he wanted to team up with his friend Mike Tyson after he got out and start a youth organization called Us First to keep kids out of trouble. The new Tupac preached anti-violence, but he often didn't practice what he preached.

The sequence of events on the night he was shot was a reflection of the almost schizophrenic contradictions in his life. On his way to perform at a Las Vegas charity event to keep kids out of trouble and off drugs, Tupac was seen beating Orlando Anderson and kicking him while he was down. Tupac played the role of the thug up until the end. Violence had become a way of life – and death – for him.

Former *Vibe* magazine senior writer Kevin Powell began interviewing Tupac during the early stages of his career and got to know him well. Powell described his relationship with Tupac as "very intense."

"I was his biographer for a while," he said. "Pac used to say to me all the time he wanted me to be his Alex Haley. [Haley] did the biography of Malcolm X.

"Sometimes I feel like a big brother to him, [like] I'm related to him. I miss him in a weird kind of way. You don't want to see anyone die. I think it was internal and external questions on Tupac that ultimately led to his demise. Internally, he could never seem to turn that corner."

The first time Powell interviewed Tupac was in 1993.

"Even then, he felt misunderstood," Powell said. "I had been following his career since 1990 when he was with Digital Underground. It was a social commentary. I liked what he was saying. He stood out in my mind. I started collecting notes way before I got the go-ahead [to write a story] from *Vibe*. I thought, 'This is a kid who's very much the '90s. He's one person who represents the hip-hop more than anybody else.'

"He was very much the period, the way James Dean was in the 1950s. He talked about dying. Always. The first piece I did with him in *Vibe*, he mentioned himself dying, and didn't want people to think he was a 'hate whitey' [person]. This kid off the bat was talking about things like that."

Powell said he doesn't know what would have become of Tupac had he lived.

"We'll never know," he said. "Tupac never really had the space to grow up, find out who he was. He was always in the public eye. The son of a famous Black Panther. He was selling drugs and trying to survive when he was young. The poverty dictated what he did. Once he had money, he was a workaholic. He never had time to take a step back. Everybody put pressure on Pac. Family, friends. He would have really had to take some time. He needed to step back and look at the source of that anger. He never, never got to do that. I was watching this documentary of Jimi Hendrix and it reminded me of Tupac. Everybody said [Hendrix] was dying out of frustration.

"I know from talking to people Tupac didn't even want to go to the Tyson fight that night. He wanted to chill in California. But he was a loyalist. He told them he would go, so he went. One thing Tupac said to me – I remember saying to him, 'Why don't you just be careful,' and he said, 'There's no place like careful. If it's time to go, it's time to go.' I think that's sad. In black America some people are just waiting for death. A lot of us are like that. I'm amazed at how much people just don't care.

"The first week in December 1995 was the last time I talked to him. I really believed, based on my conversations with him in prison, that he was going to change. He talked differently about women and racial issues. But then when I interviewed him on the set of a video, weed smoke came out of the trailer and he was flashing money. I took it personally. Sometimes as a journalist you get caught up. I thought, 'God, this guy, he's not going to change.' It depressed me. I knew it was the last time I would interview him. I didn't know he would die; I just knew it was the last time.

"I think, if there's anything we can learn from Tupac it's like, man, you cannot live your life that fast and that hard and that recklessly without thinking through every decision you make. I remember thinking the last time I interviewed him, I was wishing he had still been in jail. He would have been safe from the people who not only wanted to kill him physically, but who also wanted to kill him spiritually."

Sway, the San Francisco DJ, asked Tupac where he thought he might be in five years.

"I'll have my own production company, which I'm close to right now. I'm doing my own movies," Tupac told him. "I have my own restaurant, which I got right now with Suge and Snoop. I just wanna expand. I'm starting to put out some calendars for charity. I'm gonna start a little youth league in California so we can start playing some East Coast teams, some Southern teams. I wanna have like a Pop Warner League, except the rappers fund it and they're the head coaches. Have a league where you can get a big trophy with diamonds in it for a nigga to stay drug-free and stay in school.

"That's the only way you can be on the team. We'll have fun and eat pizza and have the finest girls there and throw concerts at the end of the year. That's what I mean by giving back."

"I see myself having a job with Death Row," Tupac continued, "being the A&R person and an artist that drop an album like Paul McCartney every five years. Not that I'm like Paul McCartney, but there's no rapper who ever did it, so that's why I use him as an example. But I wanna do it at leisure. My music will mean something and I'll drop deeper shit."

Four months after he was gunned down, Tupac Shakur was named Favorite Rap Hip-Hop Artist at the American Music Awards.

Even after death, Tupac had more than an avid following. Fans lined up for hours at record stores across the country, including in Las Vegas, awaiting the November 5, 1996, midnight release of his last album, *Don Killuminati: The 7 Day Theory*, released posthumously under his rap alias *Makaveli*. The day before, Mike Tyson, accompanied by several men, had tried to buy the CD a day early from the Tower Records Wow store on West Sahara Avenue in Las Vegas, about 10 miles from Tyson's Las Vegas mansion.

"He didn't believe us when we told him it wasn't available yet," said the store clerk who had waited on Tyson. "We told him, 'Come back tomorrow.'"

Tyson, he said, did return the next day and bought the CD.

Tupac's fourth posthumous collection, *Until the End of Time*, returned him to the top of the *Billboard* Top 200 albums chart four-and-a-half years after his death.

The double album of previously unreleased material from Tupac's vaults sold more than 426,000 copies to debut at No. 1, according to figures issued by SoundScan on April 4, 2001. The record became Tupac's fourth No. 1 album, a feat previously achieved by *Me Against the World* in 1995 and *All Eyez on Me* in 1996 while the rapper was still alive. *Don Killuminati: The 7 Day Theory* also reached No. 1.

Tupac's two other posthumous collections, *R U Still Down? (Remember Me)* in 1997 and the *Still I Rise* album with the Outlawz in 1999, peaked on the *Billboard* chart at No. 2 and No. 7, respectively. But *The Rose that Grew from Concrete*, a spoken-word album based on Tupac's poetry and featuring readings by fellow rappers, failed to break the Top 50 during its release in 2000.

8

ABOUT SUGE KNIGHT

HOMICIDE DETECTIVES WOULDN'T learn anything new about the shooting of Tupac Shakur during their questioning of Suge Knight. The interview took place a few days after the shooting. They did find out, however, what was going through Suge's mind as he made a U-turn and drove *away* from Flamingo Road instead of staying at the scene of the crime to wait for police and an ambulance. Suge told detectives his intent had been to find a hospital. Had Suge not turned around, had he kept driving east on Flamingo, he would have run into Desert Springs Hospital, practically next door to Club 662 where they were originally headed.

You have to wonder about that, at least a little. The police certainly did.

Suge, born Marion Hugh Knight in 1965, was not unfamiliar with the area. After all, he owned a house in Las Vegas. And he had spent two years at the University of Nevada, Las Vegas, also located just east of where the shooting had taken place. He played for the UNLV Rebels football team. He was there on a football scholarship.

Halfway through his college career, Suge had caught the attention of UNLV recruiter Wayne Nunnely, head coach of the Rebels in 1986, who later moved on to work for the National Football League's New Orleans Saints.

"You didn't really see that street roughness about him," he remembered about Suge. (Knight had grown up on the rough streets of Compton, California.)

A fellow player also said that rough side wasn't visible on the playing field.

Suge, according to Steve Stallworth, director of sports marketing at

UNLV and the starting quarterback when Suge played on the defensive line, "was all about the team." Stallworth said that his work ethic was second to none. "He never missed a practice. He was never even late for a practice."

Suge played for the Rebels in 1985 and '86, lettering both years as a first-team defensive lineman. He earned Rookie of the Year honors and was voted All Conference. He also was one of three player-elected captains of the team, along with teammate Eddie Wide Jr., during his senior year.

The last time Eddie Wide saw Suge was a couple of nights before Tupac was shot. They had run into each other during an evening out on the town.

"I saw him in passing," said Wide, who still lives in Las Vegas. "He was busy, taking care of business. I saw him and we talked, basically, 'How you doing, what's up.' You know, real quick."

Before that, the last time Wide had seen Knight had been in Irvine, California when the two were trying out for some Canadian football teams at a combine camp – a pro-football combination camp – where "different athletes are put together to showcase their talents," Wide explained.

"Suge was down there and a couple of other guys [from UNLV] were there, and we sat around and talked a little bit. We talked about what to do [on the field] mostly."

Wide described Knight as "a real cool guy everyone got along well with. If he had gang ties at the time, it didn't show."

"I wouldn't know about the neighborhood he came from or the kind of guy he was before [UNLV]," Wide continued. "We only met each other playing ball. What happened before that time, nobody knew. I didn't know if he was a gang member or not and I didn't care. I'm not from L.A. I was raised in Vegas pretty much all my life.

"Marion was one of those guys who could, if someone had a problem, he'd talk to them. He was the kind of guy you liked to be around because he was cool. He wasn't an asshole. He wasn't cocky. He got what he gave. Marion and I got along. We were buddies. We were the type of guys [who] might go to a club together or grab something to eat. It was mostly black guys he hung out with, but he got along with everybody.

"He's got some serious talent, as far as playing ball. Very talented. We all had the same goal, and that was to play pro ball. He did what had to be done on the field. It's a lot of work and the guys on scholarships worked hard. Marion came on a full ride [scholarship]. For somebody who was that talented, he could still be in pro ball."

As for his talent in the music business, that came later.

"The music thing, that kind of came out of the blue, because there was this one guy [on the team] named Eric Collins," Wide said. "Eric actually signed with Death Row later. Marion and Eric, these guys were both from L.A. Suge would always say how good Eric could rap. Eric *was* good. When Marion made the transition into music, I don't know. I was surprised at how big and how fast [Death Row] went up. With the guy's personality, you knew he was going to be successful at *something*. There were a lot of other guys getting in trouble in school. Some of the guys on our team are still in prison. To see Suge then and to see him now, I never would have predicted it, that he would be this kind of guy, the fact that he would have been in all the problems with the police, an outlaw. All the criminal activity, I never would have predicted."

Even while in college, with his sights set on becoming a professional athlete, Suge was moving toward becoming a businessman. While in school, Suge's favorite classes at UNLV were business-related, and his favorite instructor was a business professor. His records at UNLV have been sealed, the registrar's office said, after trying to pull up his transcripts in the college's computer system.

"I can't give out any information on that student," a school clerk said. "He has a hold on it himself so nothing about him can be given out. I can't give you any information without a signed release from him."

Suge's coaches say he left UNLV his senior year, without graduating, when the football season ended. He was drafted by the Los Angeles Rams, where he played part of a season. He crossed the

National Football League's picket line during a contract strike and played several games for the Rams before he was released.

He told *Vibe* magazine that he loved the game and still played sometimes, but that it wasn't meant to be for him. He had moved on.

Part of what Suge moved on to was trouble. In October 1987, Sharitha Lee Golden, mother of Suge's first child, obtained a restraining order in Los Angeles against her then-boyfriend that covered her, her sister, her mother, and her aunt.

"Once I refused to talk to him, he began to threaten me and my family... tamper with my car," Golden wrote in a court document.

(Suge and Sharitha later reconciled and, according to Clark County marriage license records, were married on Friday, November 3, 1989, at the Candlelight Wedding Chapel, advertised as "the No. 1 choice of recording, stage, and movie personalities in the heart of the Las Vegas Strip." Sharitha later headed Suge's management company, and they had a second child together.)

In November 1987, a month after Sharitha got the restraining order against Suge, he was arrested at his Las Vegas apartment for attempted murder, grand larceny auto, carrying a concealed weapon, and use of a deadly weapon to commit a crime. According to the crime report, Suge got into a fight with a man on Halloween night at Suge's home, at the Rancho Sahara Apartments at 1655 East Sahara Avenue, unit No. 3119.

The arrest report said that at 8:00 p.m. on October 31, "an altercation broke out between the above subject and another man, during which time Knight shot the victim twice – once in the wrist and once in the leg – with a handgun, then continued to chase him. After Knight shot the victim, he then got into the victim's vehicle, which was at the scene, a 1986 Nissan Maxima... and drove away without the victim's permission to take the vehicle."

Afterward, two LVMPD officers, Kathleen Alba and S. Stubbs, were called to the apartment complex to talk to Suge, but he wasn't there. At 10:00 p.m., a security guard called officers to tell them Suge had returned to his apartment.

Officers Alba and Stubbs returned.

"When we arrived," the officers' report stated, "we saw Knight coming out of the area of his apartment and when he saw us, he turned around and walked quickly back toward his apartment door where he removed a .38-caliber revolver from inside the waistband of his pants, which was covered up by the jacket he was wearing." The LVMPD officers confiscated the .38 Smith & Wesson Special.

Suge was arrested and kept overnight in a crowded and dirty holding cell. He was booked on November 2 into the Clark County Detention Center in downtown Las Vegas at Bridger Avenue and Second Street.

Suge Knight pleaded out to a misdemeanor in exchange for a suspended two-year sentence and was placed on three years' probation. He was fined $1,000.

Then, on June 6, 1990, Suge was charged with breaking a man's jaw in a scuffle outside a friend's house in Westside, the predominantly black area of town, when the man apparently said the wrong thing. Suge was accused of holding a gun to the man's face, while demanding an apology. The man apologized, but Suge hit him in the jaw anyway, first with his fist and then with a pistol. Suge was charged with felony assault with a deadly weapon and eventually pleaded guilty, according to the court record. He received a $9,000 fine, a two-year suspended sentence, and three years' probation. The judge also ordered Suge to complete "a temper-control counseling program."

Suge Knight was neither a rapper nor a musician and had no early connection to the music industry. He was a bodyguard in Los Angeles. While working security for rhythm-and-blues singer Bobby Brown, singer-actor Whitney Houston's husband, Suge spent time behind the scenes. He learned the ropes backstage at concerts and was sharp enough to recognize a good opportunity when it was right in front of him. After a while, he'd spent enough time around the L.A. rap scene to see its potential for making big money.

Suge became friendly with Tracy Curry, who rapped under the

stage name D.O.C. and put out albums for Ruthless Records. When D.O.C. was injured in a car accident, Suge took care of him.

"I've seen Suge do some shit to some motherfuckers that's out of this world," D.O.C. told *L.A. Weekly*. "Once, we were leaving a club and I was standing there waiting for my car to come, and some nigga run up on me like he's fixin' to hit me in the jaw, and Suge just tore his ass up – broke him down to his very components. Suge was a different nigga when he was doing his business."

In 1990 Suge began promoting shows in Los Angeles, where he became friendly with rap producer Andre "Dr. Dre" Young, whom journalist Joe Domanick in *L.A. Weekly* called "the greatest producer and best ear in the history of hip-hop music." While Dre was under contract with Ruthless Records, he was unhappy with the label. Suge talked him into forming an alliance with him.

Ruthless had been started by Eazy-E, a streetwise rapper known for his record "The Boyz N the Hood" who later died of AIDS. Suge planned to produce an album for D.O.C. and took Dre and D.O.C. to meet Dick Griffey, the chairman and founder of Solar Records and co-founder of the television show *Soul Train*. Griffey was considered a player and an insider in the record industry. Griffey and Suge reportedly intimidated Eazy-E, allegedly threatening him with pipes and baseball bats, into releasing Dre, D.O.C., and R&B singer Michel'le (once Dr. Dre's wife who later became Suge's second wife) from their contracts.

Suge denied the allegations. Still, the artists were released from their contractual obligations and Suge obtained copies of the signed releases. Subsequently, however, Ruthless Records sent out letters to major record companies telling them that the releases were signed under duress and should not be honored. As a result, no one would sign Dre, D.O.C., or Michel'le. Suge did what he had to do; he started his own label.

"We called it Death Row 'cause most everybody had been involved with the law. A majority of our people was parolees or incarcerated. It's no joke," Suge later said.

Money, as always, was an issue. A start-up record label can cost millions of dollars to get it off the ground. The company has to pay all the costs of recruiting talent, recording albums, and setting up a company infrastructure before any revenue comes in. Suge needed start-up capital.

The start-up money was secured, if perhaps from some sources that seemingly were less than legitimate. As a result, Death Row was the target of an investigation launched in 1995 by the Los Angeles Police Department, FBI, and three other federal law-enforcement agencies. The feds looked into whether the seed money had come from Michael "Harry-O" Harris, a major investor and drug dealer currently serving time on convictions for attempted murder and drug offenses. Harris's lawyer was David Kenner, who also at the time was Death Row's attorney of record. (The federal racketeering probe into allegations that Knight and his label committed acts of murder, drug trafficking, money laundering, and gun-running resulted in a pair of misdemeanor tax charges. Under a plea bargain arrangement filed Tuesday, January 15, 2002, in U.S. District Court in Los Angeles, Death Row pleaded guilty to failing to submit an income tax return. In exchange, the label paid a $100,000 fine and reimbursed the government an unspecified amount of unpaid taxes.)

Suge has stated that corporations such as Death Row's distributor, Westwood-based Interscope Records, were the source of the capital. Interscope for a time was owned by Time Warner. Time Warner sold its 50 percent stake in Death Row back to Interscope. Interscope, in turn, sold that share in 1996 to MCA Music Entertainment Group (now known as Universal) for a profit of roughly a $100 million. Funding for day-to-day operations for the label since the beginning has been by Interscope.

Wherever the funds came from, Suge Knight and Dr. Dre signed heavyweights Snoop Dogg (Calvin Broadus), Hammer, The Dogg Pound, Nate Dogg, Samm Sneed, Hug, KURUPT, K-Solo, Tupac Shakur, and others, and turned them into virtual money machines. Early on, Suge had dreams of making Death Row the Motown of the

'90s. By 1995, his record company had become the largest rap label in the world. In just a few short years, Death Row was grossing more than $100 million annually.

It's been said that signing with Death Row is like taking a blood oath. Death Row has been likened to a Mafia-like gang, with Suge Knight as the kingpin, or don.

"Death Row is a way of life," Suge told the *New York Times*. "It's an all-the-time thing. And ain't nobody gonna change that."

"Knight has successfully created a myth around himself as an executive not unlike a Hollywood mob figure who has strong-armed his way into the entertainment industry," Kevin Powell wrote in the October 31, 1996 issue of *Rolling Stone* magazine. "Many people inside the music business, afraid of his perceived power, were reluctant to speak on the record for this article."

Suge had built his reputation on intimidation tactics. As an example, to get into Death Row's studios, most visitors, including reporters, were searched for weapons; a guard at the door ran a hand-held metal detector over visitors' bodies before he'd let them in. Even reporters were scanned. If people in the music industry had appointments with Suge, he often would leave them waiting for hours, including top executives. It worked. People were afraid of Suge.

Knight, in a biographical profile released by Death Row, described himself as "12 o'clock."

"That's a street saying, '12 o'clock.' It means that I'm straight up and down. If I promise you I'm going to do something, you can believe it's going to happen. Mark my words, Death Row is going to be the record company of the decade."

Dr. Dre left Death Row to start a record label of his own. (Dr. Dre cut off any connection to Death Row; in 2001 he took out a restraining order against Suge and anyone associated with Death Row.) Distributor Interscope Records, too, severed all ties with the label, as did Time Warner. Still, Death Row had staying power. The label expanded into rhythm-and-blues, reggae, and jazz. Suge changed its name to Tha Row.

Suge defended his reputation in a *Vibe* interview, saying, "My mission is helping young black talent see their dreams happen. That's my ultimate purpose in this business, so fuck anybody who can't understand or deal with that. I know how I am and what my heart is like. I leave my judgment to God."

The music industry has been good to Suge Knight. As he made more money, he spent it lavishly. He purchased 34 vintage and luxury cars, symbols of his wealth. He also invested in real property.

On April 29, 1996, Suge purchased a 5,215-square-foot Las Vegas estate, built in 1968 and substantially remodeled in 1990. It sits on a 1.33-acre parcel overlooking a large section of Sunset Park in southeast Las Vegas. The single-story, red-brick, luxury home cost Suge $1,625,000. The estate, in the Sierra Vista Rancho Estates on Monte Rosa Avenue, sits in the horn of a cul-de-sac and beside a luxury golf course in an exclusive gated community just outside the Las Vegas city limits. It features four bedrooms, six full baths, three fireplaces, and a swimming pool and spa.

At a guard's booth to the entrance of Suge's neighborhood in December 2001, a security officer said, "Mr. Knight still lives here." Knight's name, indeed, was listed on the roster of residents. The first time he was seen at his home in several years, the officer said, "was just after he got out of prison the first time. I haven't seen him since he was released the second time [from federal prison]."

Suge's mansion is across the street from Mike Tyson's custom home. Also across the street is singer Wayne Newton's 57-acre Shenandoah Ranch, which covers the corner and more than a city block at Tomiyasu Lane, Sunset Road, and Pecos Avenue. Friends have said that Suge bought the property so he could be neighbors with Tyson and that Mike had encouraged him to move there.

Suge's house was filmed in the motion picture *Casino*. It was used to shoot the home-scene footage of Frank "Lefty" Rosenthal, a mob associate and former executive of the Stardust Hotel and Casino, played by actor Robert DeNiro.

A real estate agent, who asked that her name not be used, said that after Suge had purchased the residence, he had "redecorated like crazy." One of the first changes he'd made was to paint the sides of the pool blood red – which promptly turned orange from exposure to the chlorine and desert sun. The deck also was red, as was the master-bedroom carpet. Suge also had driven around town in a blood-red Rolls Royce Corniche.

Red is the color of the Bloods street gang.

The agent added, "The guy wears a seven-carat diamond in his ear, and I thought, 'Oh, my God, is he for real?' He and his entourage come in [to Las Vegas] once a month and throw huge parties."

On May 19, 1998, Suge's Las Vegas house was transferred into his new wife's name, listed with the county assessor's office as "Michel'le D. Toussant." The assessor's office lists Michel'le (pronounced Mish-a-LAY) as paying $1.2 million for the home, even though it was owned by her husband, whom she married while he was in a California prison.

At the time of Tupac's death, Suge had been living in Las Vegas part-time and his friends and associates had been frequent visitors, especially during boxing weekends. His rappers, including Tupac, were often spotted at Club 662.

It has been widely – and incorrectly – reported that Suge was the owner of the club, at 1700 E. Flamingo Road. In fact, Club 662, which had county business and liquor licenses pending at the time of the shooting, was owned by Las Vegas businesswoman Helen Thomas, president of Platinum Road Inc. The nightclub, originally built in 1972 on two acres, was leased to her. The club's attorney, George Kelesis, said Suge had shown an interest in buying it. The September 7 party was allowed to be held there because of a special one-time-only permit granted by the county.

Six months after Tupac's shooting, a "For Lease" sign was posted in front of the property, advertising it as a "restaurant/nightclub over 10,000 square feet." The once well-manicured grounds had weeds growing through the desert landscape that surrounded the club.

Dozens of cocktail glasses, some shattered, were strewn on the floor in the back storage area. Just months earlier it had been an exclusive, invitation-only hotspot. (Today, it once again operates as a dance club. It has been renamed the SRO Cafe and is a popular spot on the night-club circuit.)

Thanks to his success, Suge Knight's world encompassed his Tarzana studio (also done up in blood red), mansions in Encino and Las Vegas, a rented penthouse in Westwood, and a house in Compton. He often drove the 300 miles from Los Angeles, across the Mojave Desert via Interstate 15, to spend weekends in Las Vegas, going to prize fights and nightclubs.

But Suge's love affair with Las Vegas, which began when he was barely out of his teens, may have soured on September 7, 1996.

For Suge Knight, on his way to a benefit party at Club 662 with his friend and main hit-maker Tupac Shakur by his side, Las Vegas must have represented everything good about the world. A few violent moments later, as Tupac's blood spilled from fatal bullet holes, it sure-ly must have seemed like hell itself. Las Vegas is good for some and bad for others, with nothing in between.

Knight said he waited four days after the shooting of Tupac Shakur to talk to detectives because he needed time to collect his thoughts and to recover from the head wound he'd received. Two days after his meeting with homicide investigators, on the day Tupac died, David Chesnoff, one of his Las Vegas attorneys, drove Suge downtown to Sixth Street. Chesnoff said it was the FBI who had reminded Suge he needed to reg-ister as an ex-con. The 300-pound ex-linebacker walked into the finger-print section of the Metropolitan Police Department and registered for the first time with the state of Nevada as a convicted felon.

A long-time Nevada state law requires felons to register within 72 hours of arriving in the state. "Probably because of gaming," surmised Elizabeth Wright, supervisor of LVMPD's convicted-person registra-tion office. "They want to keep track of people coming into the state, the ones who have convictions."

Las Vegas police admittedly give preferential treatment to celebrities, at least when they register as felons. They're given the red-carpet treatment by the director of the section. Famous people don't have to stand in line for 30 minutes to three hours like the general public. If celebrities, or their attorneys, make a phone call in advance telling the director's office they'll be in, they're ushered through a back entrance so they don't have to mingle with the common folk. That's what Mike Tyson did when he was released from prison after serving out his sentence for a sexual-assault conviction.

Suge Knight was fingerprinted, his mug shot was taken, and he was interviewed by investigators. Police then ran his name in two national databases to see whether he had any new arrests or convictions. Seeing none, he was issued a wallet-sized convicted felon card to carry with him and he was on his way.

Death Row issued a statement following Tupac's murder. "Suge Knight and the entire Death Row Records family are saddened by the passing of our brother and star rap recording artist Tupac Amaru Shakur," the company said officially.

Unofficially, Knight told the *Los Angeles Times*: "If I could change things, I would give up Death Row, I would give up this lifestyle, I would give up a life to bring him back. Me and Tupac was joined at the hip."

Knight told reporter Jordan Pelaez that Tupac had spoken to him from his death bed. "We were in the hospital, and I was sittin' on the bed, and he called out to me and said he loved me," Suge told Pelaez.

Hospital officials, however, said Tupac never awakened from his coma and that he never spoke to anyone after he was admitted to the Trauma Unit.

To another reporter, Suge said, "I miss him. I had a lot of love for him, and I miss him."

And to *America's Most Wanted* television show, Suge said, "I loved Pac then, I love Pac now, he loved me. That's my little homey, and it's always going to be that way, you know? And nothing's going to change that.

"September 7 is a part of history. It's a sad day. It's an educational day."

However, also on *America's Most Wanted*, in an interview two months after Tupac's death, Detective Mike Franks described Suge's shortcomings as an eyewitness. "He's a hands-on witness. He's two feet farther away from Tupac, and he sees nothing," Franks said. "We spent three days just trying to get him [to talk to us]. I mean, this is a guy joined at the hip with Tupac? He's not that joined at the hip. He didn't try too hard."

Detective Brent Becker agreed, saying, "I know that some of these witnesses idolized this man. But they obviously didn't care for him enough to help bring in his murderers, and that's a pretty sad state of affairs."

Suge Knight's state of affairs definitely took a turn for the worse the fateful evening of Saturday, September 13, 1996. Rumors were already swirling about trouble at Death Row, and now he'd lost his top moneymaker and friend, Tupac Shakur. Some have gone so far as to say Death Row was on the brink of failure.

Afeni Shakur, Tupac's mother, filed a $17 million lawsuit against Death Row relating to her son's estate. After negotiations, an undisclosed settlement was reached.

Besides the FBI's investigation into Death Row's alleged ties to street gangs and the New York Mafia, a Los Angeles deputy district attorney was investigated by the California state attorney general's office for "unusual ties" to Death Row and Suge Knight.

And Death Row had reportedly fallen behind in meeting deadlines to deliver five albums that were scheduled to be released in the fourth quarter of 1996, the most profitable time of the year for record companies.

Worst of all, Suge himself had lost his freedom.

In 1995, Suge Knight pleaded no contest to assaulting two rap entertainers at a Hollywood studio, was placed on five years' probation, and warned to stay off drugs and to obey all laws. By taking part in the beating of Orlando Anderson at the MGM Grand the night Tupac was shot, a Superior Court judge ruled that Knight had violated the probation order.

In court just before he was sentenced, Suge made a statement to Superior Court Judge J. Stephen Czuleger:

"I been through a lot this year. I lost my best friend. A lot of people don't realize how it is to lose a best friend. I always wanted a little brother, and now he's not here.

"As far as the situation with the fight, I'm not trying to open up the case or go back to the incident in Vegas, but I wanna stipulate on that because it's important to me, 'cause I gotta live with this. When [Orlando] Anderson came up to testify, I'd be the first to say he's not a friend of mine. And to be honest, I felt that this guy could play with the truth and go against me just to lie. But since he was under oath, I felt he told the truth.

"Your honor, I was breakin' up the fight. I knew I was on probation. I put my freedom and my life on the line. And I feel if I wouldn't have stopped that fight – I'm not saying the same person who came and shot us later was these type of people, but if they was, instead of me getting shot in my head and one person dead, it could have been 30 people dead in Vegas at the MGM.

"And even at the end, Your Honor, when everybody say, 'It was a kick,' it wasn't a kick. I admit that I was breaking up a fight, and I admit I was frustrated, but at the same time, it's not a nine-year kick. This guy wasn't harmed. Wasn't anything broke on him. If you ask anybody that seen me fight, Your Honor, the first they'd tell you is, 'That guy wouldn't be standing there giving statements.' When I fights, sir, I fights.

"But I've changed my life to get away from fighting. And I wanna enlighten not just you, but the courtroom, because my family is here. And it might be the last time I speak to my family. I could go to jail and anything could happen. But I'm not here for the judge to feel pity for me. I'm just speaking from my heart.

"I'm not gonna waste any more of the court's time, but I just thought it was important that I get this off my chest and address the court the way I feel."

Despite his plea for leniency and his team of attorneys' earlier filings of motion after motion, on Friday, February 28, 1997, Judge Czuleger handed down a harsh sentence.

"The defendant is sentenced to nine years in state prison," he told the court. Then he turned to Knight and said, "You did blow it."

Suge's attorneys appealed the ruling and unsuccessfully tried to have Suge released. Las Vegas attorneys, David Chesnoff, described Suge as "a political prisoner," noting, "He's been punished enough."

No one else involved in the Orlando Anderson beating on September 7 was arrested or charged in connection with the scuffle. The greatest irony is that, officially, the scuffle incident never happened. Las Vegas police did not file a crime report, therefore there was no crime. Suge was sentenced to nine years of hard time for something for which no official record exists.

Suge's life in prison was a far cry from the high-flying days when the Hip-Hop Nation's largest rap label in history produced records from the top rap artist ever. On March 12, 1997, four months after his arrest, Suge was taken by a prison bus from Los Angeles county's central jail to Delano, California, where he was incarcerated at the North Kern State Prison near Bakersfield, housed as prisoner No. K43480. Suge was placed in the reception wing – DC6 unit, cell No. 229L – awaiting permanent quarters.

On May 21, 1997, Suge was transferred to the California Men's Colony East. The prison, on State Highway 101 three miles west of the quaint city of San Luis Obispo and nine miles east of Morro Bay, is a medium- to high-security facility. Two prisons there (East and West) house 6,500 inmates. Suge was placed in the East prison because of his notoriety and for his safety, according to prison spokeswoman Terri Knight (no relation). The facility has armed security and a double-fenced line surrounding it. Other celebrities incarcerated there in the past have included Christian Brando, Ike Turner, Thomas "Hollywood" Henderson (a former linebacker for the Dallas Cowboys convicted of drug-related crimes), and several members of the Charles Manson family.

In an interesting aside, the prison guard also said that officials had hung on a wall in Suge's prison module an LAPD "wanted" poster for the suspect in the Biggie Smalls's murder.

To get privileges within the prison system (such as phone use, quarterly packages from family members, and canteen privileges for snack foods), inmates must work in a prison-industry factory, making state license plates, prison-issue T-shirts and shoes, textile products and socks, work boots for forestry crews, and jackets. Inmates also have the option of going to school, but the privileges are better from the factory work.

Suge was allowed to have non-contact visits four days a week with people who were approved by the prison, including his team of attorneys.

Suge eventually worked a yard detail job at the prison. According to a guard inside the facility, "The 'gardening jobs' are pretty much a farce. The guys walk around and pick up trash for seven hours. We have no 'gardens.' We do have lots of grass, so a few of the guys in those jobs cut the grass once or twice a month in the summer, but I haven't seen Suge doing that. In actuality, the guys in those jobs work for about a half an hour a day. They check in with their supervisor a couple of times a day, then get lost for most of their work shift. The workers are very loosely supervised, if they're supervised at all, because their supervisor is responsible for lots of other custodial duties that make it impossible for him or her to actually spend much time with the yard crew."

All that ended when Suge came under suspicion by the LAPD. For his own protection, he was moved to Administrative Segregation, or "ad seg." "He only leaves his cell for showers, exercise, or non-contact visits, which take place in a small room with both participants behind glass," the prison guard told me. "He is fed in his cell. They justified it as a protective custody precaution since he is now a suspect in Biggie's death."

Once he was moved to Mule Creek prison in Ione, California, Suge was housed once again in the general population with a cellmate. Suge, according to prison spokesman Sean McCray, adjusted so well that his release date was moved up. Also, because he had no disciplinary problems, he was given more privileges at the 4,000-inmate prison. "They did an assessment," McCray said. "He met the criteria for custody reduction. That allows Mr. Knight to go out into the evening yards in the after daylight hours. He has visiting rights in the evenings as well as family visits."

Night visits were Thursdays and Fridays. Just as they had at the San Luis Obispo prison, visitors of Suge often arrived in limos. "We have several limousines showing up now and then to see Knight," Cray said. Included on his visitor list was singer Michel'le, a petite R&B singer with a squeaky Betty Boop-like speaking voice. She surprised many with her rich throaty singing style. Guards at the prison entrance of both the San Luis Obispo and Mule Creek prisons sometimes allowed Michel'le to bypass the lengthy processing of visitors.

Suge was eligible for parole after five years, which included "good-time" credits he'd earned at both prisons. Until that time, his incarceration meant he could not run Death Row Records. Knight's former wife Sharitha, from whom he amicably separated, ran the day-to-day operations in the beginning. Later, it was a group of about five Death Row employees who kept the label going.

On April 20, 2001, Suge was paroled from the Mule Creek State Prison in Ione, California, then transferred to a federal prison in Sheridan, Oregon, to finish the remaining months of his sentence. He'd been on probation for state and federal charges when he was sentenced to nine years in prison for violating his probation by taking part in the Las Vegas fight.

Federal investigators had been building a racketeering case against Death Row Records by probing alleged links to street gangs, drug traffickers, and organized-crime figures, sources told the *Los Angeles Times*. The investigation, which began shortly after Suge was jailed, involved agents from the FBI, the Internal Revenue Service, the Bureau of Alcohol, Tobacco and Firearms, and the Drug Enforcement Administration. Police in Los Angeles and Las Vegas were reportedly working on the case.

David Chesnoff, Suge's Las Vegas attorney in the federal case, had this to say about the federal probe: "Apparently there's a grand-jury investigation. There's been document production and I know they've interviewed witnesses. But that's all I know. Unlike the President Clinton grand-jury investigations, we don't get to read in the newspapers about what they [federal investigators] are doing."

According to the *Los Angeles Times* account, the feds were determining whether members of the Bloods had committed crimes while on Death Row's payroll, and whether Death Row had been launched with drug money or other illegal funds. Suge's association with convicted drug kingpins Michael "Harry-O" Harris and Ricardo Crockett, both of whom were imprisoned, was also being looked at by federal agents. Suge admitted knowing the men but said he did not take money from them to launch Death Row. Because Harris was serving time for, among other things, a narcotics conviction, they believed drug money may have been used by Knight.

According to a federal grand-jury indictment filed in Las Vegas in 1993, Suge Knight was listed as the 34th defendant, along with Crockett, in a drug-distribution ring in which cocaine was brought in from Los Angeles and sold in Las Vegas. The indictment alleged that Crockett ran the operation, selling the cocaine to his sub-distributors for further sale in the Las Vegas area between July 1992 and May 1993. The indictment also charged that Crockett and others had used guns to protect the operation or to rob other narcotics dealers of money and drugs. Suge ended up with a gun-possession conviction in the Crockett case and received probation. Crockett was convicted of drug charges and sent to a penitentiary.

The feds were also reportedly looking into Suge's investment in the now-defunct Club 662 for links to organized crime. On February 13, 1997, a federal grand jury subpoenaed the financial records of

Suge, his attorney David Kenner, Death Row Records, and 36 companies, including Club 662, and individuals who had done business with them.

One of Suge's many lawyers is John Spilotro, attorney of record for Suge's 1987 attempted murder charge in Las Vegas. Spilotro was the nephew of the late Chicago mobster Anthony "Tony the Ant" Spilotro, an "enforcer" and the muscle behind the mob in Las Vegas in the 1970s.

From L.A. County Jail where he was incarcerated at the time, Suge vehemently denied the federal allegations of ties to organized crime, saying he was being targeted because of his race.

"This is the most outrageous story I have ever heard," he told the *Los Angeles Times*. "A black brother from Compton creates a company that helps people in the ghetto, so what does the government do? They try to bring him down."

Suge's company attorney, David Kenner, also strongly denied allegations of mob ties to the New York Genovese family, telling reporters, "Suge wouldn't know a member of the Genovese crime family if he tripped over him."

Oscar Goodman, a famous Las Vegas attorney who made a successful career of representing mob figures and later became mayor of Las Vegas, was in court in L.A. as a consultant on Suge's case. Goodman is also partners with David Chesnoff, Suge's federal attorney of record.

"I went down to Los Angeles as a consultant on [Suge's] revocation case," Goodman told me. "I went down there for one court proceeding and counseled with the lawyers who actually made the presentation. The judge [Superior Court Judge Stephen Czuleger], in my opinion, went through the charade of pretending to afford Knight due process and gave the decision. The presentation by defense attorneys couldn't have been better. They walked beautifully through their presentation to the judge. They shouldn't have wasted their time and effort. The judge, I think, enjoyed the media attention, and it was a foregone decision. It was a done deal. Before they even made their presentation, the judge's mind was already made up. The decision was made and the judgment typed up.

"On the federal case, if there ever was any federal case, if anything ever came to light federally, I would probably be involved."

In a standard FBI-style non-denial, Special Agent John Hoose with the FBI's Los Angeles bureau told me, "We've neither confirmed nor denied there's an investigation."

But George Kelesis, another Las Vegas lawyer who has represented Suge, said he got a call from out-of-state FBI agents after Tupac was shot, questioning the lawyer about Suge's business dealings. He said he believes the feds unfairly targeted Suge.

"He was definitely a target," Kelesis said. "I think it has more to do with the image, the image that they manifest. I can tell you I have not seen a shred of tangible evidence that would indicate to me that he is involved in a criminal enterprise. And I'm not blowing smoke and hot air."

On Monday, August 6, 2001, Suge Knight was released from a federal prison in Sheridan, Oregon. He boarded a plane for Los Angeles and went straight to the studio to work. At his headquarters in Beverly Hills, a huge billboard above his offices greeted him with the words "Welcome Home Suge."

In January 2002, Suge was acquitted of all federal racketeering charges leveled against him while he was in prison.

Today, he's a free man. His record company has been renamed Tha Row. From all appearances, Tha Row and Suge Knight are thriving. In April 2001, Tha Row, while Suge was still incarcerated, released *Until the End of Time*, an album with some of Tupac's previously unreleased songs. It debuted at No. 1 on *Billboard*'s Top 200 list.

9

THE MURDER OF YAFEU "KADAFI" FULA

YAFEU "KADAFI" FULA (also called Yak) was gunned down in the hallway of a federal housing project in Irvington, New Jersey, two months and two days after Tupac Shakur was fatally shot.

Yaasmyn Fula, one of Afeni Shakur's best friends and Kadafi's mother, lost her only son in the shooting. Las Vegas police lost their only willing witness to Tupac's murder.

Yafeu Fula was born on Sunday, October 9, 1977, and raised in Irvington, New Jersey. Like most of his fellow rappers in the back-up group the Outlawz, Kadafi had led a troubled youth growing up in the ghetto.

Kadafi looked up to Tupac like he was his big brother. Tupac, after all, had mentored him. Many of Fula's friends believed that he and Tupac were half-brothers. They weren't. While their mother's were close friends, they were not related.

At the time of his death, Yafeu was living in Montclair, New Jersey.

Kadafi had toured with the Outlawz, first called Thug Life, then Outlaw Immortalz, a quartet who regularly backed Tupac in concert and appeared with him on the first album he cut for Death Row, *All Eyez on Me*. All of the back-up singers, including Kadafi, had had the words "THUG LIFE" tattooed, like Tupac, across their mid-abdomens. Tupac planned to produce records for the group under his newly formed company, Euphanasia. Tupac hired Fula's mother Yaasmyn to manage his Beverly Hills-based company.

Yafeu, just 19-years-old, was an unwitting player in the events surrounding Tupac's murder. He was a passenger and eyewitness in the Lexus that was directly behind Suge's BMW when Tupac's shooting occurred. Bodyguard and former peace officer Frank Alexander was driving the Lexus; neither he nor the other passenger, rapper Malcolm Greenridge, who performed in the Outlawz as E.D.I., would immediately admit to seeing Tupac's assailant. Only Yafeu told police at the time that he thought he could pick out Tupac's shooter from a photo line-up. He was the only witness that night who exhibited a willingness to help investigators.

"Yafeu Fula was the only one who gave us an indication in the [initial] interview he could identify the gunman," then-homicide Lieutenant Wayne Petersen said. "His statement was, 'Yeah, I might be able to recognize him.'"

But in the aftermath of the shooting, detectives were frustrated by not being able to schedule an interview with Kadafi. Once Fula left Las Vegas, detectives were referred to Death Row attorney David Kenner, one of the lawyers they'd dealt with in their attempt to interview Suge Knight.

Before a meeting could be arranged, Fula was murdered.

On Sunday, November 13, 1996, at 3:48 a.m., Fula was fatally shot in the face at point-blank range with a handgun while in a hallway of a federal housing project on Mechanic Street in Orange, New Jersey, where his girlfriend lived. Found slumped against a hallway wall on the third floor, he was taken by ambulance to University Hospital in Newark. Efforts to save his life were futile, and he was pronounced dead at 1:00 p.m. Yafeu Fula was born on a Sunday, and he died on a Sunday.

There were reports that Fula had been wearing a flak jacket when he was shot. Bruce "Fatal" Washington, a fellow rapper in the Outlawz, told reporters that Fula and the other members of the group frequently wore bullet-resistant vests for protection, especially in the wake of Tupac's murder.

Like Tupac, Fula was shot following a Tyson heavyweight prize fight, slain just hours after Mike Tyson-Evander Holyfield fight in Las Vegas.

Within two days of the murder, Orange police arrested and charged an Irvington, New Jersey teenager in connection with the murder. A few hours later, on the afternoon of November 14, 1996, a second suspect surrendered to investigators working for the Essex County prosecutor's office. Nine months later the teenagers' identities were revealed as Kaseem Nadier Way and Rashad Clark. Their names weren't released earlier because they were minors.

Orange Police immediately claimed the Fula case was not related to Tupac's murder. Publicly, Las Vegas investigators, too, insisted there was no link. LVMPD's Sergeant Manning attributed Fula's death, in part, to the general nature of being a young black male in this country today, with the odds against him.

Another officer close to the case agreed, comparing it to Tupac's murder. "Just because Tupac was famous," he said, "does not mean we're going to assign more detectives than usual [to the case]. Tupac was a young black man in America, and young black men get murdered."

Statistics show that black-on-black gun violence has been the leading cause of death for black youths aged 15- to 19-years-old since 1969. From 1987 to 1989, the gun homicide rate for black males aged 15 to 19 increased 71 percent. Of the roughly 20,000 murders committed each year in the U.S. between 1991 and 1995, 50 percent were cases involving black victims.

Privately, Las Vegas police say that while their sense is that the Fula case probably *is* related to Tupac's, they have to go on the evidence, not a gut feeling. The criminal-justice system demands that when police submit a case to the district attorney's office, the evidence must be strong enough for it to be approved for criminal prosecution. Manning said he couldn't go on instinct and he couldn't go on a gut feeling. Still, it's hard to imagine that a possible star witness to a murder who gets gunned down just two months later isn't in some way connected to the crime he witnessed.

Having been intimately involved with this story for months, I recognized the connection the minute I heard about it and broke the story.

I was working on Monday, November 14, making my beat rounds on the phone as I did every morning. Since I was working at the time for an afternoon daily, I was on deadline each morning for that day's edition. I made a routine phone call to homicide to see whether there was anything new in the Shakur investigation. I was told that detectives had sketchy information that a witness in the case had been murdered back East; homicide had gotten a message overnight on its answering machine. The investigator didn't know how to spell Yafeu Fula's name. He didn't know the name of the city where the witness was murdered. He did know that it had happened somewhere in New Jersey.

I hung up and immediately relayed what little I knew to the city desk and was told to see what I could get in 30 minutes. In the meantime, the news desk freed up space on the front page just in case the story panned out.

I picked cities at random, phoned directory assistance for the numbers, and then, one by one, called about 10 police departments; the last one had heard there'd been a murder in Orange, New Jersey. I called the police department there and asked for the homicide division. An officer confirmed that there had been a murder the day before. The captain who could tell me about it, however, was in a meeting, unavailable to speak with me. No one else there was authorized to talk to the press. The officer invited me to attend an afternoon news conference. I told him that I was in Las Vegas and needed information for that day's paper. He said he'd heard the homicide got a brief routine mention in one of the area's newspapers, but he didn't know which one. He also said that no mention was made that Fula was an eyewitness in Tupac's murder and that police had been trying to schedule an interview with him. I called the papers. Within a few minutes, I reached a reporter at the *Star-Ledger* in Orange who faxed me a copy of an article.

The newspaper reported that Yafeu Fula had been shot to death. Wire services had not moved the story overnight.

The connection had not been made – nor reported – that Fula was a key witness in Tupac's murder and that now he, too, was dead.

Orange Police Captain Richard Conte called me a few minutes later with the details. The captain told me he had not been made aware that Fula was a witness to a murder.

My paper, the *Las Vegas Sun*, bannered the story on the front page, above the fold. The article began, "A key witness Metro Police have been trying to interview since the fatal shooting of rapper Tupac Shakur has been murdered in New Jersey." The Associated Press picked up the piece and it was the lead story on local and national TV news programs that evening.

Officially, Las Vegas and Orange police claimed that Fula's murder was not connected to Tupac's slaying. "It doesn't appear at this time to be involved with the Tupac Shakur killing," Captain Conte told reporters who followed up on the story.

When I pressed him about a Las Vegas connection, Conte said Fula knew the two people who shot him and that it may have been drug-related.

"From what we understand right now," the captain said, "one has nothing to do with the other. I think it's more or less a lifestyle-related homicide, as opposed to Death Row versus Biggie and all that. The availability that people have of drugs and guns – I think he died because of that, not because he saw Tupac Shakur killed. It was a lifestyle thing. [Fula] was going out with a girl there. He was at her apartment."

Conte noted, "In talking to California and Las Vegas detectives, I do not believe [Fula's death] was related to either Tupac Shakur or gang affiliation. With the evidence at hand, I can say it's not gang-related."

LVMPD's Sergeant Kevin Manning, as well, maintained there was no evidence to link Fula's killing with his being a witness in Shakur's murder. "Based on the information we received from Orange Police, we don't think there's a connection," Manning told me. Las Vegas homicide detectives never went to New Jersey to interview the murder suspects. They based their opinions on Conte's.

Manning, did, however, express defeat. "It just kind of adds to our frustration about this whole investigation," he said. "It's another dead end for us. He spoke to us the night of the shooting, and based on what we got from him that night, we wanted to speak to him again. We wanted to show him some photographs."

Both suspects in the murder pleaded not guilty. One of them was a blood cousin of Outlawz member Mutah Wasin Shabazz Beale, who uses the moniker of "Napoleon."

Kaseem Nadier Way and Rashad Clark remained in custody at the Essex County Youth House until their cases were processed by the judicial system.

After the arrests of Way and Clark, Captain Conte said, "Basically, the case is over." Prosecutor Clifford Minor, however, said the investigation into Fula's death was continuing and that it was too early to speculate on a motive.

On Wednesday, October 14, 1998, according to Essex County court records, the indictment against Kaseem Nadier Way was dismissed by the court after a motion was filed by the prosecution. A court administrator said the dismissal was for lack of evidence. Kaseem was released from custody.

Rashad Clark was offered a plea bargain to a lesser charge of manslaughter in the Fula case. He accepted it. On October 9, 1998, Rashad was sentenced by Judge Richard Camp to seven years in prison, with a three-year parole eligibility.

A motive in the murder has never been made public.

After four years of silence about the shooting, in 2001 members of the Outlawz talked about Yafeu's death, in magazine interviews. They said that Napoleon's cousin was playing with a gun when he exchanged words with Yafeu. The gun, they said, accidentally went off in Yafeu's face. The police investigation never mentioned an accident and the rap group's take on the shooting has never been corroborated.

Since Tupac and Kadafi's deaths, the Outlawz have remained together. They originally signed with Death Row Records in March 1997. But after a contract dispute, they left to record under an indie label.

10

THE MURDER OF BIGGIE SMALLS

ON SUNDAY, MARCH 9, 1997, East Coast rap superstar Biggie Smalls, also known as Notorious B.I.G., was attending a star-studded party in Los Angeles to celebrate the 11th Annual Soul Train Music Awards. He'd been in Los Angeles for about two weeks doing West Coast interviews and had canceled a flight to Europe so he could attend the post-awards get-together. The party, held at the Petersen Automotive Museum in the mid-Wilshire district of Los Angeles and sponsored by *Vibe* magazine, Qwest Records, and Tanqueray gin, was supposed to have been private, but by the time Biggie and his associates and friends arrived, about 2,000 people had filed into the museum.

Biggie, six-foot-three and weighing 350 pounds, wore a long-sleeved black-velour shirt and faded blue jeans. It was too warm for a jacket. Around his neck on a heavy gold chain hung a large gold Jesus Christ pendant, not the prized Bad Boy Entertainment gold medallion and logo with a baby wearing a baseball cap and work boots. Biggie also wore one of his trademark hats, a bolo riding cap.

Biggie was a presenter at the awards ceremony at the Los Angeles Shrine Auditorium. He was booed as he walked on. It didn't daunt his enthusiasm, though. He bent over the mike and said, "Whad up, Cali?" He felt honored to be a presenter. He was in good company. Also appearing throughout the evening were co-hosts Gladys Knight, LL Cool J, and Brandy, along with fellow presenters Snoop Dogg, Aaliyah, Immature, Tisha Campbell, and Heavy D.

The night's biggest award, for Best R&B/Soul or Rap Album, went posthumously to Biggie's onetime rival, Tupac Shakur, for his multi-platinum double disc *All Eyez on Me*.

The night also marked the end of a lengthy recording session in L.A. as well as a big promotion opportunity for Biggie's *Life After Death* album, to be released in just two weeks. All Biggie wanted to do that night was relax with his friends.

The guest list for the party included Heavy D, Busta Rhymes, Chris Tucker, Da Brat, Yo-Yo, Jermaine Dupree, and, of course, Biggie Smalls and his friend, record producer, and owner of Bad Boy Records, P. Diddy Combs. Also attending was Kidada Jones, Tupac's girlfriend at the time of his death.

A noteworthy, if not a surprise, attendee was Orlando Anderson, the reputed Crips gang member all but accused of having something to do with Tupac's murder. Also with Orlando was his uncle, Keefee D, or Dwayne Keith Davis, an alleged Crips member. LAPD homicide detective Fred Miller, a lead detective in the Biggie Smalls murder case, later told me that Orlando's appearance had "no significance" for investigators and that they had ruled out Orlando as a player in the murder-scene scenarios. Orlando had been trying to break into the music business and had built a studio in a garage behind his Uncle's Compton house, where he lived.

At about eight o'clock the guests began arriving at the auto museum on Museum Row on the Miracle Mile in the Wilshire District near Hollywood.

At the post-awards party, the DJ played a single, "Hypnotize," from Biggie's new album. Biggie talked about the new release in an interview with Black Entertainment Television. "If you thought the [first] album was a fluke, hold your head, 'cause this next one, man, it's all. It's all like you never thought. The next album is called *Life After Death*, and we ain't takin' no prisoners."

By 9:30 p.m. the party began to take off. It was about that time, witnesses later recalled, that Biggie was seen enjoying himself, talking and laughing. He sat at a table on the edge of the dance floor, directly in front of a classic German car, with Combs and record-producer Jermaine Dupri.

Russell Simmons, president and CEO of Def Jam Records, stopped by Biggie's table. Actor Wesley Snipes and singer Seal, among others, were sitting nearby. Women danced for Biggie at his table. Biggie, who was using a cane, couldn't get up and dance with them because he had broken his leg in a car accident and was still recovering. He signed autographs. He appeared to be having a good time.

More people crowded onto the second floor of the museum. By midnight, the room was overly packed. About 30 minutes later, at 12:35 a.m., Los Angeles fire marshals, already standing by for the special event, announced they were breaking up the party. By that time, an estimated 2,000 were in attendance. Two hundred fans milled around outside hoping to catch a glimpse of a celebrity. The building needed to be evacuated, fire marshals said.

"This party is over!" barked a fire marshal's voice over a loudspeaker. "Please leave in an orderly manner. Immediately!"

As people left, Biggie and Puffy Combs stayed upstairs waiting for the crowd to disperse. Biggie had to take it slowly because of his leg. While they waited, they posed together for a last-minute photo. It would be the last photograph taken of Biggie alive.

By 12:45 a.m., the guests spilled onto the street. Biggie and Puffy emerged from the building. They talked with friends and made arrangements to meet at a private after-party at the home of Interscope Records executive Steven Stoute.

Biggie and his group left the parking garage and walked to the street, where their SUVs were parked. Biggie climbed into the front passenger seat of his rented GMC Suburban (he didn't have a driver's license and never drove himself). Biggie's driver, a bodyguard and friend identified only as Greg, got behind the wheel.

Just like Tupac six months before him, Biggie was sitting shotgun. He was a perfect target.

On the bumper of Biggie's Suburban was a sticker that read "Think B.I.G. March 25, 1997," which was a promotion for his upcoming CD release. Damien "D-Roc" Butler and Lil' Cease got in the back seat. Another Suburban, carrying Combs and others, pulled into the street. Biggie's Suburban followed. Falling in behind Biggie's vehicle was a Chevy Blazer. The Blazer carried the group's personal bodyguards –

all off-duty cops from the Inglewood Police Department, the same pool of moonlighting cops from which Suge Knight had drawn. One of those off-duty cops was behind the wheel of the Blazer.

The convoy headed down Fairfax Avenue toward Wilshire Boulevard. All three SUVs stopped at a red light at the Wilshire intersection, about 100 yards from the entrance to the museum. Just then, a dark-colored sedan pulled up next to the second GMC's passenger side and stopped. The sedan's driver, a black man in his early twenties wearing a suit, dress shirt, and bowtie, stuck a 9-millimeter silver-colored handgun out the window and opened fire. More than a half-dozen rounds were pumped from the semiautomatic. Biggie, who for a moment had a look of surprise on his face, was hit seven times in his chest and abdomen. He was the only one injured.

Damien and Lil' Cease saw enough of the shooter to help police draw a composite sketch of him. Damien told the *Los Angeles Times* that Biggie, for a fleeting moment, appeared to recognize the shooter.

Puffy Combs said he heard the crack of gunfire. "I jumped out of my car and ran over to his," he told the *New York Daily News*. "I was saying the Lord's Prayer and Hail Marys. I was begging God to help him out. I was touching him and talking to him in his ear."

Biggie lost consciousness almost immediately. He was slumped over in his seat.

The shooter, in the meantime, simply drove away. The off-duty Inglewood Police Department officers moonlighting that night as security for Biggie and Puffy took off in their Blazer after the gunman. Their efforts were unsuccessful. The shooter had sped away into the night. The off-duty cops did not get a license-plate number.

Lil' Cease, Damien, and Puffy tried to move Biggie, but he was too heavy. Instead, they propped him up in the passenger seat and closed the Suburban's door. Lil' Cease and Damien got in the back. Puffy followed behind in his Suburban. They left the scene of the crime and headed for Cedars-Sinai Medical Center, less than two miles away.

When they arrived at the hospital, they helped emergency personnel lift Biggie's lifeless body onto a stretcher.

Biggie Smalls was dead on arrival. Hospital officials said Biggie probably died immediately after being shot.

He'd suffered massive injuries from the seven shots he'd taken in his chest and abdomen. He'd lost a lot of blood from internal injuries. Still, for about 20 minutes, doctors and emergency-room personnel tried to resuscitate him. But he had been mortally wounded. "They tried everything in the hospital to revive him," said Voletta Wallace, Biggie's mother. "Everything."

At 1:15 a.m., 24-year-old Christopher George Latore Wallace was pronounced dead at Cedars-Sinai, the same hospital where Eazy-E had died of AIDS the year before.

"He died in my arms," Biggie's friend Damien told the *Los Angeles Times.*

Biggie was buried on Tuesday, March 18, in his native New York City. With thousands cheering along the route, his casket was driven through the impoverished streets of Bedford-Stuyvesant where he was raised. Some onlookers jumped onto parked cars and began dancing to his music, blaring from ghetto blasters. Ten people were arrested for disorderly conduct.

The similarities in the lives and deaths of Tupac Shakur and Biggie Smalls are striking.

Like Tupac, Christopher Wallace was born in Brooklyn and grew up on the streets of Bed-Stuy. They were both raised by single mothers. Biggie's mother, Voletta Wallace, a Jamaican national, was a preschool teacher. His father, also Jamaican, left when Christopher was two. But unlike Tupac's troubled and impoverished childhood, Voletta said she tried to raise her son in a stable wholesome environment.

Mrs. Wallace said that her son was once an honor-roll student at Queen of All Saints Middle School.

"According to what I've read, he's some hooligan from a single-parent household in a run-down ghetto walk-up. There are plenty of intelligent good-hearted kids from single-parent homes, and I always had a beautiful apartment. He has never gone hungry. He never went without."

Tupac, too, had been a good student.

Despite his mother's best efforts, Biggie succumbed to the lure of the street. He dropped out of high school at 17 to sell drugs. So did Tupac.

"When he quit school, I wanted to kill him," Voletta said. "Finally, when he was 18, I said, 'If you can't live by my rules, you can't live under my roof.' I don't care if I was cold. If I had to do it all over again, I would."

At that age, Biggie was cocky. "I was full-time, a hundred percent hustler," says one of Biggie's rap songs. "Sellin' drugs/Waking up early in the morning/Hitting the set selling any shit till the crack of dawn/My mother goin' to work would see me out there in the morning/That's how I was on it."

Biggie and Tupac each lived the life of a street gangsta before either had broken into the music business. Biggie had gone from the street to the studio. He made his debut on Mary J. Blige's remixes of "Real Love" and "What's the 411?" He appeared in Supercat's video, "Dolly My Baby." His first single was "Party and Bullshit." His first album, *Ready to Die*, went platinum for Bad Boy Entertainment, selling more than one million copies. He was honored as Rap Artist of the Year at the 1995 *Billboard* Awards.

"He was the king of rap on the East Coast, definitely, without a question," said rap music promoter Peter Thomas, during a *Prime Time Live* interview.

Like Tupac, Biggie had trouble with the law (although not nearly as onerous).

In August 1996, Biggie was charged with gun and marijuana possession. Police had staked out Biggie's Teaneck, New Jersey condominium, then raided it. Undercover officers confiscated a rifle with an infrared sighting scope. Besides that, according to a police report, officers netted a cache of marijuana, a submachine gun, several semiautomatic handguns, a revolver, and a large quantity of ammunition, including hollow-point rounds.

Then, on September 15, 1996, two days after Tupac died, Biggie was caught smoking marijuana while sitting in his parked luxury car on a Brooklyn street. For the second time in a month, he was charged with drug possession.

Most bizarre, however, was that both Biggie and Tupac had predicted their own deaths in their last albums, both of which were released posthumously. In his song "You're Nobody," Biggie raps, "You're nobody/Till somebody kills you." Both Tupac's *Makaveli* and Biggie's *Life After Death* albums sold out the first week. Biggie's final album surpassed the Beatles' last album in record sales.

As in life, so too in death.

Both Tupac and Biggie were gunned down in drive-by shootings – Tupac was 25 when he was killed; Biggie was 24. Both had hired off-duty cops to guard them the night they were killed. Lieutenant Ross Moen of the Los Angeles Police Department's Wilshire division, which first handled Biggie's murder investigation, said the Blazer carrying Biggie's security guards chased after the gunman's vehicle for a few blocks, but lost it before they could get a license-plate number. The same thing happened after the Tupac shooting; several cars chased the Cadillac, police said, but none was able to catch it or get a plate number. Or, if they did, they didn't report it to the cops.

When Tupac was shot, record-label owner Suge Knight had driven with him away from the crime scene, ostensibly headed for a hospital. When Biggie was shot, his record-label CEO, Sean Combs, told his bodyguard to drive away from the scene and head to the hospital.

Also similar to the Tupac shooting, Biggie's murder was witnessed by scores of people. Biggie's estranged wife Faith Evans, dozens of partygoers, security guards, and parking attendants witnessed the shooting. But just as in the Las Vegas investigation, police initially said they had no description of the gunman and that witnesses were afraid to talk. And just like in Tupac's drive-by, no one took down the license-plate number of the get-away car.

"It's frustrating," Detective Raymond Futami, one of 20 investigators assigned to the Biggie case, told reporters. "I'm sure there's a little bit of an intimidation factor because of the reputation of some of the people who are involved in the case."

Two witnesses in the Smalls case were able to help police. Unlike the members of Tupac's entourage, two of the men sitting with Biggie in his Suburban that night provided enough information for a police artist to sketch a detailed composite drawing.

The first composite drawing was rendered one day after the murder. It shows a black man with a heart-shaped face, a light trimmed mustached, and a receding hairline. He was wearing an Oxford shirt and a dark bowtie. LAPD Lieutenant Moen described the suspect as a "young male African-American in his early twenties." The second drawing, done 18 days after the shooting, shows a thin, older, light-skinned black man, that was circulated to media and police departments nationwide.

However, the first composite sketch, drawn a day after the murder, didn't make it into the hands of the media until it was slipped to reporters at the *Los Angeles Times* 36 months later. Because the murder had been committed with such precision and ease, an easy deduction was that it involved a professional, perhaps even a copy.

The reason for two composite sketches, one released to the media, the other held, was never disclosed.

Detectives began looking at one of their own. Not until the *Los Angeles Times* wrote a story breaking the fact that ex-police officer David Mack and Suge Knight were under investigation and suspected by police of orchestrating the hit was the composite sketch released to the public. Neither composite resembled Mack.

Attorneys for both Mack and Suge strongly rejected the notion that their clients were involved in Biggie's murder. Robin J. Yanes, Suge's attorney, said this: "A year ago it came up and now they're recycling it to cover their butts."

As in the Tupac shooting, police said they believed the gunman had an accomplice.

Early on, investigators considered the theory that Biggie Smalls's death may have been payback for Tupac Shakur's slaying.

"We believe it was gang-related," Lieutenant Moen said. "We believe that it was premeditated, that he was targeted for the purpose of killing him. The way it went down, it was a targeted hit."

One of the scenarios was that Biggie was rumored to have gone the week before his murder to South Park, a hangout for the South Side Crips, and that Crips members had tried unsuccessfully to get money from him.

Lieutenant Moen added during a news conference: "We're investigating possible connections to other murders in New York, Atlanta, and L.A. We can't ignore the fact that there have been a number of murders involving rap singers recently."

In another development, about two weeks after the shooting, L.A. police seized a videotape in Houston that they felt could help them find Biggie's assailant.

"We expect the tape to give us some key information. We're hoping the tape is going to assist in having people come forward to identify the shooter for us," Moen told the *Houston Chronicle*. A Houston woman, who spoke to the newspaper on condition of anonymity, told the *Chronicle* the tape was filmed by a group of Houston residents who were in Los Angeles for the Soul Train Music Awards. In a telephone interview, Moen said he couldn't reveal what detectives had learned from viewing the videotape, because it was evidence in the ongoing investigation.

L.A. Homicide Detective Harper (who wouldn't give his first name), said, "The tape is just one in a million things we're doing in the investigation." In the end, the tape didn't provide any evidence.

There were rumors that Biggie was under federal surveillance just before the shooting, but they were unsubstantiated and probably "not true," said Lieutenant Pat Conman.

"I have no idea what the feds are doing, but to my knowledge, that's not true," Conman said in a telephone interview. "I have no knowledge that Biggie Smalls was under surveillance by the feds."

But the *Los Angeles Times* reported that undercover officers from New York were in the vicinity at the time of the shooting as part of a federal investigation of criminals thought to have connections to Bad Boy Entertainment. And it was rumored that at least one member of a federal task force investigating the rap industry was at the Petersen Automotive Museum the night of the party.

Conman also said that members of LVMPD's homicide team investigating Tupac's murder had been in touch with LAPD detectives about Biggie's murder, "but just in the normal course of business. I believe detectives have had some conversations with them. They're following the case."

Unlike investigators in Tupac's murder case, Los Angeles police early on were optimistic about cracking Biggie's slaying and publicly stated that they expected to make an arrest.

"I can tell you we are going to make an arrest," Lieutenant Moen said at a news conference two weeks after Biggie's slaying. "I cannot tell you when we are going to make that arrest. There's a lot left to be done yet in this investigation."

But six weeks after Biggie's death, homicide Lieutenant Conman admitted that there was nothing new in the case. "We have just a few leads we're following up," Conman told me. "There's nothing startling to report."

Detective Harper pointed out that "people are afraid and don't want to talk to us. People [rappers] have careers to look after."

In stark contrast to the Tupac investigation and LVMPD's three-man homicide team, LAPD assigned a team of 20 investigators, who identified and interviewed nearly 200 witnesses. "We didn't need any more," LVMPD's Manning said. "They [L.A. police] gathered as much information in their case, with all their people, as we did in ours. The more people involved, the more things get lost. You have a communications problem."

Six months later, 20 officers were still involved in Biggie's investigation. Nearly six years later, though, two detectives, a sergeant, and a lieutenant were assigned to the case, one of many in their total work load.

Biggie and Tupac once counted each other as friends. Biggie's childhood friend, Abraham Widdi, told me that he, Biggie and Tupac sometimes drank beer and threw dice together at Hodgie's corner saloon on Fulton Street in Brooklyn's Bed-Stuy. But the two had a falling out after Tupac accused Biggie of copying his style and, later, of setting him up in the 1994 shooting at Quad Studios in Manhattan.

San Francisco DJ Sway, in a telephone interview from his San Francisco radio studio, had this to say: "The Biggie thing, Tupac told me, is what he heard. He knew Biggie didn't pull the trigger [at the Manhattan studio]. There were allegations in the air that Biggie had something to do with it, but I don't think Tupac knew who did it."

When Tupac was in prison, people sent him letters saying Biggie's homeboys had something to do with the shooting. In Tupac's mind, that scenario grew stronger as more and more people told him that. From that moment on, the two were at odds with each other. Their record labels were rivals during the same time. As early as 1994, Biggie told the *Chicago Tribune*, "I'm scared to death. Scared of getting my brains blown out."

By then bitter enemies, Tupac and Biggie taunted each other, and they used their music to do it.

After accusing Biggie of stealing his lyrics, Tupac stole Biggie's wife, Faith Evans, or at least he claimed to have slept with her.

Tupac rapped, "I fucked your bitch/You fat mothafucka/You claim to be a playah/But I fucked your wife." (Biggie and Faith were separated at the time; Biggie was seeing other women, including rapper Lil' Kim, or Kimberly Jones, when he was killed.).

Biggie rapped right back in his solo album, "Dumb rappers need teachin'/Lesson A/Don't fuck with B-I-G/That's that." But Biggie claimed the lyrics had nothing to do with Tupac.

In a Miramax documentary titled *Rhyme or Reason*, Biggie talked about his dispute with Tupac and said it was just a coincidence. "We two individual people, you know what I'm saying?" he explained. "One man against one man made a whole West Coast hate a whole East Coast, and vice versa."

The situation with Tupac was "blown up to much more than it was," he told *The Source* magazine. "They'd gone and made a personal beef between me and [Tupac and Death Row] into a coastal beef,

East against West. And that's crazy. That's bananas right there." He said he still planned to go to California because "they got the women, the weed, and the weather."

Biggie blamed the media for the hype.

"I never did nothin' wrong to nobody," he said. "I ain't never did nothin' wrong to Tupac, I ain't never did nothin' wrong to Faith... And I kept quiet. I kept my mouth shut. I figure if I had been the one sittin' here riffin' it'd seem like I'd had a point to prove. I know I ain't done nothin' so it don't make no sense for me to say nothin'. I just let everybody do they thing."

After Tupac was killed, Biggie told *Spin* magazine's Sia Michel, "I had nothing to do with any of that Tupac shit. That's a complete and total misconception. I definitely wouldn't wish death on anyone. I'm sorry he's gone. That dude was nice on the mike."

Biggie's mother, Voletta Wallace, said, too, that her son had nothing to do with Tupac's death. She was also adamant that her son's murder had nothing to do with Tupac's death. "I don't think my son's death was connected to Tupac. And I don't think Christopher had anything to do with Tupac's death," said Mrs. Wallace, who told me during an interview from her New Jersey home that Biggie's friends had told her that.

"The other thing I heard was that the shot was not meant for my son. The shot was meant for Puffy. My son was supposed to leave for London the same day he was killed. Puffy [Combs] asked him to stay. He didn't want to stay [in L.A.]. He had to go to a party he didn't want to go to. The only reason he was in L.A. was to help Puffy finish an album."

For his part, Tupac, in a *Vibe* interview, once described Biggie as his brother.

"Regardless of all this stuff – no matter what he say, what I say – Biggie's still my brother. He's black. He's my brother. We just have a conflict of interest. We have a difference of opinion," he said.

"I don't want it to be about violence. I want it to be about money. I told Suge my idea: Bad Boy make a record with all the East Coast niggas. Death Row make a record with all the West Coast niggas. We drop the records on the same day. Whoever sell the most records, that's who the bombest. And then we stop battling. We could do pay-per-views for charity, for the community.

"That's as together as we can get. For money. What about getting together as black men? We are together as black men – they over there, we over here. If we really gonna live in peace, we all can't be in the same room."

Writer Kevin Powell said he thought Biggie was an unfortunate innocent bystander in the Death Row-Bad Boy feud.

"Suge definitely encouraged that," Powell said. "It sells records, definitely. What record label – think about it – when in the history of music has a song like 'Hit 'Em Up' been put out? People heard the record. It was ridiculous. Tupac says he slept with Biggie's wife, Faith. There's a song on Biggie's new album. It's called 'Notorious Thug.' He says, 'I have a so-called beef with you-know-who.' He doesn't even say Tupac's name.

"I really feel deep down in my heart that Biggie just happened to be an innocent bystander and he caught the brunt of it," Powell said in an interview from his Brooklyn home. "Black kids, the young black people on the East Coast, are very different from the West. I can go to Harlem, I can go to Staten Island or Queens. It's not like a big deal. We've never claimed East Coast like they claim West Coast in California. New York is not the East Coast. You have Connecticut, Florida, other states. I know for a fact that a lot of kids in the East love West Coast music. I do. Biggie was the first East Coast artist in a long time who was able to transcend those boundaries. People here are petrified of going to California at this point. No one knows where it's coming from. The running joke is, whoever is mentioned in Tupac's last album, they are scared to death. You don't know who's doing the killings. You don't know where it's coming from. It's scary, man."

KMEL's Sway said, "The media has done a very poor job of reporting the truth and kind of printed what they wanted to print in order to sell papers. There's no such thing as an East-West war. There are individuals who had conflicts. It's not the coast of a country against a coast of a country. It's easier to print that. The coasts are divided by the media."

"It's a sad world," commented Peter Thomas, a rap music promoter, "where you can't even go out and enjoy a party like everyone else because you think somebody's going to kill you. You're not just talking to an individual. You're talking to a complete community, and in that community there's a lot of people who have absolutely no sense, but they do have a .45."

"For a rap superstar," wrote Sia Michel in *Spin* magazine, "Biggie's dreams were almost embarrassingly small: his ideal future, he said, was 'to quit the game and just chill and watch my kids grow up – live the life of a normal rich person.' That became an impossibility the day Tupac Shakur declared war on [Biggie]..."

Just before he was killed, Biggie told *The Source* magazine he'd thought about quitting the game of rap, commenting that he was laying low because, "I could fuck around and get murdered out in these streets."

"It's a headache... Sometimes as of late," he said, "I've really been talkin' about quittin'. I really want to stop. If I was financially stable, I would. I figure if I was to make like a cool $10 or $15 million, I could; probably just chill and put my artists out on my label and help them out more, but just not make any more music. I would quit."

He talked about relocating, from the East Coast to the South, "where I can just move at my [own] pace and not really have anybody movin' at the same pace as me. Or where I can just do what I want to do and it wouldn't seem strange to other people. I just wanna be in a calm area. I just wanna be able to relax."

The beef with Tupac was wearing on him.

Sway conducted one of Biggie's last interviews on the air. Sway said, "Biggie talked about Puffy being instrumental in him finding God in his life. He talked about his child. He had a baby. He talked about music and trying to be one of the best rappers. It was real important that he get respect as an emcee. I don't think he had no idea what was going to hit him. He wouldn't have been parading around like that in L.A. if he did."

No arrests have been made and the murder of Biggie Smalls remains unsolved.

11

MURDER IN COMPTON

FOURTEEN MONTHS AFTER the Biggie Smalls murder and 19 months after Tupac Shakur was gunned down, another black-on-black killing took place, leaving the man widely suspected of being connected to Tupac's murder dead on a Compton, California street.

It was just after 3:00 p.m. on a spring afternoon on Friday, May 29, 1998, when a car drove up to a crowded car wash on a street corner in the heart of Compton, on Alondra Boulevard and Oleander Avenue. An argument broke out between two groups of men. Moments later, the sound of gunfire erupted. When the smoke cleared, four men were sprawled on the ground, bleeding from gunshot wounds. Two were dead. A third died early the next morning. The fourth man was charged with three murders.

Although a shooting in a white rural school is cause for a national outcry (as witnessed by a rash of killings in schools in the late 1990s and early 2000s), a black-on-black gun battle in an African-American ghetto barely raises an eyebrow. The bloodshed at the car wash would have been quickly forgotten with little mention, but for the notoriety of one of the dead 23-year-old Orlando Napoleon "Little Lando" Anderson, a second-generation member of the Los Angeles street gang known as the Southside Crips.

The shooting of Orlando Anderson was another in the string of ongoing murders that blighted the reputation of rap culture and the image of young black men. Perhaps most intriguing, Orlando was the man widely suspected of pulling the trigger a year-and-a-half earlier and killing Tupac Shakur.

After police in Las Vegas and Compton had all but named

Anderson, a Lakewood resident, as Tupac's killer, Orlando's family released a statement denying his connection. The statement read: "Tupac Shakur, the talented musical genius, fell at the hands of a violent cruel drive-by shooter or shooters in Las Vegas. That's a fact. That person, however, is not Orlando."

In March 1997, *MTV News* reported that Tupac's murder had touched off a gang war in Compton and that Compton police informants had heard that Orlando was the trigger man.

The day after the MTV story aired, Orlando's attorney arranged for him to appear on CNN to dispute the accusation to a national audience. Orlando, who sat quietly on a studio set next to his attorney, spoke briefly to the CNN reporter. "I just want to let everybody know that I didn't do it," Anderson said.

Orlando also told CNN that he was afraid for his life and rarely left his house for fear of retaliation for being accused of killing Tupac. What critics couldn't forget, however, was the look on his face as he spoke to CNN. It looked like he was smiling. Was it out of shyness, embarrassment, or guilt?

To the *Los Angeles Times*, Orlando said, "I wish they would hurry up and catch the killer so my name could be cleared."

Ironically, while some may have wished Orlando ill, believing he was a passenger in the Cadillac from which the gunman fired, his murder was unrelated to Tupac's, according to Captain Danny Sneed with the Compton Police Department. "Apparently, one of the guys involved in this owed Anderson some money," Sneed said. "An argument ensued; guns came out. It had nothing to do with Shakur's murder. Anderson was a known gang member. [But] as it related to this case, it had nothing to do with gang affiliation or Tupac Shakur."

Orlando Anderson's usually guarded demeanor was down when he left his house that day; he was unarmed when he was killed, but only because his friend, police later said, had taken his gun away from him. It was his childhood friend, Michael Reed Dorrough, 24 at the time, who, while sitting in the passenger seat of Orlando's black sports-utility vehicle, started the gunfight, Sneed said. Sneed conceded that "Anderson was a known gang member. But as it related to this, it had nothing to do with gang affiliation. But he *is* a gang member, I can tell you that."

What happened that Friday afternoon was that Orlando drove his friend Dorrough to a hamburger joint, across the street from a car wash, located at the center of Compton and down the street from a high school. While at the hamburger place, they saw Michael Stone, who owed Orlando money. Stone, 41, had left his vehicle at the car wash so it could be hand-detailed. Anderson and Dorrough, tipped off that Stone would show up there, sat in Orlando's SUV, eating their hamburgers and patiently waiting for Michael Stone to return for his car.

Just after 3:00 p.m., Stone arrived. Anderson and Dorrough thought Stone was alone, but a few feet away stood Stone's nephew, 24-year-old Jerry Stone. As Michael Stone walked to his car, Orlando drove up next to him, and the three began to argue. Then Dorrough, from the front passenger seat, started firing, Captain Sneed said. Jerry Stone, who was standing a few feet away, returned fire, blasting Orlando's SUV.

"When one man began firing his weapon, another returned the fire with a handgun. Four people were shot," said Sneed, who said he was at the scene of the shootout minutes after it happened.

Orlando Anderson, 23, tried to drive away from the spray of gunfire. Bleeding from several gunshot wounds, he managed to drive about 200 yards down the street. When Compton police officers arrived, they found Orlando's SUV on a curb and against a pole. Orlando was slumped over the steering wheel, dying. Dorrough was still in the SUV. Both were taken by ambulance to Martin Luther King Hospital. Orlando Anderson was dead on arrival.

Suffering from minor injuries, Dorrough, the one whom police said started the gunfight, was taken to St. Francis Hospital, where Compton police took him into custody.

Michael Stone also was taken by ambulance to Martin Luther King.

He died the next day. Jerry Stone, who was taken to the same hospital by a friend, died of his wounds a short time after his arrival.

Michael Dorrough initially was booked on two counts of murder and one count of attempted murder. After Michael Stone's death the next day, Dorrough's charges were upgraded to three counts of open murder.

At the completion of the police investigation, Sneed issued this press release, dated Wednesday, July 22, 1998:

On May 29, 1998, at 3:11 p.m., the Compton Police Department received several 911 calls of shots fired at a car wash located in the area of Alondra Boulevard and Oleander Avenue. Upon officers arrival in the area, they discovered three gunshot victims. Compton Fire Department paramedics responded and administered treatment prior to transporting victims to local area hospitals. Victim Jerry Stone was located at Martin Luther King Hospital, after having been transported to the hospital by private vehicle.

The investigation has revealed that four subjects became involved in an altercation over a previous monetary dispute. Suspect Dorrough removed a handgun and began shooting. Victim Jerry Stone removed a handgun and returned fire. Numerous shots were fired and all four subjects involved were shot.

Anderson drove off, with Dorrough as the passenger, and both were found by police a short distance away. Dorrough was treated and released for minor injuries and booked at Compton Police Department. Anderson, Jerry Stone, and Michael Stone died at Martin Luther King Hospital.

Although this incident did occur near a high school, this was in no way connected to the high school or its students. No persons injured or involved were connected to the high school in any way.

Although gang members may have been involved, this does not appear to be gang-related.

A team of homicide and gang detectives have concluded an investigation in this matter. Suspect Michael Dorrough has been charged with three counts of murder and is awaiting trial. Anyone having information regarding this shooting is encouraged to call the Compton Police Department at 310- 605-6505.

SUSPECT: Michael Reed Dorrough, male African-American, DOB 2-9-74, resident of Long Beach.

VICTIMS: Orlando Anderson, male African-American, DOB 8-13-74, resident of Compton, DECEASED. Michael Stone, male African-American, DOB 12-18-56, resident of Compton, DECEASED. Jerry Junior Stone, male African-American, DOB 8-20-73, resident of Compton, DECEASED.

Even though Michael Dorrough didn't personally shoot all the victims, he was charged with all three murders because police contended he was responsible for the deaths. "He started the gunfight," Captain Sneed told me. "That's why he's being charged with all the murders."

Investigators with the LAPD confiscated Orlando Anderson's utility vehicle, hoping it would help them in their investigation of the Biggie Smalls murder. "We stood by while LAPD recovered the car," Sneed said. That was the first anyone had learned that Orlando was being investigated in Biggie's murder, not just Tupac's. Later, after the LAPD crime lab didn't turn up any evidence connecting Orlando to Biggie's case, the LAPD returned the vehicle to Compton police, Sneed said.

The Compton gun battle marked an end to a stormy 19 months for Orlando Anderson. During the time between Tupac's death and Anderson's, police ended up twice seizing materials from Orlando's uncle's house, which was owned by "Keefee D" Davis. Davis was never charged with a crime. At the time, Orlando denied living in the house.

An affidavit filed in court by Compton police also contended that Orlando was seen several days after Tupac's shooting carrying a Glock 40-caliber handgun, the same type of semiautomatic weapon said to be the kind used to kill Tupac. Others said Orlando had bragged about his involvement.

Gilbert D. Sanchez, an expert in gang violence at Cal State University, Los Angeles, and himself a former gang member, said, "I heard the Crips did it [Tupac's murder], but I'm not in a position to say for sure. Usually a person doesn't brag at all. He may be trying to look good in front of someone else."

Orlando Anderson's family continue to deny that Orlando had anything to do with Tupac's death. Although Orlando had earlier links to the Crips and he was anything but a Boy Scout, he didn't come across as an archetypal gang-banger. He graduated from high school and even attended Compton College for a semester. He was never convicted of a crime. His half-brother, Pooh, graduated in 1999 from the University of California at Berkeley.

Also, friends said that Orlando didn't drink, didn't take drugs, didn't smoke, and didn't sport tattoos.

Orlando had two girlfriends simultaneously and had fathered four children by the time he was 23. He didn't appear ever to have been gainfully employed, and never filed a federal tax return. He lived a lower-middle-class life despite having no obvious means of support. In an interesting twist, Orlando was starting his own record label at the time of his murder.

The probable-cause affidavit from Compton police for Orlando's arrest at his uncle's house was thrown out of court. Thus, Orlando was never prosecuted. In it, however, Orlando was identified by Travon "Tray" Lane as being at the scene of an L.A. murder. In addition, he was once suspected of killing Edward Webb in April 1996. He was also identified as being behind a retaliatory attack on Bloods following the murder of Bobby Finch, a bodyguard who grew up with the Southside Crips, the sect Orlando was said to belong to. Finch was shot to death in the bloodbath that erupted in the days after Tupac was shot and was believed to have been a passenger in the Cadillac used by the assailant who'd murdered Tupac.

Meanwhile, three Bloods members were fired on and wounded in two separate shootings. On September 13, the day Tupac died, two more Bloods were shot and killed by an assailant who fled on foot.

And as the gang war raged, police in Compton and Las Vegas continued to receive tips that "Keefee D's nephew" or "Baby Lane" (aka Orlando Anderson) was the one who had shot Tupac.

Armed with this information, Compton police were confident in resolutions to both their April 1996 murder and Tupac's September 1997 killing. However, Los Angeles County District Attorney Janet Moore refused to hold Orlando because she believed there was not enough evidence to indict him in the April 1996 Compton murder. And Las Vegas police said there wasn't enough evidence to hold Orlando in the Tupac killing.

After Tupac's death, Orlando Anderson filed an assault charge against Tupac's estate, claiming he was assaulted by Tupac at the MGM Grand Hotel (during the infamous scuffle following the Tyson bout). Tupac's mother, Afeni Shakur, filed a countersuit against Anderson for wrongful death in her son's murder.

After Anderson was himself shot to death, his estate claimed that only hours before Anderson was killed his attorney was told by Tupac's attorneys that he would receive a $78,000 settlement from Shakur's estate. When no money was paid, a breach-of-contract suit was filed on behalf of Anderson's family. Later, A. Ammar Kharouf, an attorney for the Shakur family, confirmed that a settlement had eventually been reached and the lawsuit subsequently dismissed. Kharouf and Anderson family attorney Renee L. Campbell would not disclose the amount.

12

GANGSTA RAP AND THE
RECORD INDUSTRY

RAP BEGAN AS A beat in the streets and word play. It draws its roots from the Jamaican art form known as "toasting." Early rapper DJ Kool Herc said that "the whole chemistry of rap came from Jamaica."

"I was born in Jamaica," he has said, "and I was listening to American music in Jamaica. In Jamaica, all you needed was a drum and bass. My music is all about heavy bass."

In the early days, when rap was just getting started, the rhyming was added. Its authentic from-the-street lyrics were crucial to rap's success. Rap developed into an East Coast cultural phenomenon, which included graffiti and break dancing.

"[For me] the rhyming came about because I liked playing lyrics that were saying something," DJ Kool Herc said. "I figured people would pick it up by me playing those records, but at the same time I would say something myself with a meaningful message to it."

Herc identifies the first rappers, besides himself, as Coke La Rock (whose first stage name was A-1 Coke), Timmy Tim, Clark Kent, and Bo King, American rappers all. Artists such as James Brown, the Last Poets, and Gil Scott Heron helped influence rap's early years.

Surfacing in the '70s, rap was a vibrant provocative new musical form from America's urban black community. It has progressed into different sounds and different avenues. Its free-style music, a form of electro funk – music with a beat in the background and an emcee, or a rhymer, rapping to it in front.

The first real hip-hop song, "Rapper's Delight" by Henry "Big Banle" Hanle, broke into the mainstream in 1979 under the first hip-hop label, Sugarhill Gang. Hanle was a club bouncer who started out emceeing and rapping in a New Jersey pizzeria. Early hip-hop rappers were Melle Mel, Grand Master Flash, and Rakim. Rakim was one of the first to rap about the living conditions of blacks and Latinos. (The trend continues today. Tupac Shakur often said his music showed how he and others like him *really* lived the ghetto and street experience.)

In 1987, the music industry for the first time recognized rap music by giving it a separate category at the American Music Awards. It was a monumental move that put rap into the mainstream.

Hip-hop became the term for the culture surrounding rap music. True hip-hop, purists in the music industry contend, evolved from beebop in the 1950s. Rapping (or emceeing), scratching records, break dancing, and graffiti are a part of the hip-hop culture. How the rappers act, walk, look, and talk is also a large part of the scene; without those elements, rappers say, the music is colorless. Like rap, hip-hop was popularized in the mid 1970s, particularly in the South Bronx section of New York City. It has thrived within the African-American and Puerto Rican communities in New York. It's referred to today as the culture of the Hip-Hop Nation.

In the late 1980s, "gangsta" rap splintered off from the larger hip-hop/rap culture. The lyrics borrowed heavily from the '60s and '70s themes of sex, drugs, and rock'n'roll – with primary focus on gangs, weapons, and violence. Infused in the style were new words and phrases, such as "gats" (19th-century Gatling guns), gang wars, bitches and ho's, "blunts" (fat marijuana joints or cigars), 40-ouncers (bottles of malt liquor), and "25 with an L" (a prison sentence of 25 years to life). Gangsta rap had become about as "street" and hard-core as any other music before it.

Some credit Philadelphia's Schooly D as being the original hard-core gangsta rapper. Others claim the hard-core rap style was officially launched with Ice-T's 1987 *Rhyme Pays* album.

On the East Coast, Def Jam's LL Cool J, Public Enemy, and the Beastie Boys (who are white) elevated gangsta rap into a prevailing musical influence. Conversely, it was Compton's N.W.A. (Niggas With Attitude) who pioneered gangsta rap on the West Coast. Dr.

Dre, who would later found Death Row with Suge Knight, was an early member of N.W.A.

Gangsta rap, which chronicles the bleak and often violent way of life of the residents of the nation's toughest black neighborhoods, has increasingly sparked controversy since it emerged in the late 1980s and early '90s. Much of the controversy has centered on the violence-packed lyrics. The music industry, defending its artistic freedom and arguing that music doesn't cause violence, rode out a storm of criticism. Some of the criticism was prompted by a practice of the record companies in hiring rappers with criminal backgrounds.

The gangsta rap rivalry developed when West Coast rappers grew more popular, surpassing the record sales of East Coast rappers. But Biggie Smalls, who built his gangsta rap persona around a troubled past that included admitted crack dealing, albeit short-lived, was credited with reviving the East Coast scene (thus rivaling West Coast sales) in 1994 on the Bad Boy label, which was launched in 1993 by entrepreneur Sean "Puffy" Combs (now known as P. Diddy), then a 22-year-old college student.

According to the Recording Industry Association of America (RIAA), since 1996 record sales for rap total more than $1 billion. Rap/hip-hop in 2000 was among the favorite genres of 29 percent of music consumers, up six points from 2000, the RIAA reported. Industry statistics indicate Death Row Records alone generated $100 million; its hard-core recordings by Tupac Shakur and Snoop Dogg ranked as the most successful. Bad Boy Entertainment sold about $75 million worth of albums in 1996 from such artists as the Notorious B.I.G., Faith Evans, Craig Mack, and 112.

Early on, Sean Combs developed a reputation for cockiness and arrogance, and Suge Knight, in turn, developed a dislike for Combs. After Tupac joined Death Row, he too openly criticized Bad Boy rappers, particularly the Notorious B.I.G. And Tupac fanned the flames with his public pronouncements on rap.

In Tupac's own estimation, no one could rap like Tupac.

"Nobody can talk about pain like Tupac," he told *Vibe* magazine about himself. "No one knows it like me. It separates me from other rappers. All the pain I'm talking about in my rap, you can see it." Tupac prided himself in embodying the thug-life aspect of gangsta rap.

When asked why he had adopted a thug persona, Tupac said, "Because if I don't, I'll lose everything I have. Who else is going to love me but the thugs?"

Tupac – and, no doubt, Suge Knight – knew that the harder the lyrics, the larger the sales. Tupac had both "THUG LIFE" and "OUTLAW" tattooed on his body.

Writer Kevin Powell said being an outlaw in music was nothing new. "In black culture, the outlaw figure has always existed, beginning with Chuck Berry," Powell said. "Sometimes people will put on the persona. A lot of times Pac wasn't the person he was rapping about; he *became* it. A lot of people in this generation have an 'I-don't-give-a-fuck' attitude.

"Hip-hop music is really a reaction to the failures and the fallacies of the so-called civil-rights movement. A lot of these people say, 'We can vote now, we can sit in the bus, in the restaurant, but we don't own the bus, we don't own the restaurant. So we say, "Fuck it."' That's why you see a lot of people, white or black, frustrated. White kids are alienated too. They identify with rap and the hip-hop culture. It is the most cutting-edge, most aggressive music out there. It's very rebellious. Historically, white youth have always identified with cultures that were rebellious. Tupac, like me, like Kurt Cobain [a grunge rocker from the Seattle musical movement who committed suicide], represented the bleak outlook on life that this generation, our generation, feels."

Prior to the September 11, 2001 attacks on American soil and the U.S. war on terrorism, Powell said this: "I definitely understand why all these records are being sold. It's like the '60s, except there's no political movement. It's like an anarchy. [For] a bunch of young people – black, white, straight, gay – it's like an individual revolt. Look at him. On one hand, Tupac was this superstar, but on the other he was another young black man in jail."

Americans have long been fascinated with the connection between criminal life and pop culture – Frank Sinatra and his alleged mobster pals, for example, were immortalized in the *Godfather* saga. "Beneath all the ethnic specificity, these rappers are really imitating the lifestyle of white gangstas," the Reverend Jesse Jackson Jr. said after Tupac and Biggie were killed. "They have chosen white role models."

According to police, gangsta rap isn't organized enough to imitate the real mob.

"Gangs are considered disorganized-organized crime," homicide Sergeant Kevin Manning said. "[The Mafia] has a hierarchy. It's very organized. Everybody knows who reports to whom. It's not that way with gangs. They're organized in their own way. It's very fleeting. Everything they do seems random, but they are very powerful and violent."

Retired Sergeant Bill Keeton, who worked for 11 years in LVMPD's organized-crime unit, said that the violence rap singers have brought with them from the streets "is a cultural thing."

"Even though they make a lot of money," Keeton said, "you can take the kid out of the street, but you can't take the street out of the kid. It's not organized crime. They're brought up around armed robberies, [and] they're pulling guns on each other."

Manning agreed, saying, "These guys come up from the streets and make millions of dollars. You've got somebody with a [gang] mentality who has a talent, but he can't handle it."

Gangsta rap focuses on the young-black-male segment of society that has historically been ravaged by crime. Gangsta rap also has been described as a form of release for those living in the ghetto, imprisoned and unable to lift themselves out. Still, it's mostly the young people from the suburbs who buy the music, according to statistics. Rhymes from Tupac and other rappers have become a mantra of sorts for youth of all colors.

"Is the hip-hop generation all about violence and degradation?" CNN commentator Farai Chideya asked in a *Time* magazine piece published shortly after Biggie Smalls's murder. "Are we collectively doomed to go the way of Tupac Shakur and Biggie Smalls? I hope not, because I'm a member of that generation. In the weeks to come, as we try to make sense of the deaths of two of the youngest, richest, best-known black men in America, we'll probably succumb to a natural temptation to divide the 'good kids' from the 'hip-hop kids.' I'm not buying it. I grew up listening to hip-hop. In elementary school I tuned my radio to the techno-influenced chant of 'Planet Rock' and innocent party jams like 'Rapper's Delight.' By high school and college, hip-hop was everything from the pop female braggadocio of Salt-N-Pepa to the black nationalism of Public Enemy. Today, in addition to music that ranges from alternative rock to techno, I listen to rough-edged rappers [like] the Wu Tang Clan – and, yes, Biggie and Tupac as well...

"Who's pushing the rawest rhymes to No. 1 on the charts? For years now, the largest volume of hip-hop albums has been sold to white suburban kids who've deposed heavy metal and elevated hip-hop to the crown of Music Most Likely To Infuriate My Parents. The suburban rebellion – its record-buying tastes, its voyeurism of what too often it views as 'authentic black culture' – has contributed to the primacy of the gangsta-rap genre.

"The music may be in white America's homes, but the violence is in black America's neighborhoods. That's why we, the hip-hop generation, bear the ultimate responsibility for reshaping the artform we love. Hip-hop used to lift us above the struggles we faced; then it tried to inform us about the struggles we faced; now it's *become* one of the struggles we face. I used to tell myself that the 'thug life' portrayed in the music was just fiction. Now it's incontrovertible fact. We can do better than this. If we don't, we're little more than voyeurs of our own demise."

While the murders of Tupac and Biggie spurred record sales, the long-term effects initially weren't good for business. After the rappers' murders, the larger record companies and distributors asked themselves whether business should continue as usual. The music industry has weathered a storm of criticism for backing gangsta rap and its violent lyrics, especially when those lyrics became self-fulfilling prophecies.

Some industry executives wondered if it was ethical to be in business with characters with questionable backgrounds, just so they could cash in on the lucrative market of gangsta-rap record sales. The financial stakes are high, and the answers are seemingly contradictory. To survive, the hip-hop music industry needed to turn its bad-boy image around, while also maintaining its street authenticity.

When then-Senator Robert Dole, an outspoken moral crusader, singled out Death Row for producing albums with lyrics that he said were unfit for the youth of America, Time Warner, Death Row's distributor at the time, severed its ties with the label.

The white corporate world of the record industry is what Suge Knight, Puffy Combs, and other black record producers had to penetrate to get their rappers into middle-class America. One rap insider described Combs and Knight as "middle men, liaisons between corporate America and black rappers."

But, according to other insiders, the bloodshed following Tupac's death alarmed corporate bigwigs backing the rap record labels, so much so that they took a harder look at who was being allowed to run their labels. "There is an uneasiness with gangsta rap even among the black executives and artists," the *New York Times* wrote in a feature about rap published before Tupac was killed.

That sentiment has been enhanced by the escalation of violence on the heels of the murders of Tupac Shakur and Biggie Smalls. Some prominent industry executives privately questioned whether greed was blinding record companies to the body count connected to gangsta rap. A decision to tone down the music could have had enormous financial ramifications – less money for record companies.

With the deaths of Tupac and Biggie, the futures of the heads of Death Row and Bad Boy were uncertain. After all, Suge was in prison; Puffy was free but frightened.

As Death Row's battleship sank into an ocean of bad publicity, some of it's stalwarts abandoned ship. In 1996, Dr. Dre split acrimoniously with Death Row, telling the *Hollywood Reporter* only days before Tupac's shooting, "Gangsta rap is definitely a thing of the past. I've just moved on."

In the end, rappers, by the turn of the 21st century, had cleaned up their lyrics. The beat went on, but a little softer.

Death Row unsuccessfully attempted to sell the car in which Tupac was shot. After learning that Primadonna Resorts in Primm, Nevada, had purchased the bullet-riddled car in which Bonnie and Clyde Barrow were killed in a 1934 shootout, a representative from Death Row contacted the casino company. Aaron Cohen, a spokesman for the resort, said they told Death Row casino executives weren't interested in buying the car.

Cohen explained: "It's not a piece of American history the way the Bonnie and Clyde car is. Maybe in 20 years it will be."

Likewise, the rental-car company that owned the vehicle in which Biggie was shot briefly flirted with raising money from the bullet-riddled door of the car Biggie was killed in. On Sunday, April 27, 1997, LAPD returned Biggie's 1997 GMC Suburban to Budget Rent A Car of Beverly Hills, which had rented the Suburban to the Los Angeles production company FM Rocks. At the time, police told co-owner Corky Rice they were finished with their analyses of the Suburban. Shortly thereafter a story ran across the Associated Press wire that the bullet-riddled door from the vehicle's front passenger side was about to be offered on the auction block to raise money for charity. The passenger door was the only part of the vehicle damaged during the shooting.

"We haven't decided when or where to auction the door," Rice told reporters at the time. "We don't want to be tacky. We want to be in good taste. We don't want to make any profit at all. Everybody's telling me the door must have some value. We'd like to somehow find a way to sell the door to the highest bidder and then donate the money to charity. I'm trying to figure out how to turn this terrible incident into something good. If you put the money to good use, I don't think it's in bad taste."

But police intervened before the door hit the auction block: LAPD detectives returned on April 30 and once again confiscated the door.

"They said it was for evidence," Rice said.

In the end, neither the BMW Tupac was murdered in nor the door from the Suburban in which Biggie was shot were sold.

On top of everything else, on January 7, 1997, Suge, David Kenner, and Death Row were sued in Los Angeles Superior Court by American Express Travel Related Services. American Express claimed that Suge, Kenner, Kenner's wife Erica, and Death Row Records owed the credit card company upwards of $1.5 million. American Express alleged a breach of contract and sought payment in full, plus court costs, attorneys' fees, and prejudgment interest.

The court documents itemized Death Row's expenses, including those charged while Tupac Shakur lie in a coma at University Medical Center, a paper trail that led to limousine services, pricey hotel rooms, and private planes.

Kenner held both gold and platinum American Express accounts. Erica Kenner was also a signatory on a credit card. Suge and Death Row employees were authorized to make charges on the platinum account, but only with Kenner's approval, the weekly alternative newspaper the *New Times* in Los Angeles reported.

American Express stated in its suit that "all parties had customarily used and paid for charges before October 1996 on Kenner's cards with no objections." Kenner had paid for his and his wife's expenses "regularly and promptly," the credit card company said. Death Row debts were paid for with checks from Death Row's corporate account, which was administered by Kenner, according to a civil suit filed against Suge by Dr. Dre.

Kenner told the *Los Angeles Times* that the disputed charges "were put on these cards without the authorization of Mr. Knight or myself for expenditures that had nothing to do with us."

Some of the charges, however, did include fight tickets for the Tyson-Seldon match on September 7, 1996. The American Express bills were sent directly to Kenner's Encino, California, law offices, the *New Times* reported.

Thirteen pages in the suit itemized the expenses charged from June to September 1996.

Kenner's wife had charged $3,763.69 to Dial-a-Mattress, Bed Bad & Beyond, Nobody Beats the Wiz, and the NYU Book Center in New York, and Ralph Lauren and Barey's in Beverly Hills. Also included was airfare to New York City. At face value, the charges appear to be personal and household items to outfit Erica Kenner and her home at the expense of Death Row Records.

Las Vegas-related expenses included chartered jets – at a cost of $42,279.86 – from Jetwest International on September 4 and September 17, plus jet refuel charges of $23,042.88 from Spirit Aviation. Kenner also reportedly charged airfare of $122,303.44 to Bel Aire Travel. On September 19 there was another Bel Aire Travel charge of $108,294.95. Limousine services were charged to CLS Transportation on September 12 and September 13, the day Tupac died, for $160,000.

The records also show that Suge booked 27 separate hotel rooms at Luxor Hotel for $50 per night (or $1,584.21) and spent $666.45 at the Tinder Box in Las Vegas for cigars. A charge of September 12 was made to CLS Transportation for $50,000. A transaction on September 21 was made at the Beverly Hills Hotel for $2,738.82. Besides the actual expenses, American Express tacked on an additional $25,787 late fee.

A Luxor Hotel executive, who asked not to be identified, said that only two hotel rooms, both suites, were booked by Suge Knight that week, and that Knight had been billed just for those two rooms.

In perhaps the strangest turn of events, Suge Knight was accused by a former accountant for Death Row Records of assaulting him, in what the *Wall Street Journal* termed a "horrifying encounter." The behavior of accountant Steven Cantrock, however, seemed even more bizarre.

On the morning of Saturday, October 12, 1996, Cantrock, Death Row's accountant and a principal in the Los Angeles office of Gelfand, Rennert & Feldman, a division of Coopers & Lybrand, went to his boss.

He told him that he had attended a meeting with Suge Knight the night before and claimed that Suge had "assaulted him, forced him to his knees, and made him sign a trumped-up IOU," the *Wall Street Journal* reported.

In the IOU, Cantrock confessed that he had stolen $4.5 million from Knight, his client. "The coerced statement, he assured his shocked Coopers associates, was false and absurd," the newspaper's Alix M. Freedman and Laurie P. Cohen wrote.

Troubling questions soon emerged, and Cantrock eventually left the firm with his story in doubt. Coopers declined to comment, other than to say that it had "several ties with both accountant and client."

Coopers' association with Death Row and Suge Knight began in November 1993 when Cantrock landed the account with the record label, which had been looking for someone to manage the financial end of the business. Cantrock was given sole authority to write checks for the rap label.

"Mr. Knight and his roving entourage were huge spenders, even by Hollywood standards," the newspaper reported. "Rather than rein them in, Mr. Cantrock went with the flow... When the Death Row clan was on the road, Mr. Cantrock saw to it that stretch limousines were lined up outside their hotels 24 hours a day, as Mr. Knight desired. The accountant signed off on their impulse purchases of Rolex watches, Lexus cars, yachts, and jewelry."

One thing Cantrock wasn't able to accomplish, however, was organizing Death Row's financial affairs; the rap label was perpetually short of cash.

Suge told the *Wall Street Journal*, through his attorney, that he "was in the dark" about money problems and believed "everything was fine."

Suge began to realize there was a problem when Cantrock started to lose clients at Coopers & Lybrand. Suge started paying more attention, and he quickly suspected that Death Row funds were missing. He confronted Cantrock for the first time on June 4, 1996, the newspaper reported, asking about the missing money, including a refund of

$25,000 for the down payment on a Las Vegas house Suge had decided not to purchase. Cantrock reportedly admitted taking the money. Suge told him, "Just stop stealing, pay me back, and get on the ball with putting the business in order."

But by the end of June 1996, Death Row's financial situation was already a shambles. Suge said he wasn't getting an accounting of the books from Cantrock and was still being kept in the dark. So Suge called a meeting, attended by several people, including Suge's attorney David Kenner, at a San Fernando Valley home. An IOU was written and signed by Cantrock. Those present in the room during the confrontation disputed Cantrock's claim that he signed the IOU under duress.

On February 7, 1997, Coopers issued a statement that it had "asked for and received [Cantrock's] resignation" for violating the firm's policies.

Death Row did not try to collect the $4.5 million it said it was owed, although Kenner said at the time that he was contemplating a lawsuit against Coopers & Lybrand and Cantrock.

13

VIOLENCE IN RAP AND GANGS

SINCE NOVEMBER 30, 1994, the day Tupac Shakur was shot the first time, in the lobby of Quad Studios in Manhattan, six people directly involved in the rap-music business have been murdered. Besides Tupac, there were the murders of Randy Walker, Yafeu Fula, Jake Robles, Biggie Smalls, and Alton "Bungry" McDonald. In addition, at least another dozen people known to be affiliated with the Bloods and Crips gangs have been wounded or killed in drive-by shootings. In most of the cases, homicide and gang detectives involved in the investigations (other than Compton police, who called the rash of violence a "bloodbath") say the assaults and murders are not connected.

People in the music industry thought otherwise. For years many people in the rap music industry were worried, wondering who was next.

Snoop Dogg, at the time a rapper for Death Row, postponed a music tour a week after Biggie Smalls was killed. Snoop delayed the Lollapalooza tour for a month, he said, out of respect for Biggie, but others said it was out of fear for his life. Indeed, he had rented an armored bullet-proof vehicle (said to be equipped with holes for weapons) instead of riding the tour bus with the crew.

"Tupac has been killed, and six months later [Biggie was] killed, and he doesn't want to be next," Jeff Bowen, booking and marketing director at Winston-Salem's (North Carolina) Lawrence Joel Veterans Memorial Coliseum, told the Associated Press. Bowen said Snoop was expected to begin his tour – the Doggfather East-West Fresh Fest 1997 World Tour – sometime in April 1997. His revamped tour was to include a film tribute to Biggie and Tupac. Instead of opening in Winston-Salem, it opened May 1 in San Diego, closer to Snoop's L.A.

base, and included the film tribute to his slain fellow rappers.

"Snoop is the only one left," J. Howell, owner of C&J Concert Promotions, told a reporter. "He will take it to the forefront and let people – let kids – know that it's not all about [violence]. He's coming out with a band and talking about peace and unity, whether you're white, black, green, or yellow."

Snoop Dogg wasn't the only one who was scared off. Warren G's record-company execs postponed a promotional tour for his new album, *Take a Look Over Your Shoulder*, because they feared for his safety.

Havoc, a rapper with the band Mobb Deep, told reporter David Bauder that the violence can't be ignored.

"We're talking targets because we're rappers, we're entertainers. We've got to be careful," he said.

Ice-T agreed, telling Bauder, "This is the first time I ever felt unsafe."

Luke, a rapper formerly with the band 2 Live Crew, concurred that many rappers were nervous. "It's unsafe for Snoop to come to a concert in New York, for Nas to go to a concert in L.A., because there ain't nobody finding these people who are killing everybody."

On June 28, 1997, Snoop Dogg attended the Evander Holyfield-Mike Tyson heavyweight rematch bout at the MGM Grad in Las Vegas. Many witnesses said that shots rang out inside the casino (LVMPD denied it). An ensuing stampede injured several dozen people, but Snoop escaped unharmed. He was seen being guarded by Nation of Islam security officers (who are easily identified by their bowties).

On September 24, 1995, 10 months after Tupac was shot the first time in New York, Jake Robles, a close friend to Suge and an employee of Death Row, was shot at an Atlanta nightclub. Robles died a week later. Suge blamed Sean Combs and Bad Boy Entertainment's associates for Jake's death.

Then, on November 30, 1995, a year to the day after the first attempt on Tupac's life, rapper Stretch Walker, a key witness to the

New York shooting, was murdered. Walker, a close friend of Tupac's, was shot by three assailants during a high-speed chase in Queens. Walker had rapped with Tupac on his *Thug Life* album and Tupac wrote lyrics about him, saying, "Big Stretch represent the real nigga." As with the majority of the other "unrelated" murders involving gangsta rappers, Walker's murder remains unsolved.

After the April 1996 Soul Train Music Awards, someone pulled a gun during a heated exchange in the parking lot between associates with Bad Boy Entertainment and Death Row Records associates.

On July 3, 1996, Biggie Smalls, Lil' Cease (of Junior M.A.F.I.A.), Lil' Kim, and DJ Enuff narrowly escaped a possible hit attempt, the *Village Voice* reported. Biggie had gone to Atlanta to represent Combs and Bad Boy at a concert. But during his set, Tupac's crew began taunting Biggie and shouting, "Tupac! Tupac! Tupac!"

Afterward, Biggie and his crew were followed to their hotel by people in a van they believed were trying to kill them. With the groups' Glock 9-millimeters locked and cocked, one of Biggie's bodyguards told the *Village Voice*, the driver of Biggie's car made a series of radical maneuvers leading to the interstate. The people following them apparently realized "they'd been made," the guard said, then pulled in front of Biggie's car. Biggie's crew thought they might have to shoot their way out.

"Face it," the bodyguard told the *Village Voice*, "there wasn't no questions gonna be asked. You knew it was on and what you had to do right then."

The van and a truck continued shadowing them as they drove on the interstate and around the suburbs of Atlanta.

Biggie, the bodyguard said, wanted to find out who they were. "Pull over and see what they want," he told the driver. He did. With that, the truck and van sped off. Biggie and his entourage returned to their hotel without learning the identities of the occupants of the van.

"The next day we found out that Tupac did come into town that night and he stayed in the hotel across the street from where Biggie was staying, and he left that morning," the bodyguard told the *Village Voice*.

Then Tupac and Biggie were killed in drive-by shootings and Yafeu Fula was executed gangland-style. The alleged killers of Fula have been arrested, but the gunmen who murdered Tupac, Biggie, Robles, Walker, and McDonald have gotten away with murder.

One thing police have not disputed is that all the shootings have been executed in gang-style drive-bys.

As for police claims that the murders were all unrelated, it's a difficult sell. It was common knowledge that Randy Walker was a witness in the November 30, 1994, shooting of Tupac in Manhattan. Tupac and others said they believed Walker was murdered because of that, and that his death was not a random act of violence.

Many in the music industry feel the same way about Yafeu Fula's death. He was a witness to Tupac's fatal shooting, so he, too, had to be executed to eliminate the possibility that he'd drop a dime and talk.

Then, when Biggie Smalls was murdered in a scenario similar to Tupac's slaying, talk that it was retaliation for Shakur's death was widespread.

Still, police from coast to coast have been hesitant to say any of the killings are related. Even now, after all these years, it's anyone's guess as to whether the murder connections, if any, are real or perceived. Could they be, as police have suggested, just gang-bangers doing their thing, in random shootings, coincidentally hitting witnesses to other murders?

If the murder of Jake Robles, Randy Walker, Tupac Shakur, Yafeu Fula, and Biggie Smalls are gang-related, the fatal results of a war between the Bloods and Crips, people in the gangsta-rap business say they won't be the last.

In the past, gang members carried Saturday Night Specials. Today's black gangs are armed with sophisticated paramilitary weapons such as semiautomatic rifles, Uzis, Glocks, Mac-10-type submachine guns, and 9-millimeter and .45-caliber pistols.

There are several stories about the origins of the Crips, but the most commonly accepted version is that the gang was started in the neighborhoods of West Los Angeles. The smaller neighborhood gangs consolidated and joined forces, forming the larger, and more powerful, Crips gang. An influential gang member named Raymond Washington started the Crips, which gradually built a reputation for being the strongest force among the black gangs of West L.A. Soon, other gangs started renaming themselves, incorporating the word Crips into their new names, gangs such as the Main Street Crips, Kitchen Crips, 5 Deuce Crips, and Rollin' 20 Crips appeared on the streets.

The development of the Bloods has been similar to that of the Crips. Black men in their late teens and early twenties living in rival neighborhoods in Compton formed the Bloods. In the early '70s Sylvester Scott and Vincent Owens formed the Compton Pirus, named for West Piru Street in the city of Compton. The Compton Pirus rose to power quickly and became extremely powerful. As the recognition given to the Compton Pirus spread throughout L.A. County, other Piru gangs, which later changed their name to Bloods, were formed. Today, the Bloods are the most formidable rivals of the Crips.

Numerically, the Bloods are outnumbered by the Crips, according to Compton and Los Angeles police. But what the Bloods lack in numbers, they make up for in violence.

Sometime in the early '70s, police began to notice that the black gangs were dividing into Crips and Bloods. But although many of the gangs fall under the loose umbrella defined by the two best-known names, the smaller sets are still identified by the local streets, landmarks, parks, or neighborhoods, which are incorporated into their names – the Donna Street gang in North Las Vegas, for example, and the 18th Street gang in Las Vegas. Today, Crips often have altercations among their own subsets or factions. Bloods, on the other hand, don't seem so inclined.

In the Compton area, police have seen different Crips gangs unite to enhance their criminal enterprises. The Crips gangs began calling themselves C.C. Riders (Compton Crip Riders). They've spread to other Western states, including Nevada.

(In the late 1980s, southern California gang members began traveling into Las Vegas, one of the hottest spots in the nation and, to the gangs, a ready mark. The gangs had a similar M.O.: takeover robberies of banks and casinos. Gang members considered casinos, especially, an easy score, according to gang unit detectives. They were able to grab a large sum of money in just a couple of minutes. When casinos were hit, some of the money was later found by Los Angeles-area police in gang sweeps. The disturbing thing for officers, however, was that the takeover robberies seemed to serve as an initiation ritual for new Los Angeles-based gang members. The police swooped in on the early perpetrators and slowed the practice down a bit. But they couldn't stop it completely.)

Crips gang members identify with the color blue, and usually have a blue rag in their possession or wear some blue article of clothing (such as blue shoelaces, blue hat, blue hair rollers, or blue canvas belt). In Las Vegas, they wear light blue. Members generally write their graffiti in blue, tagging their gang name on walls in the 'hoods to mark their territorial boundaries and to publicly taunt their enemies or rivals. They use terms like "Crip," or "BK" or "PK" (which means Blood Killer or Piru Killer). Crips refer to one another as "Cuzz" and use the letter "C" to replace the letter "B" in their conversations and writings, such as "Meet me at the cusstop" and "That guy has crass calls."

Pirus and Bloods identify with the color red and refer to one another as "Blood." A Piru usually carries a red rag and wears red clothing. Bloods write their graffiti in red and use the terms "Piru" and "CK" (for Crips Killer).

Black gang members once eschewed tattoos, but that's changed; now, members are tattooing themselves in the same manner as the traditional Hispanic gangs.

In the black street gang, there is little structure in terms of hierarchy and rank. No one member is in charge of everyone. Some members have more influence than others, but the term "leader" is seldom used. Age, physical stature, arrest record, and behavioral background are the main factors that determine an individual's influence upon a gang. Gang members gain respect, influence, and power within a particular group by demonstrating their nerve and daring.

Each gang's level of violence is determined by the dominant member's ability to incite the others. The dominant members are generally the most violent, street-wise, and knowledgeable in legal matters, which is especially useful in the event their members are arrested. They might participate in a violent act, or simply encourage others to commit it. They're usually well-liked and respected by their fellow members, as well as by outsiders.

Are black gangs becoming the new mob? Claims of "disorganization" not withstanding, some cops think so. Police say that black gangs and the mob now overlap, with players from organized crime hiring gang members as their hit men.

"I compare [black gang members] to the early days of the mob," said North Las Vegas Police Lieutenant Chris Larotonda. "They're doing the exact same things. Then it was bootleg whiskey. Now it's drugs. But you have to make yourself look legitimate even though your money may be coming from other [illegal] sources. Some of the gangs are expanding in just the narcotics sales and [otherwise] trying to legitimize themselves. We've seen them try to branch out into more legitimate-type businesses."

Even U.S. Senator Harry Reid, D-Nev., has likened Nevada's street-gang members to mobsters. Reid told a Judiciary Committee considering an anti-gang measure that "we've got sophisticated crime syndicates turning out cities and towns into war zones."

The basic differences between traditional organized crime versus street gangs "[usually comes down to] access to political influence," said Lieutenant Bill Conger from LVMPD's gang unit. "The street gangs aren't organized enough for that – yet."

Black street gangs are alive and well in Las Vegas. Although L.A. gangs still influence them, they now stand alone.

"We have our own Crips and Bloods," said Conger. "There was

some Los Angeles influence early on, but Las Vegas is its own town, and we have our own [gang] problems."

Indeed, 2001 ended up "the bloodiest year ever," said North Las Vegas Sergeant David Jacks. Two street gangs were in open combat, with an onslaught of shootings taking place on the border between Las Vegas and North Las Vegas. One street separated the rival street gangs, both of which originated in Los Angeles, Jacks said. "We refer to [the area] as 'Crips city.'"

14

MOTIVES

THERE ARE SEVERAL motives.

According to police sources and talk on the street, the killing of Tupac Shakur (and, to an extent, Biggie Smalls) was a byproduct of one of three pre-existing situations: one, the fierce competition between East Coast and West Coast music factions to sell records and dominate the gangsta rap world; two, Tupac Shakur and Suge Knight's connections to the street gang the Bloods and its rivalry with the Crips; and three, a conspiracy of top record-company executives to kill their own superstar rappers as a way of boosting sales.

Each of the three theories has also spawned related sub-theories. One relating to the third scenario is that Suge Knight was behind the deed, an accusation that Knight has vehemently denied and one that has never been substantiated with evidence. Conversely, it has been suggested that Suge, not Tupac, was the intended victim.

Still, others who have followed the saga contend that it was nothing as sinister as a deep-rooted conspiracy, but more likely a case of personal retaliation (stemming from the fight at the MGM Grand), or a semi-random act of violence, *semi*-random to the extent that the rival-gang consideration would be involved if that were the case.

One music industry insider said, "The only scenario that fits is somebody thought they were doing Pac a favor [by killing Biggie]. I don't know who killed Tupac. I'm tired of the speculation."

Tupac himself has been named in speculation that there was no killing, that the whole thing was an elaborate dodge staged to fake his own death.

Let's take a look.

"R-E-S-P-E-C-T," Aretha Franklin sang 20 years ago. And that's exactly what Suge Knight, Tupac Shakur, Biggie Smalls, and Puffy Combs all said they wanted. Could the vicious and bloody rivalry between record companies be as simple as that?

Some sources say that the rivalry has, indeed, been as simple as that – respect as rappers and songwriters, as businessmen, and as gangstas.

"The rumors [about a feud] are helpful, but not true," Suge told *Vibe* before Tupac was killed. "They get me additional respect, and this business is about getting the respect you deserve so you can get what you want. I don't worry about all the talk."

Tupac also spoke to *Vibe* about being respected for his music, while at the same time appearing to be willing to fight Suge's East Coast battles with him.

"My homeboy Suge gave me the best advice that I could ever get from anybody," Tupac said. "When people ask Suge if he's beefing with Bad Boy and Puffy, he says, 'It's like me going to the playground to pick on little kids. That's like me being mad at my little brother 'cause he's getting cash now. I'm not mad at that; I'm just mad at my little brother when he don't respect me. And when you don't respect me, I'm a spank that ass.' I don't give a fuck how rich you got on the block, I'm your big brother. That's my only point. I feel as though he wrong, he got out of hand. He got seduced by the power not because he's an evil person, but because money is evil if it's not handled right."

"Why is it mandatory that I get respect?" Tupac said to writer William Shaw. "I know other people who are just as successful as me and you can call *them* a bitch... but if somebody calls me a bitch, I don't care if we're in court, we're going to fight." In his world, he told Shaw, "All good niggas, all the niggas who change the world, die in violence. They don't die in regular ways. Motherfuckers come take their lives."

Some observers maintained, however, that the bicoastal feud was more about money and women than personalities, that it was these tangible status symbols that led to the professional jealousies.

Producer Jermaine Dupree, a friend of Puffy Combs, told *Newsweek*: "This industry has a problem with people thinking there isn't enough room for everyone. It's the attitude that, 'If you got it, I can't have it, so I am going to take it.' That's why these deaths are happening."

But of course, the rivalry motive was far more involved than that. Deep down, Tupac wondered whether Biggie really *had* set him up to get robbed and shot at Quad Studios in 1994. Though he occasionally denied it, Tupac told San Francisco DJ Sway two months before he was killed, "Strangers, niggas in jail told me, 'Hell, you don't know who shot you? Biggie's homeboys shot you.'"

"Tupac really believes Biggie and them shot him," veteran rapper Ice-T said in a *Vibe* magazine interview. "If somebody thinks they shot them, it's on for life."

Biggie responded to Tupac's accusations. "The rumor that's spreading is all this shit like we set him up – you know what I'm saying? – and that's crazy," he told MTV.

Biggie asked for but never got an apology from Tupac. "It's real niggas in the streets thinking, 'That's fucked up what Big did to Tupac.' I think that should be erased," Biggie said. "As far as with me, he always gonna be my man... But he need to just check himself. And I want an apology, 'cause I don't get down like that."

Instead, after Tupac signed with Death Row, he responded by publicly attacking Biggie, even bragging that he'd had sex with Biggie's wife Faith Evans. Then in 1996 at the Soul Train Awards in Los Angeles, Biggie's armed bodyguard got into a fight with an armed associate of Tupac backstage at the Shrine Auditorium. That's when the rivalry started being referred to as an East Coast-West Coast rap war.

On the other hand, Tupac's cousin, Chaka Zulu, told a reporter, "I don't think [the feud] came out of Pac's camp. I think it came from people that are caught up in the hype of the East Coast-West Coast thing."

Biggie and his friends continued to vociferously deny the accusations. Lance "Un" Rivera, Biggie's partner in the Brooklyn record label management company Undeas Recording, said in a published interview that the accusations were unfounded.

"He and Tupac didn't have no beef," Rivera told *Rolling Stone* magazine. "They was real close friends. Tupac developed a hate for him. [Biggie] couldn't understand what it was, but he never responded. He said, 'I'm not going to feed into it.'"

Biggie, in his last interview, published in *The Source* the week after his death, again insisted that the rift between him and Tupac was blown out of proportion. But no one has ever said whether Biggie had an alibi for either – or both – the Manhattan and Las Vegas shootings of Tupac. When asked, the police said they didn't know, because Biggie was never a suspect.

The rivalry wasn't relegated just to Tupac and Biggie. It went right to the top. Suge Knight's Death Row Records had been battling Puffy Combs's Bad Boy Entertainment for control of the multimillion-dollar rap music industry for a few years, and the rivalry heightened further, some say, after the 1995 *The Source* Awards in August at the Paramount Theater in Manhattan, when Suge criticized Combs on stage, making fun of his appearances on videos with Bad Boy artists. Suge was an award presenter. Before he left the stage, he said, "If you don't want the owner of your label on your album or in your video or on your tour, come sign with Death Row."

This was an obvious shot at Combs, who occasionally appears in his rappers' videos and often raps on their albums. Puffy was shocked by Suge's blatant and public disrespect. Some say a battle to the death began that night. A few months later at a party for producer Jermaine Dupree, a Death Row employee and Suge's close friend Jake Robles was shot. When he died a week later, Suge blamed Puffy Combs, calling it a hit. No one was ever arrested and Puffy has denied any involvement.

Movie actor Warren Beatty became friendly with Suge while researching a movie project set in the rap world. Beatty dismissed talk that Suge would retaliate against Puffy for Jake's death.

"It's sort of hard to keep up with the apocryphal on Suge," Beatty told the *New York Times*. "I mean, Puff Daddy, Muff Daddy, whatever. I know Suge was very close to the man who died. And I know he was very upset. The apocryphal is just talk, even when it's pungent."

Still, rumors persisted, and if they had any substance, the feud had escalated. Now people were being marked for death. What may have started out as hype to sell records had turned violent.

Steve Jackson, a rap music producer who was with Biggie the night he was killed, told the *Village Voice*, "You know as well as I know that people wanna avenge Biggie's death, man, because they are very sad over the fact that he was set-up. They have friends and their friends have friends and their friends want revenge. You still have Suge Knight, you still have Puffy Combs, you still have their friends. You still have the East, you still have the West."

"Now everybody is scared," Jackson continued. "I don't think it would be in the best interest of Puffy to go back to L.A. any time in the future. I don't think he should go back, period. I think they're definitely going to try to kill him. Somebody is out to kill him, just as they killed Biggie Smalls."

It's a war that neither Death Row nor Bad Boy can contain," *Village Voice* reporter Peter Noel wrote on March 25, 1997. "Combs, Knight, and Snoop Doggy Dogg are undoubtedly concerned for their own lives."

Dominique DiPrirna, a DJ at L.A.'s KKBT, expressed shock at the violence surrounding rap. "What you have are two of our biggest stars killed – shot down – within six months," he said. "This is out of control."

While the East-West record-label rivalry was an early theory for a motive in the shooting, many blamed another, more obvious, one: rivalry and the ongoing battle between the Bloods and Crips street gangs. In the days immediately following the shooting, rumors ran rampant that Tupac had taken a bullet intended for Suge, that Tupac had died in a war involving gang members from Suge's old Compton neighborhood.

Vibe Editor-in-Chief Alan Light saw it this way: "[I] wouldn't be surprised if it didn't have anything to do with Tupac, but is more related to Suge," Light told me in a telephone interview. "There have been up to three contracts on [Suge's] life at any given moment. He's very public... about his gang affiliation. There are a lot of people with a lot of issues with him."

In a photo taken just minutes before Tupac was shot, Suge is pictured holding a blood-red rag in his hand, a well-known sign of Bloods affiliation. Meanwhile, Orlando Anderson, roughed up by Tupac's crew at the MGM Grand the night of the shooting, was, according to Compton police, a reputed member of the Southside Crips.

According to a police affidavit, two months before Tupac was killed, there was a confrontation between some Crips and Bloods at the Lakewood Mall near Compton. Travon Lane, aka Tray Dee, a Mob Piru member and rap singer, was in the mall's Foot Locker store with Kevin Woods, also a known Piru, when they were confronted by about eight Southside Crips members. The two crews fought and Tray's diamond-laden Death Row pendant was stolen.

On September 7, Tray was in Las Vegas for the Tyson- Seldon fight with Suge, Tupac, and Death Row associates. After the boxing match, Tray told his friends he'd recognized Orlando Anderson as one of the Crips who stole his pendant. Tupac, Suge, and the crew stomped and kicked Orlando, which was captured on the now-famous MGM Grand surveillance videotape. Police in the L.A. area were given this information from L.A. gang-member informants.

Vegas police have said that since the night of the Tupac shooting they have not been able to speak with Travon Lane, who, the Compton Police affidavit asserts, was involved with in the first scuffle with Orlando Anderson at the Lakewood Mall, pointed out Orlando to Tupac at the MGM Grand, and was overheard at Club 662 hours after the shooting identifying Orlando Anderson as the shooter. Efforts to talk with Travon Lane were unsuccessful.

Could Orlando have caught up with Suge and Tupac later that evening and taken his revenge? Did Orlando Anderson have an alibi at 11:10 p.m. on September 7? Las Vegas police won't say. "We usually don't comment on statements made by potential witnesses and suspects," Sergeant Kevin Manning said.

The random (or semi-random) theory supposes that rival gang members simply happened upon the Death Row caravan at Flamingo and Koval. And, finding themselves in a serendipitous position, perpetrated a spontaneous attack.

George Kelesis, the Las Vegas attorney who'd organized the benefit at Club 662 the night of the shooting, told me, "I never really have reconciled it. I've heard so many stories... It could have been, in my mind, as simple as just some gang-banger trying to make a name for himself. The possibilities are infinite. To buy into the story that it was [planned], how in God's earth did they pull it off? Tupac drove into Las Vegas at the last minute. Plans change.

"I was supposed to go in the limo with Suge, but people started lining up at Club 662 at five o'clock. I couldn't leave the benefit, so Suge went in [Tupac's] car. Everything that happened prior to the fight was all last minute. The plans were changed at the last minute and nobody, not even us, knew it. Suge was going to come late and a lot of stars were coming late. I think the shooting was happenstance. If it was a plan to kill him, then those guys were good, because they had to have a crystal ball to figure it out."

The theory that Tupac's death was the result of a random shooting simply doesn't hold up. There is too much evidence to point to a gang-related shooting.

Still, in either the retaliation or the random scenarios, it's possible that it wasn't Tupac who was specifically targeted. Killing Tupac or Suge would have sufficed, and circumstances (the traffic pattern) resulted in Tupac's side of the car taking the brunt of the attack.

If nothing else, any version of the gang motive provides an easy out for investigators. "In my opinion, it was black gang-related, probably a Bloods-Crips thing," Metro gang detective Chuck Cassell told Kevin Powell. "Look at [Tupac's] tattoos and album covers – that's not the Jackson 5... It looks like a case of live by the sword, die by the sword."

At the hospital the afternoon Tupac died, Patricia Cunningham, the radio reporter for Sheridan Broadcast, who'd spent the week in the hospital with Billy Garland, Tupac's father, and Kidada Jones, Tupac's girlfriend, hinted that there would be retaliation for Tupac's death. "You're not going to hear any talk about retaliation here. That'll come later," she said to me as she stood inside the trauma center's lobby.

Marcos, a friend of Tupac who had met him on the set of a video 18 months earlier, sat on the hood of a white BMW parked outside the trauma center 30 minutes after Tupac was pronounced dead. Marcos was wearing a collarless, crisp white shirt and white shorts. A couple of his friends stood stoically beside him. They all had the "L.A. look" with their clothing style and jewelry. As Marcos began talking to reporters, his friends backed away.

When asked, "Why are you here?" Marcos looked down and answered quietly, "Man, to show my respect to Tupac. To show respect to his family and his mother. We're here for her. We're here for Pac."

After the reporters were done with Marcos, I stuck around and asked him if friends of Tupac knew who Tupac's assailant was. He said, "Yeah, we know. We know who did it."

Then I asked why, if they knew who the shooter was, didn't they tell the police?

He replied, "Nobody wants to help the police. What for? What are they gonna do? They can't bring him back."

When I asked whether the assailants eventually would leak information that they shot Tupac, he said, "They already have." He declined to say who. All he'd say was, "They're not from Las Vegas."

Finally, could Suge have possibly ordered Tupac hit to sell more records? Some observers don't think it's as far-fetched as it sounds. As one insider put it, "Think about it. Tupac's worth more dead than alive."

According to a police source, Suge Knight had been considered a possible suspect from the beginning, especially in light of rumors that a hefty life-insurance policy had been taken out on Tupac before his death. According to the rumors, after Tupac signed with Death Row, a $4 million insurance policy was written on him, naming Death Row, not Tupac's family, the beneficiary.

Richard Fischbein, Afeni Shakur's attorney who also represents the Tupac estate, said he, too, had heard talk about the insurance policy, but said, "We haven't been able to substantiate it."

Las Vegas Police Sergeant Kevin Manning said that no one, including Suge Knight, had been eliminated as a potential suspect. But when asked what Knight could have gained financially with Tupac gone, Manning said, "I have no comment about the money."

However, a search for such an insurance policy came up empty. A representative for the State of California's Office of Insurance said no claims of fraud and no investigations had been opened in the Shakur case. It's not known which company, if any, wrote a policy.

"Death is a commodity, you know?" commented Ramsey Jones, a clerk at Tower Records in Greenwich Village, New York, explaining to the Associated Press why he couldn't keep Biggie's CDs on the shelf (they were selling quicker than he could stock them).

A music-industry insider who asked not to be identified had this to say. "Here's my theory. [At first], these rap artists are small-time investments. They're lucky if they make one album. When they start getting up to four albums, they're big investments. Then they become a liability. [And they remain] a liability as long as they're alive. They lead lavish lifestyles and get in trouble. Tupac Shakur and Biggie Smalls, they got themselves in trouble a lot. They had big mouths. The record companies had to bail them out all the time, get them out of trouble. They had to keep throwing money at them for their lifestyles – their cars, their cribs, their women.

"But if they're dead and they've already cut their albums, the record companies are just selling their albums. They're not giving the money to them any more. They don't cost them anything. The green keeps coming in, but they don't have to spend anything to get it, you understand? Green comes in and nothing goes out to the rappers because they're dead."

That's not exactly accurate. In both the Tupac and Biggie cases, their estates continue getting royalties, long after they've been buried. At the time of his death, Tupac had some 200 songs recorded – potentially worth hundreds of millions of dollars. Worth more dead than alive? Unlikely. Still, by all accounts, he'd certainly taken on the posture of a liability. Tupac's star was still on the rise; however, his interests appeared to be shifting slightly, broadening to include a (time-consuming) movie career. Worse yet, Tupac reportedly was putting out feelers for a new record company to produce his albums once he fulfilled his three-album contract with Death Row.

"A few days before he was killed he [Tupac] formally sent a letter telling David Kenner that he no longer could represent him, basically firing him," said Rick Fischbein.

On top of that, Tupac may have been beginning to make noises about money. Death Row Records said that at the time of his death Tupac owed $4.9 million to the record label, even though he sold more than $60 million worth of albums for them. The money Tupac owed, Death Row claimed, was for services rendered – including Tupac's jail bond money.

But Afeni Shakur has said that her son questioned where all the money his albums were generating was going.

Fischbein said that Suge would throw money at Tupac periodically to keep him happy. "He asked over and over again for accountings of the things that he did, the monies that came in, and he never got it. When he screamed loud enough, I'm told, they would – someone would bring over a car and say, 'Tupac, here's a Rolls Royce,' and he'd drive it around. Then when he died the family found out none of it was his."

Also brought into question has been Suge's decision to leave the scene of the shooting and head in a direction away from area hospitals. It's a mistake easily dismissed given the confusion of the moment. Much more interesting is George Kelesis's statement that a planned effort would have required a "crystal ball" because nobody knew the night's plans until the last minute. Suge knew.

But reality takes hold when you consider the actual course of events. It seems inconceivable that Suge would risk putting himself in the path of 13 shots sprayed from a semiautomatic weapon, and, in fact, take a bullet in the head to distance himself from Tupac's murder. If he'd known what was coming, you'd think he would have at least worn a bullet-proof vest that night to help ensure his safety. He didn't.

In an interview with Lena Nozizwe on *America's Most Wanted*, Suge said as much, calling speculation that he had arranged the shooting ludicrous. "If you look at any interview that Tupac did, if you look at any video, any TV show he did, one thing he always did was praise Death Row. And me and him praised each other. 'Just shoot me in my head, make sure you hit me in my head, so it can look good.' That's crazy."

The theory that Suge had something to do with the death of his top rapper also pales when you consider Suge's Bloods gang affiliation. Why would he hire a rival Crips member (Las Vegas and Compton police have speculated that Crips were the shooters) to kill Tupac? It simply doesn't make sense. Though some might argue that it provides the perfect cover, it also creates several additional possibilities for leaks.

Yet another music insider insisted, "The trail clearly leads to money. Who benefits?" the source asked. Whatever motive you buy into, "the green" is certainly flowing into the record companies: Tupac's posthumous *Don Killuminati: The 7 Day Theory* (recorded under the pseudonym *Makaveli*), released six weeks after Tupac's death, sold 664,000 units in the first week, and 2.5 million copies by April 1997. And Biggie's posthumous double album, *Life After Death*, sold 690,000 copies in its first week, topping the *Billboard* charts with the best first-week sales since the Beatles' double album *Anthology I* was released in 1995; stores couldn't keep it stocked.

What's more, the money in the beginning didn't appear to be flowing too fast in Afeni Shakur's direction. At the time, she contended she was owed money by a music industry that continued to profit heavily from her son's music.

"The entertainment business is a business of prostitution and thievery, and that was rampant around my son's talent," Afeni told ABC's *Prime Time Live*. "He absolutely thought he was quite rich and that his family would, you know, be rich forever. Please remember that my great-grandmother was a slave, my grandmother was a sharecropper, my mother was a factory worker, and I was a legal worker, do you understand? And so this represents the first time in our life, in our memory ever, that we have been able to enjoy the American dream, and that's what Tupac brought to his family."

But her son had no assets in his own name. Instead, Death Row Records had doled out money and expensive merchandise – cars, clothes, jewelry, a condo, Afeni's house, cash – to Tupac, but none of the assets were in his name.

After Tupac's death, Afeni arranged to meet with Suge to settle her son's estate, she said during the same *Prime Time Live* interview.

"I kept telling Rick [Fischbein], 'We're just going to – we'll meet with Suge. He'll tell you everything. We'll meet with him first.' But he didn't even show up."

In December 1996, Afeni filed an infringement lawsuit against Death Row Records for selling hats, T-shirts, and sweatshirts connected with Tupac without her permission. After the lawsuit was filed, Death Row and two companies that made and distributed the merchandise agreed during a hearing in U.S. District Court in Los Angeles to a sales moratorium. They also promised to deposit potential royalties in a court-monitored account – more than a half-million dollars total.

Also, three record producers in March 1997 agreed to delay the release of an album containing two early recordings by Tupac. The move came as a federal judge in Sacramento, California, was to rule on a restraining order requested by Afeni Shakur's estate attorney. The three Sacramento-area producers were accused in court documents of "intentionally infringing upon [Tupac's] valuable trademark and publicity rights." The complaint continued, "...[the trio is] profiting from their illicit conversion of songs that he authored and performed in or about 1990, before he became famous, and which belong to Shakur's estate... [The producer's actions] are especially predatory and harmful at this critical point in time, when Shakur's recordings and film appearances are receiving widespread, critical acceptance before a mainstream audience."

Celeste Chulsa, Fischbein's assistant, told me in a telephone interview from New York City that Afeni had also sought rights to previously unseen home videotape of Tupac that was reproduced in the biographical film, *Thug Immortal*. The movie stayed on the *Billboard* Top 20 list for several weeks after its release.

Conversely, in February 2002, Frank Alexander's documentary, *Before I Wake*, which made Amazon.com's top seller list, was welcomed by Tupac's mother. "She called me and we both cried on the phone. I have her blessings," Frank said.

Earlier, Afeni had accused Death Row of not giving her any money from her son's estate since his death. She told *Prime Time Live* that Suge had told her at the hospital at her son's deathbed that he would take care of her and her family. When asked if Suge Knight had done that, Afeni answered, "No."

Suge, however, told reporter Lena Nozizwe with Fox's *America's Most Wanted* that Afeni was, in fact, paid. "When I was in jail, I gave her a check for $3 million," Suge said. "Plus ... I think in four or five months Tupac spent $2.4 million, $2.5 million."

Afeni contended that the $3 million had come from Interscope, not from Suge like he'd promised her.

Besides the money, she said the masters of the 200 unreleased songs Tupac had recorded were missing. "We don't know where the masters are because we can't get an accounting from Death Row Records," she said.

Suge's long-time attorney, David Kenner, echoed Suge's comments that Death Row had made numerous advances to Tupac and that all of his money had been properly accounted for and paid in a timely manner.

Suge responded to Mrs. Shakur's accusations during his final appearance in court. "I'm not mad, but I'm disappointed at Tupac's mother," Suge said during his sentencing speech. "People tell her that the songs I paid for and marketed is her songs. And she made statements saying that he never got any money. I got signed documents where he received over $2.5 million, even before he was supposed to receive money. And beyond all that, when he was incarcerated, I gave his mother $3 million. But when the media gets it, it turns around that I left him for dead, I left him with zero, and that I'm this monster."

"If I was so bad I would have no success," Suge told *Prime Time Live*. "I know business. I know how to take my artists and give them superstar status, and [let] them get what they deserve."

Death Row Records countersued after Afeni filed suit against the record company. Death Row claimed Tupac's estate owed the record company $7 million for advances and expenses paid out to Tupac.

Attorney Rick Fischbein, who at the time I spoke with him was in the middle of negotiating a settlement for Tupac's mother with Death Row Records, said a sizable settlement was "imminent."

"We're close to a settlement," Fischbein said in July 1997. "It's a substantial settlement, if it happens. We're certainly all working to try to settle it."

Fischbein also indicated that Death Row had complied with providing an accounting, and that the settlement would not be one lump sum, but a percentage of future sales of Tupac's works. "We now have an accounting," Fischbein said. "What's being discussed is not just a single payment. Music is odd in that it doesn't really matter who owns it. The real question is, who gets the money for releasing it or playing it? Owning it is an interesting issue, and it might lead you to get those other rights, but those rights could be separate. These issues are all being discussed."

Police won't commit to saying which of the motive scenarios they believe is most likely. Years after the primary investigations, it's still anyone's guess. No one was ever arrested, but, as Metro P.D.'s Sergeant Kevin Manning pointed out, no one was ever ruled out as a suspect, either.

And no one means no one. One final theory transcends all the others, and implicates the white record-company power brokers themselves. Death Row is a black-owned label, but it was financed by white corporate bosses who, it's long been alleged, have profited by exploiting young black men from the ghetto. Use 'em up and throw 'em away is the charge. Tupac Shakur's legal problems alone had become a public-relations nightmare for Death Row's parent corporation. Add to that the public attack on Time Warner over gangsta-rap lyrics (Time Warner eventually sold its stake in Interscope), and you have the foundation for a monster conspiracy scenario, the proportions of which dwarf anything previously discussed. Backers of this motive conclude that the murders of Biggie Smalls and Yafeu Fula were crafted to look like gang retaliation to cover tracks.

Writer Kevin Powell said rappers and people in the music business are afraid to speculate about who killed Tupac Shakur. "That's the talk, to be honest, on the streets," Powell said. "It may have been gang members who pulled the trigger. People believe there may be people behind it, people bigger than gang members. People are afraid to even speculate. It's much more profound than Death Row-Bad Boy. Will we ever know who killed John F. Kennedy or Martin Luther King?"

15

THE AUTOPSY

OUT OF THE 9,250 people who died in 1996 in Clark County, 5,528 were reported to the coroner's office and 3,138 were accepted for investigation. Of those, 978 were autopsied, including Tupac's body. Coroner Ron Flud at the time had a staff of 17 investigators, including Dr. Ed Brown, who went to the hospital and confirmed Tupac's death, toe-tagged him, put him in a body bag, and arranged to have his body taken to the office for an autopsy.

Flud, who in 1996 had been with the Clark County Coroner's Office for 12 years, was born in Muleshoe, Texas, a small Western town. He moved to Las Vegas to attend UNLV. After earning a bachelor's degree in criminal justice, he became a patrol officer for the North Las Vegas Police Department. He later obtained a graduate degree from Golden Gate University in San Francisco. He started as an investigator with the coroner's office until he was elected to the coroner's post, in 1983. At the time of Tupac Shakur's death, Flud was earning $100,000 a year (not including benefits).

The coroner's offices, on Pinto Lane, have been expanded since Tupac's death. Before that, the quarters were crowded and cramped.

The close quarters led to inefficiencies in performance. For example, the discrepancy in Tupac's body weight and height written on the coroner's report. Human error was at fault.

Today, offices of the coroner and medical examiners are in a new, state-of-the-art facility. The Clark County Coroner is the administrative head of the office, overseeing three divisions, with a staff of about 40 people, including forensics, investigation, and administration. The office performs an average of 1,100 autopsies a year.

In the old building, medical investigators sat just one foot from each other and a few steps away from the scale on which bodies were weighed.

After the examiners had finished the autopsy of Tupac's body, a worker made a red checkmark next to the name "Lesane Crooks" on a wall board hanging near the examination room, indicating that the autopsy of the body had been completed.

In February 1997, I visited the Clark County Office of Vital Statistics and viewed Tupac Shakur's original death certificate. They would not give me a copy, but they allowed me to look at the original and take notes, with an employee sitting next to me. The only copy released was to Tupac's mother, Afeni Shakur.

The original document remains on file with the county. I read the certificate, which was in a binder filed in a cabinet at the county office. It stands as the official notice of death. It should be noted that it is against Nevada Revised Statute to fake, forge, or sign a public document, including death certificates. Tupac Shakur's death certificate includes the following:

* Tupac Amaru Shakur was pronounced dead by Dr. Lovett at 4:03 p.m. on Friday, September 13, 1996, at University Medical Center's Intensive Care Unit.
* The one-page death certificate was filed with Clark County's vital records section by County Coroner Ron Flud on September 18, 1996. Dr. Ed Brown with the Coroner's office signed the certificate.
* Afeni Shakur made a positive identification of her son's body at 5:00 p.m. at the hospital. His body was then taken by Davis Mortuary to the morgue, three blocks away. An autopsy was performed and the official cause of death was respiratory failure and cardiopulmonary arrest in connection with multiple gunshot wounds.
* Shakur's occupation was listed as "rap singer" and the company he worked for was shown as "Euphanasia" in Los Angeles, California.
* A Clark County seal was stamped on the certificate, making it an official and legal document.

***

The mortuary van carrying Tupac Shakur's body drove from the hospital to the morgue. The driver maneuvered the three blocks without being noticed, or so he thought. But fans did eventually make it there and pounded on the back door. Because of that, Coroner Ron Flud decided not to wait and do the autopsy the next day, but to do it that afternoon. Flud was worried about fans breaking in to get a glimpse of Tupac's corpse.

An autopsy was done the evening of September 13, 1996, according to authorities.

While the autopsy report is not deemed by Nevada state law to be public information, the coroner's report is available to the public. However, after I bought a copy for $5, an office employee later said it had been given to me in error, and that they would not be releasing it to anyone because of the ongoing homicide investigation. To my knowledge, I am the only reporter to have a copy of that report. Six 35-millimeter photos taken during and after the autopsy are on file at the coroner's office, along with the report.

According to statements on the four-page coroner's report, Tupac Shakur's remains were positively identified by his mother, Afeni Shakur. The autopsy determined that Tupac had no illegal drugs in his system. He was, however, heavily sedated during his hospital stay, it says. He was shot in his right hand, right hip and right chest just under his right arm.

"I interviewed the decedent's mother, Afeni Shakur, and she stated that the decedent was not married and he had no children," coroner Investigator Ed Brown wrote in his report. "She stated that Tupac A. Shakur was his name. She was not able to give any more information than this."

When Tupac arrived at University Medical Center's trauma center, immediately following the shooting, he was wheeled into the recovery area and "was resuscitated according to advanced-trauma-life support protocol," the report said, and "a full trauma activation was called."

He was placed on life support machines. Two liters of blood that had hemorrhaged into his chest cavity were removed. His pulse was "very thready and initially he had a minimal blood pressure, which rapidly declined."

In a conversation with Ed Brown at the hospital following Tupac's death, the surgeon told Brown that Tupac's injuries included a gunshot wound to his right chest with a "massive hemothorax" and a gunshot wound to the right thigh with "the bullet palpable within the abdomen." Tupac also had a gunshot wound to a right finger with a fracture. The preoperative diagnosis was a gunshot wound to the chest and abdomen and post-operative bleeding.

He was taken immediately to the operating room for operative intervention and further resuscitation. His right lung was removed.

Tupac underwent two surgeries. The first began at 6:25 p.m. on September 8 and lasted an hour. The surgery "consisted of exploratory" procedures, the surgeon wrote. He also noted that it appeared Tupac had had some prior surgery for bullet wounds in his upper right chest area.

The second operation at University Medical Center consisted of "ligation of bleeding" and removal of a bullet from his pelvic area. It was done at midnight on September 8 and completed at 2:35 a.m. on September 9.

The one bullet remaining in Tupac's chest was not removed during surgery, but during the autopsy, Coroner Ron Flud told me. It then became evidence, he said.

Tupac was pronounced dead at 4:03 p.m. September 13 by Dr. James Lovett at University Medical Center. Clark County Coroner Investigator Ed Brown was called to the hospital at 4:15 p.m.

"Upon my arrival... I found no apparent life signs, and trauma was observed to the right hand, right hip and right chest under the right arm, apparently caused from gunshots."

16

DEAD OR ALIVE?

EVEN THOUGH Tupac Amaru Shakur was gunned down on the streets of Las Vegas in front of at least a hundred people, there are those who refuse to believe that he died from the wounds he suffered that hot September night. "Dead or alive?" is the question that has surfaced again and again concerning the 25-year-old gangsta rap artist and film star.

Some people, no matter what they hear or see, have chosen to believe that Tupac is still alive, sequestered somewhere in Cuba, with sightings in Manhattan, Arizona (perhaps because of its close proximity to Las Vegas), South America, and the Caribbean.

New conspiracy theories claiming Tupac is still alive cropped up, for at least a couple of years after his death, every day; the World Wide Web remains cluttered with their rationalizations. Internet chat rooms are full of dialogue discussions of whether he did, in fact, pass away. They often ignore logic and facts, opting instead for their own "explanations."

For those who refuse to accept Tupac's death, each time a new song or video is released, they assert it's proof of Tupac's existence. They can't seem to comprehend the fact that he recorded the music *before* his death. If the track was released after the shooting, in their minds, it must have been *recorded* after the shooting. Therefore, to their way of thinking, he was still alive and well.

Also fueling the rumors was a song titled "God Bless the Dead." It begins with Tupac shouting, "Rest in peace Biggie Smalls." The Notorious B.I.G., aka Biggie Smalls, of course, was killed after Tupac. The Biggie Smalls mentioned in the track was a lesser-known California rapper, an old friend of Tupac, who was killed in a drive-by shooting. Puffy Combs once explained it to a reporter like this: "There was another rapper called Biggie Smalls, so we couldn't use that name. [Christopher Wallace] wanted to call himself 'Notorious.'" To prevent confusion with the other Smalls, Biggie devised a new moniker by simply adding "Notorious" in front of his nickname "Big." He still, though, referred to himself as Biggie Smalls, but did not use it as a stage name, because it was already taken.

At the top of the "alive" list is the seven-day theory (Tupac was shot on September 7; the numbers in his age, 2-5, add up to seven). Rapper Chuck D, who sings with Public Enemy, has posted "Chuck D's 18 Compelling Reasons Why 2Pac is not Dead" on the internet. They include the "Makaveli theory" – named after the Italian philosopher Machiavelli, who talked about faking his own death in his works. Tupac was introduced to Machiavelli, including his book *The Prince*, first in high school and later in prison. He often made references to Machiavelli to friends. He named his last album *Makaveli: The 7 Day Theory*, thus the Makaveli and seven-day theory.

Another of Chuck D's "compelling reasons": "The cover of [Tupac's] next album has 2Pac looking like Jesus Christ. Could he be planning a resurrection?"

Chuck D also claimed that "Las Vegas is still very much a mob town. No one gets killed on the Strip. You have to pretty much get permission in order for something like this to happen. Who was calling the shots on this one?" (Chuck D has since changed his stance and backed away from the theories he helped get started.)

Much of the speculation has maintained that medical examiners never did an autopsy, that, naysayers say, Tupac's remains weren't cremated as the funeral home employees confirmed they were, and that his mother had helped him secure a new identity so he could spend the rest of his days out of the limelight in the solitude of Cuba.

So prominent were the rumors, the police and county officials were forced to comment on them. Metro Police Lieutenant Wayne Petersen told an Associated Press reporter, "The public believes he staged his own death, for whatever reason."

University Medical Center, where Tupac died, was deluged with telephone calls. "[The rumor] started probably a couple of weeks after he died," Dale Pugh, a hospital spokesman, said. "It kind of escalated for a while, [then tapered off], but we still get an occasional call. Apparently there's a lot of stuff on the internet claiming he's still alive, and that may be refueling the rumors.

"I have a son in high school, and he comes home and tells me that he hears Tupac is still alive, that his death was a hoax, and that there was this giant conspiracy to allow him to escape to a more favorable environment. We get calls from people saying they hear the doctor who cared for him has been arrested by the FBI and that the FBI is investigating a conspiracy. It's gotten pretty wild."

"There's the big rumor," said Ron Flud, the Clark County coroner, "that's taken on a life of its own. TV called me and said, 'We understand that Tupac's not dead.' I told them, 'Well, I can guarantee you he's not down at Kmart with Elvis.'"

Theories aside, the fact is that Tupac is dead. Here's the proof.

First, for Tupac to have faked his own death, he would have had to have the cooperation of not only his family, friends, and associates; but of the Clark County Sheriff; the Las Vegas Metropolitan Police Department's patrol, traffic, and bike cops, general-assignment and homicide detectives, criminalist investigators, lab technicians, dispatchers, and its public affairs officer; Nevada Highway Patrol troopers and dispatchers; Mercy Ambulance paramedics and dispatchers; Clark County Fire Department firefighters, paramedics, and dispatchers; University Medical Center nurses, doctors, and administrators; the Clark County Coroner and his entire staff of examiners, technicians, and clerks; not to mention reporters and photographers who were on the scene shortly after the shooting. In other words, it would take a conspiracy of epic proportions.

Much of the speculation seems to stem from the air of secretiveness surrounding post-mortem activities. Dale Pugh of University Medical Center, said, "Personally, and I've thought about this a lot – I suspect one of the reasons this still goes around is the media never saw the body leave the hospital, because we didn't want to turn that into some sort of circus. His body went out another exit from the hospital, from the back. That was our decision based on respect for the patient and based on respect for the family and based on the large number of people outside the hospital. We were uncertain as to what might happen and felt that it would be better to take another approach. And we did. As soon as he passed away, we called the media. And as soon as the body was out of the hospital, we again notified the media."

Friends and relatives were allowed to see Tupac in the intensive-care unit at University Medical Center, where he lay for six days in a coma until his death on September 13, 1996. After he succumbed to his wounds, Tupac's mother, Afeni, positively identified her son at the hospital. His body was quickly moved to the coroner's office, where the autopsy was performed.

"At a typical autopsy," coroner Ron Flud said, "the people normally in the room are the pathologist, forensic technician, the crime-scene analyst, and the detectives assigned to the case. Look at the number of people who would have had to be involved in this to say that there's some kind of conspiracy or cover-up to facilitate Tupac. I'd never even heard of Tupac [before the shooting]."

The coroner's office in Las Vegas keeps busy. In the fastest-growing city in America, with 4,000 to 6,000 people moving to the Las Vegas Valley each month and more than 30 million tourists visiting each year, the crime rate has grown nearly as rapidly as the population. Murders in the Las Vegas Valley skyrocketed to an all-time high in 1996; Tupac was one of 207 people murdered in Clark County in that year.

After Tupac's body was taken by a mortuary ambulance to the morgue, a decision was made by both Clark County Coroner Flud, along with a sergeant and two detectives from homicide, to go ahead with the autopsy that evening. It's not unusual for the process to move quickly in Las Vegas. Examiners often perform autopsies on victims the same day their bodies are brought in, especially in homicide cases. In this case, for security reasons, the coroner didn't want the body to stay in the morgue overnight. Too many people knew where the coroner's offices were – around the corner from the hospital where a 24-hour vigil had begun six days earlier, following the shooting. Hundreds of people had flocked to the hospital when they heard the news. It was too risky to keep the body until the next day.

Often, homicide detectives follow the coroner to his office so they can witness the autopsy not long after a homicide is committed. Homicide's Sergeant Manning and Detectives Becker and Franks met the ambulance at the coroner's office. The investigators were in the coroner's examining room as medical examiners performed Tupac's postmortem exam.

The coroner finished with his examination, autopsy, and coroner's report, and handed over Tupac's body to Davis Funeral Home, across the street from the hospital, at 2127 West Charleston Boulevard. No doubt Afeni chose the mortuary because of its close vicinity to both the hospital and coroner's office. Also, it wasn't far from the Golden Nugget downtown where she had been staying all week. The mortuary employees, in turn, cremated Tupac's body, at Tupac's mother's request.

It's no small task, making arrangements to move a body from one state to another. That had to have played a role in Mrs. Shakur's decision to have her son's remains cremated with his ashes scattered, instead of burying his body.

Following a brief memorial service in the Las Vegas funeral parlor with a few friends and family, Afeni Shakur boarded the plane that returned her home to Stone Mountain, Georgia, near Atlanta. It was a little more than 24 hours after her only son – and oldest child – had been pronounced dead.

The ashes of Tupac's body were later scattered over a grassy area in a park in Los Angeles, where Tupac had spent the last years of his life. A small group of family members and friends were invited to the private, informal ceremony. There was no pomp and circumstance for the fallen rapper; the brief ceremony honoring him was conducted with quiet dignity. Afeni Shakur is not a woman who dwells on tragedy; rather, she has devoted her life to the empowerment of the human spirit; its ability to survive and soar.

Keith Clinscates, an executive at *Vibe* magazine, issued a statement about the rumors surrounding the rapper's death. "Tupac had a huge presence in the community that loved and respected him. [His death] was a human tragedy," he said, calling such rumors cruel and unkind to the Shakur family. "These [rappers] are not comic-book heroes. These are real people."

Tupac, unfortunately, did die. Those who claim otherwise argue that no photographs showing Tupac's injuries were ever seen. But photos were taken, plenty of them; they just never made it to the press. Any photo of Tupac Shakur in the hospital or in the coroner's office would have fetched a tidy sum from tabloid periodicals, so they were – and still are – kept under lock and key.

Lieutenant Brad Simpson, who oversees Metro's criminalistics unit, which includes the photo lab, said his office's photos of the Tupac Shakur investigation have been locked up.

"The only copies of homicide photos that we keep," he said, "are one set kept with the crime-scene reports and one with homicide. There was interest from some of the tabloids in getting some of those photos. The tabloids offered a lot of money, but they didn't get any photos. They made the offer to the coroner's office. We knew that after the Jon Bonet Ramsey case in Boulder, Colorado, we had to be careful. We have tighter controls here."

County Coroner Ron Flud was surprised when he received a mysterious phone call from a man who told the receptionist the call was "personal."

Flud took the call in his office. "The person was being clandestine and said he represented a client who would like to purchase something and would like to meet with me. I told him, 'I don't meet with people.' He said, 'Well, you have some photos.' I knew at that point where he was headed. I stopped him and said, 'No.' At that point, he hung up on me."

Flud said he assumed the man calling him was from a tabloid publication, but he didn't stay on the phone long enough to find out. He knew about reports of other calls to LVMPD offering as much as $100,000 for a photo.

"Because of the *Globe* and the *National Enquirer*, [the photos] are under lock and key," Brad Simpson agreed. "It's a policy violation. We'd probably fire the son-of-a bitch too."

Tupac's former bodyguard, Frank Alexander, said the offer was for even more.

"There was an offer going around that a photo of Tupac either dead or hooked up to machines would pay $250,000," Frank said during an interview from his Ontario ranch in southern California. "We weren't going to allow that to happen. That's why there are no photos of him in the hospital. I was on duty that morning, the day he died. From the very beginning, he always had a bodyguard there in addition to the hospital security guards."

Photos, however, were taken of Tupac's body during and after his autopsy, taken by a number of different people. All but one have been accounted for and secured. The one that got away is published in the center photo spread of this book. The photo is explicit. It's not easy to look at. That's because it's real. It's the image of Tupac Shakur lying on a gurney at the morgue, with his chest opened; that's what coroners do when they autopsy bodies. A skull and crossbones tattooed on his right arm are clear and recognizable. The incision doctors made a few days earlier to remove his right lung is visible just above "Thug" on his lower chest. However graphic and gruesome it may be, the photograph in this book should forever dispel any theories that Tupac faked his own death.

Journalist Veronica Chambers, who interviewed Tupac while he was on the set of the film *Poetic Justice*, wrote in *Esquire*, "Of all the rumors and conspiracy theories I've heard since Tupac died, only one has reverberated inside my head: 'I've heard that Tupac isn't really dead.' A friend said, 'Why did they cremate the body right away? In Las Vegas, where they had no family or friends?'

"I shrugged. I make it a point never to argue down conspiracy theories.

"'What I heard is that Afeni has had Tupac's identity changed, and shipped him to Cuba.' As I listened to my friend, what surprised me was how my heart leaped at the thought of Tupac alive...

"[On the set] I asked [Tupac] if he didn't think that staying in the Valley, instead of going out and instigating all the trouble he did, would make him live longer. He looked at me as if I were crazy. 'It would be an honor to die in the 'hood,' he said solemnly, as if he were reciting the Pledge of Allegiance. 'Don't let me die in Saudi Arabia. These motherfuckers are rushing with a flag to die on foreign soil, fighting for motherfuckers that don't care about us. I'd rather die in the 'hood, where I get my love. I'm not saying I want to die, but if I got to die, let me die in the line of duty, the duty of the 'hood.'"

Snoop Dogg, a fellow emcee with Tupac at Death Row Records at the time, perhaps said it best.

"People need to let him rest in peace, let that rumor rest in peace," he told reporters. "Because it's a hard pill to swallow, people don't want to accept it. So they gonna keep that myth or that philosophy goin' on as long as they can because his music lives on and he's a legend, you know what I'm sayin'? When you make legendary music, people don't want to believe you're gone, like Elvis. They keep sayin', 'Elvis ain't dead,' but it's just all about the individual himself. He was a legend, and everybody don't wanna let it go."

EULOGY

SINCE HIS DEATH, Tupac has been called a black prince, a revolutionary, an icon for Generation X, a hip-hop Lazarus, a brother for black America.

Some see only the tattoos and the jewelry – the body language – as a way of describing him. Or the angry words and the defiant message. They can't get past his persona.

Still others see Tupac as the young Malcolm X, speaking for young black America, the voice they couldn't find for themselves.

And others see him as the most talented singer to ever take the rap-music industry by storm.

To many, Tupac Shakur was a figure of violence, who became a victim of the same violent gang culture he glorified – shot down on the streets of Las Vegas in a gangland-type killing.

His friend, boxer Mike Tyson, told *Playboy* magazine five years after Tupac's death that he remembered him mostly for his "misplaced loyalty."

"He was around people who were into drugs," Tyson said, "but that wasn't who he was. He was a good person. He got a lot of bad rap. I've never seen a good rapper with a good image. They're good guys, though."

Those who knew Tupac best saw him as a force moving toward the truth, cut down too soon, before he could mature and reach his full potential, before he'd had a chance to come into his own. He was young, not yet matured, they said. They felt his anger, his frustration, his pain. They have called him the '90s Elvis, or have likened him to John Lennon, or Jimi Hendrix, or Jim Morrison, or Sammy Davis Jr., or any other famous singers who were symbols of something larger than themselves.

"To me, I feel that my game is strong," Tupac told writer Tony Patrick. "I feel as though I'm a shining prince, just like Malcolm, and feel that all of us are shining princes, and if we live like shining princes, then whatever we want can be ours." Tupac considered his music spiritual, like the old Negro hymns. "Except for the fact that I'm not saying, 'We shall overcome,'" he explained, "I'm saying, 'We *are* overcome.'"

Many people believe Tupac was a promising talent who wound up a casualty of a society that destroys black youth, males in particular. It's not just a belief among many that the black man in America today is an endangered species. Statistics back it up. If the drugs don't get them, the violence will. And if the violence doesn't get them, cops and the justice system eventually bring them down.

Writer Kevin Powell elaborated: "There's a perception in the black community that if you're young and black and male, and happen to be making lots of money, you are vulnerable to attacks from the system or the powers that be."

"You know what I think?" E-40, a San Francisco rapper who once recorded with Tupac, asked *Spin* magazine. "Tupac is looking down on us, saying, 'Y'all don't know what you're missing up here.' We the ones in hell."

The killing of Tupac Shakur heightened the debate about whether gangsta rap promotes violence or is just a reflection of the ugly mood on the streets. A dark aura of violence looms over the hip-hop music industry. To some, Tupac, with his tattoos that promoted firearms, had it coming. To others, his songs spoke against the gun culture of the ghetto.

In "Young Niggaz," he sang, "Don't wanna be another statistic out here doin' nothin'/Tryin' to maintain in this dirty game/Keep it real and I will even if it kills me/My young niggaz stay away from dumb niggaz/Put down the gun and have some fun, nigga."

After Biggie Smalls was shot to death, Quincy Jones, who might have become Tupac's father-in-law had Tupac survived, wrote in *Vibe* magazine, "When will it end? When will the senseless killing of our hip-hop heroes cease? I thought Tupac's death was going to be the end of it, but the psycho-drama keeps going. The murder of Christopher Wallace... is the latest in what is becoming a pathetic string of deaths in and around the rap community. And the speed with which the media turned this unnecessary tragedy into evidence of a 'Rap War,' a 'Slay Revenge,' makes me worry that we haven't heard the last shots ring out yet.

"I love hip-hop. To me, it is a kindred spirit to beebop, the music that started my career. But I also know history. The gangsta lifestyle that is so often glorified and heralded in this music is not 'keeping it real'; it is fake, not even entertainment. A sad farce at best and a grim tragedy at worst.

"'Real' is being shot five times with 'real' bullets. 'Real' is having a promising life ended at 24 years of age by somebody you might call 'brother.' If that's keeping it real, it is up to all of us to redefine what 'real' means to the Hip-Hop Nation... Ultimately, love is real."

In another statement, this one a news release issued the day after Biggie's death, Quincy Jones said he was "absolutely stunned."

"This death, as well as the death of Tupac Shakur, Eazy-E [from AIDS], Marvin Gaye [murdered by his own father], and so many more young people who we never hear about, are senseless acts that should never have happened.

"I spent my formative years growing up in 'Gangsta Central' on the Southside of Chicago, so I am no stranger to random violence. If life continues to imitate art this way, it will result in self-inflicted genocide. We all need to re-evaluate what our priorities are or else we have nothing to look forward to except more of this madness."

He said he had developed a "close personal relationship" with "the superstar rappers" over the last ten years. "It's witnessing their genius and compassion that makes incidents such as these particularly disturbing to me," he said.

***

No public funeral service was ever held for the slain Tupac Shakur.

This was at the request of his family, who said he would not have wanted one. In fact, the family told reporters that Tupac had talked about his death and had specifically stated that he did not want a funeral if he were to die. In high school he told friends they could snort his ashes and get high off of him. His mother took his ashes home to Georgia to the house Tupac had bought for her (through Death Row). Later, she scattered them over a neighborhood park in Los Angeles.

Spontaneous celebrations of Tupac's life were held all over the country. At the Civic Center in Atlanta, Georgia, friends remembered him shortly after his death. They called it "Keep Ya Head Up! The Celebration of Tupac Shakur," a three-hour tribute of speeches, poetry readings, dance, and music.

"I know people are sad, but I am here and we are here to celebrate Pac and continue on with his spirit," Afeni Shakur said of her son.

"Shock G and Money-B, members of Digital Underground where Tupac's professional music career began, issued this statement:

"If you want to mourn, do it for your own personal loss. Don't mourn for Pac. Remember him for his art and don't be sad for his death. Pac lived a short, fast, concentrated, and intense life. He lived a 70-year life in 25 years. He went out the way he wanted, in the glitter of the gangsta life, hit record on the chart, new movie in the can, and money in the pocket. All Pac wanted was to hear himself on the radio and see himself on the movie screen. He did all that – and more."

Tupac was also mourned at his boyhood church, the House of the Lord Pentecostal Church in Brooklyn, New York, which he joined at age 15 with his mother and sister. Tupac left Brooklyn in his teens, but was still listed as a member of the congregation until his death.

"Who will weep for Tupac Shakur?" the Reverend Herbert Daughtry asked mourners at the memorial service. "I will weep for Tupac. I will weep for all our youth.

"He had the genes, he had the ability. Could we have provided the society that would have made him blossom?"

Daughtry said that Tupac's self-proclaimed ambition to be a revolutionary against injustice to blacks "was just as real as Martin's and Malcom's," referring to Martin Luther King and Malcolm X.

"I know that there are those who say he went about it the wrong way, joining the 'gangsta' culture he glorified in his lyrics," Daughtry said. "But it's not for me to judge."

Mikal Gilmore, in a *Rolling Stone* article shortly after Tupac's death, wrote that he suspected "Shakur's death will be cited as justification for yet another campaign against hard-core rap and troublesome lyrics."

"So a man sings about death and killing, and then the man is killed," he wrote. "There is a great temptation for many to view one event as the result of the other. And in Tupac Shakur's case, there are some grounds for this assessment. He did more than sing about violence; he also participated in a fair amount of it. As Shakur himself once said, in words that *Time* magazine appropriated for its headline covering his murder: 'What goes 'round comes 'round.' Still, I think it would be a great disservice to dismiss Shakur's work and life with any quick and glib headline summations. It's like burying the man without hearing him."

Writer Kevin Powell put Tupac's life and death in perspective when he eulogized Tupac in the same issue of *Rolling Stone*.

"He was a complex human being; both brilliant and fooling; very funny and deadly serious; friendly and eager to please, but also bad-tempered and prone to violence; a lover of his people and of women, but also a peace divider and a convicted sex offender; generous to a fault but also a dangerous gambler when it came to his personal and professional life; incredibly talented but at times frivolously short-sighted. To me, Shakur was the most important solo artist in the history of rap, not because he was the most talented (he wasn't), but because he, more than any other rapper, personified and articulated what it was to be a young black man in America.

"But the demons of Shakur's childhood – the poverty, the sense of displacement, the inconsistent relationship with his mother, the absence of a regular father figure – haunted the rapper all his life. In his song, 'Dear Mama,' he sings, 'When I was young, me and my mama had beefs/17-years-old, kicked out on the streets.'

"Now that Tupac Shakur is gone, some will charge that it was the music that killed him or that he had it coming because of the choices he made in his life. Those are cop-out, knee-jerk responses. Shakur, in spite of his bad-boy persona, was a product of a post-civil rights, post-Black Panther, post-Ronald Reagan American environment. We may never find out who killed Tupac Shakur, or why he did the things he did and said what he said. All we have left are his music, his films, and his interviews. Shakur lived fast and hard, and he has died fast and hard. And in his own way, he kept it real for a lot of folks who didn't believe that anyone like him (or like themselves) could do anything with his life."

Keisha Morris, Tupac's ex-wife with whom he remained friends, told *People* magazine, in an issue released while Tupac was still in a coma, "He's an entertainer, not a gangsta. As a person, Tupac is very misunderstood." After his death, Keisha told *Rolling Stone*, "I thought he was going to walk out of the hospital just like he did before."

"At the end... you kind of had that feeling he was going to die, according to his preaching," writer Tony Patrick said in *Thug Immortal*. "He seemed to have taken up power and weapons, his posse lifestyle, as his deity. Tupac went from one extreme to the other. There was really no middle ground with him. It was age without maturity, knowledge without wisdom, order turning to chaos. Tupac Shakur should stand as a living testament in the Hip-Hop Nation as the pinnacle of greatness achieved, but at the same time, the frailties of human weakness and tragedy."

His stepfather, Mutulu Shakur, penned a letter, "To My Son," from inside a Florence, Colorado, federal penitentiary, the night Tupac died. Excerpts were reprinted on the internet by Double J Productions.

"I love you whenever, forever. Tupac, so much I needed to say, so much you wanted to say. Many conversations between us within the ether...

"The pain inflicted that scarred your soul but not your spirit gave force to the rebellion. Many couldn't see your dreams or understand your nightmares. How could they, Tupac? I knew your love and understood your passion. But you knew of your beginning and saw your end, racing towards it.

"You taught and fought through your songs and deeds. *Ratt-tatt-tatt* of words penetrating the contradiction of our existence...

"Who cares? We cared, Tupac. The Shakurs have been guided by struggle, prepared or not, whenever, forever. We've exposed our existence, naked from fear, to those who would hear the positive. Who would witness the stress, wear and tear of this lonely path? You couldn't have evaded the effect or the changes. You inherited it; it was in your genes.

"Friday the 13th didn't mean a thing. Life is for living and dying well... You understand the pain of disappointment in the ones we love. You pushed so many away. Burnt so many bridges so they wouldn't follow you into battles against the demons you were facing. Knowing well to what lengths you would go. This battlefield of reality is littered with many meaningless casualties.

"You never yelled out, 'Somebody, save me!' You only asked for your soul to be free, whenever, forever. You told us to keep our head up, knowing the pain was coming. Knowing to look for the strength in the heavens. Set your soul free, Tupac Amaru.

"The victories – we will teach your mission. We are thankful for you. We love you, Tupac Shakur. We ain't mad at you. We'll be better because of you.

"So now I give you my tears so I might assimilate your loss and I can live on in peace.

"Knowing I will feed your spirit with my unconditional love, knowing you will need it on your next journey. May Allah bless you for your deeds and forgive your errors. Tupac, come to me and give me strength.

"Love always,

"Your father, friend, comrade, Mutulu."

Billy Garland, Tupac's biological father, said in an exclusive interview with Kevin Powell for *Rolling Stone* that his son did not deserve to be criticized.

"My son is dead, and he don't deserve to be talked about like some common criminal," Garland said. "He wasn't perfect, but he did do some great things in a little bit of time."

After Suge Knight's release from prison, nearly five years after his star performer was killed, Suge had this to say, to the BBC: "Tupac is what you call a superstar. There's a difference between being an artist and a superstar. You get guys on other labels [who] could probably go and sell some records, but they're not a star. Tupac was a star. When he walked in a room, the room lit up. He could still be a thug and still talk about thuggish things, but he can still take his shirt off and be a pillar to the women. There's a difference between being a thug and a street punk. Tupac is and always will be a legend. Even when he was alive he was a legend, because he had his own spiritual flava, his own vibe, and that's one of the best things you can look for in a guy like Pac.

"There isn't ever going to be another Tupac. There will be a lot who imitate it, but not duplicate it. He's in a class by himself."

And, finally, Tupac Shakur's mother Afeni spoke about her only son.

"Tupac has always been the person who's made up the game – always," she told *Vibe* magazine before his death and after one of Tupac's many court arraignments. "He would have make-believe singing groups, and he would be Prince, or Ralph in New Edition. He was always the lead."

And after his death, she told a *Vanity Fair* magazine reporter, "From the moment he was born, I measured his life in five-year periods. When he was five, I was so grateful. When he was 10, I thanked God he was 10. Fifteen, 20, 25. I was always amazed he'd survived. He was a gift."

The killing of Tupac Shakur remains unsolved.

And the retaliation killings continue.

APPENDIX

Official Coroner's Report

REPORT OF INVESTIGATION
OFFICE OF THE CORONER MEDICAL EXAMINER, CLARK COUNTY, NEVADA
1704 Pinto Lane, Las Vegas, Nevada 89106

DECEDENT SHAKUR, TUPAC A.   **AKA** LESANE PARISH CROOKS **Status** S **DOB** 06/16/1971
Residence Address 8489 W. 3RD ST., STE. 1038, LOS ANGELES, CA 90048
Tel No. (213) 653-3515   **Desc: Sex** M **Race** N **Age** 25   **SS #** 546-47-8539 **Height** 72.00
Weight 215.00   **Hair** BROWN   **Eyes** BROWN

Scars/Tattoos & Other identifying features
TATTOOS: SKULL - RIGHT SHOULDER, THUGLIFE - STOMACH, NUMEROUS OTHER TATTOOS ON BODY.
Rigor Mortis NONE   **Livor Mortis** NONE   **Decomposed?** No
Clothing NONE
Drugs & Medications
NONE NOTED

Occupation RAP SINGER   **Employed by** EUPHANASIA
Agency Reporting UNIVERSITY MEDICAL CENTER   **Date & Time Reported** 09/13/96 16:15
Location of body UMC TRAUMA ICU
Type of Death V   **At Work:** N

CIRCUMSTANCES	DATE	TIME
Reported to Agency by		
Name & Address		
Last Seen Alive by		
Name & Address		
Found Dead by		
Name & Address		
Pronounced Dead by	09/13/96	16:03
Name & Address	DR. LOVETT	
Body Viewed by	09/13/96	16:15
Name & Address	ED BROWN, CCCME	
Identified by	09/13/96	17:00
How Identified	VIEWING	
Name & Address	AFENI SHAKUR, MOTHER	
Witnesses		

Law Enforcement Agency LVMPD   **Event #** 960907-2063
Officers   SGT. MANNING, SGT. ANDERSEN
        OFC. DENSLEY P#3577, OFC. DEBECKER P#3917, CSA LEMASTER
Property Receipt # 50389
In Custody of NO PROPERTY TAKEN
CUSTODY OF BODY: Removed by DAVIS   **To** CCCME
Driver   SONNY THOMAS
Assisted by   TROY FARRELL
Requested by FAMILY

DEATH NOTIFICATION
N.O.K. AFENI SHAKUR   **Relationship** MOTHER
Address 883 RAYS ROAD, STONE MTN., GA 30083   **Tel No.** (404) 508-8599
Other #1   **Relationship**
Address   **Tel No.**
Other #2   **Relationship**
Address   **Tel No.**
Means   PERSONAL CONTACT AT THE HOSPITAL
Notification Made by   ED BROWN, CCCME   **Date** 09/13/96 **Time** 17:00

VEHICULAR DEATHS: Deceased was   **Seat Location**
Vehicle   **Lic No**   **State**
Accident location   **Date**   **Time**
SAFETY EQUIPMENT USED: Seat belt   **point** **Air bag**   **Other**

ABOUT THE AUTHOR

Cathy Scott is a full-time police reporter for the *Las Vegas Sun*. A reporter for over a decade, Scott has received more than a dozen journalism awards. Her articles have appeared in the *Los Angeles Times* and the *New York Times*. Scott covered the Los Angeles riots, Operation Restore Hope in Somalia, and the Republic of Panama's drug interdiction program. She holds a bachelor of science degree from the University of Redlands.

Also by Cathy Scott

The Notorious B.I.G.: The Murder of Biggie Smalls

Biggie Smalls is now the subject of a major movie, *Notorious.*

Biggie Smalls, aka The Notorious B.I.G., exploded onto the hip-hop scene with his platinum-selling album *Ready to Die* in 1995. A war of words with Tupac Shakur ensued, then within six months they were both dead. Following Tupac, Biggie's death shocked the rap music industry and a media storm followed as millions of loyal fans mourned his passing. Cathy Scott has interviewed those involved with Biggie Smalls and reviewed court documents and police reports in order to bring us the real story of his murder.

ISBN-13: 978-0-89565-307-7
ISBN-10: 0-85965-307-2

£9.99